The Communicator's Commentary

Job

THE COMMUNICATOR'S COMMENTARY SERIES
OLD TESTAMENT

I *Genesis* by D. Stuart Briscoe

II *Exodus* by Maxie D. Dunnam

III *Leviticus* by Gary W. Demarest

IV *Numbers* by James Philip

V *Deuteronomy* by John C. Maxwell

VI *Joshua* by John A. Huffman, Jr.

VII *Judges, Ruth* by David Jackman

VIII *1, 2 Samuel* by Kenneth L. Chafin

IX *1, 2 Kings* by Russell H. Dilday

X *1, 2 Chronicles* by Leslie C. Allen

XI *Ezra, Nehemiah, Esther* by Robert M. Norris

XII *Job* by David L. McKenna

XIII *Psalms 1–72* by Donald M. Williams

XIV *Psalms 73–150* by Donald M. Williams

XV *Proverbs, Ecclesiastes, Song of Solomon* by David A. Hubbard

XVI *Isaiah* by Ernest J. Lewis

XVII *Jeremiah, Lamentations* by John Guest

XVIII *Ezekiel* by Douglas Stuart

XIX *Daniel* by Sinclair B. Ferguson

XX *Hosea, Joel, Amos, Obadiah, Jonah, Micah* by Lloyd J. Ogilvie

XXI *Nahum, Habakkuk, Zephaniah, Haggai, Zechariah, Malachi* by Lloyd J. Ogilvie

Lloyd J. Ogilvie
General Editor

The Communicator's Commentary

Job

David L. McKenna

WORD BOOKS, PUBLISHER • WACO, TEXAS

Library of Congress Cataloging in Publication Data
Main entry under title:

The Communicator's commentary.

Bibliography: p.
Contents: OT12. Job / by David L. McKenna.
1. Bible. O.T.—Commentaries. I. Ogilvie, Lloyd John. II. McKenna, David L. (David Loren), 1929–
BS1151.2.C66 1986 221.7'7 86–11138
ISBN 0–8499–0418–8 (v. OT12)

Printed in the United States of America

5 6 7 8 9 9 AGF 9 8 7 6

Sharing Job's Joy

"When my children were around me;
. . . my steps were bathed with cream,
And the rock poured out rivers of
oil for me!"

Job 29:5–6

The book is dedicated

to

OUR FIRST SEVEN GRANDCHILDREN

David Loren McKenna II
Anne Patricia McKenna
Edward Orville Blews III
Christine Elizabeth Blews
Patrick Douglas McKenna
Marshall Jackson Kinzer
Lauren Marie Blews

OUR FIRST GODCHILD

Ashleigh Lauren Graves

AND THOSE TO COME!

Contents

Editor's Preface

God has called all of His people to be communicators. Everyone who is in Christ is called into ministry. As ministers of "the manifold grace of God," all of us—clergy and laity—are commissioned with the challenge to communicate our faith to individuals and groups, classes and congregations.

The Bible, God's Word, is the objective basis of the truth of His love and power that we seek to communicate. In response to the urgent, expressed needs of pastors, teachers, Bible study leaders, church school teachers, small group enablers, and individual Christians, the Communicator's Commentary is offered as a penetrating search of the Scriptures of the Old and New Testament to enable vital personal and practical communication of the abundant life.

Many current commentaries and Bible study guides provide only some aspects of a communicator's needs. Some offer in-depth scholarship but no application to daily life. Others are so popular in approach that biblical roots are left unexplained. Few offer impelling illustrations that open windows for the reader to see the exciting application for today's struggles. And most of all, seldom have the expositors given the valuable outlines of passages so needed to help the preacher or teacher in his or her busy life to prepare for communicating the Word to congregations or classes.

This Communicator's Commentary series brings all of these elements together. The authors are scholar-preachers and teachers outstanding in their ability to make the Scriptures come alive for individuals and groups. They are noted for bringing together excellence in biblical scholarship, knowledge of the original Hebrew and Greek, sensitivity to people's needs, vivid illustrative material from biblical, classical, and contemporary sources, and lucid communication by the use of clear outlines of thought. Each has been selected to contribute to this series because of his Spirit-empowered ability to help people live in the skins of biblical characters and provide a "you-are-there" intensity to the drama of events of the Bible which have so much to say about our relationships and responsibilities today.

The design for the Communicator's Commentary gives the reader an overall outline of each book of the Bible. Following the introduction, which reveals the author's approach and salient background on the book, each chapter of the commentary provides the Scripture to be exposited. The New King James Bible has been chosen for the Communicator's Commentary because it combines with integrity the beauty of language, underlying Hebrew and Greek textual basis, and thought-flow of the 1611 King James Version, while replacing obsolete verb forms and other archaisms with their everyday contemporary counterparts for greater readability. Reverence for God is preserved in the capitalization of all pronouns referring to the Father, Son, or Holy Spirit. Readers who are more comfortable with another translation can readily find the parallel passage by means of the chapter and verse reference at the end of each passage being exposited. The paragraphs of exposition combine fresh insights to the Scripture, application, rich illustrative material, and innovative ways of utilizing the vibrant truth for his or her own life and for the challenge of communicating it with vigor and vitality.

It has been gratifying to me as Editor of this series to receive enthusiastic progress reports from each contributor. As they worked, all were gripped with new truths from the Scripture—God-given insights into passages, previously not written in the literature of biblical explanation. A prime objective of this series is for each user to find the same awareness: that God speaks with newness through the Scriptures when we approach them with a ready mind and a willingness to communicate what He has given; that God delights to give communicators of His Word "I-never-saw-that-in-that-verse-before" intellectual insights so that our listeners and readers can have "I-never-realized-all-that-was-in-that-verse" spiritual experiences.

The thrust of the commentary series unequivocally affirms that God speaks through the Scriptures today to engender faith, enable adventuresome living of the abundant life, and establish the basis of obedient discipleship. The Bible, the unique Word of God, is unlimited as a resource for Christians in communicating our hope to others. It is our weapon in the battle for truth, the guide for ministry, and the irresistible force for introducing others to God.

A biblically rooted communication of the Gospel holds in unity and oneness what divergent movements have wrought asunder. This commentary series courageously presents personal faith, caring for individuals, and social responsibility as essential, inseparable dimensions of biblical Christianity. It seeks to present the quadrilateral Gospel in its fullness which calls us to unreserved commitment to Christ, unrestricted self-esteem in His grace, unqualified love for others in personal evangelism, and undying efforts to work for justice and righteousness in a sick and suffering world.

A growing renaissance in the church today is being led by clergy and laity who are biblically rooted, Christ-centered, and Holy Spirit-empowered. They have dared to listen to people's most urgent questions and deepest needs and then to God as He speaks through the Bible. Biblical preaching is the secret of growing churches. Bible study classes and small groups are equipping the laity for ministry in the world. Dynamic Christians are finding that daily study of God's Word allows the Spirit to do in them what He wishes to communicate through them to others. These days are the most exciting time since Pentecost. The Communicator's Commentary is offered to be a primary resource of new life for this renaissance.

It has been very encouraging to receive the enthusiastic responses of pastors and teachers to the twelve New Testament volumes of the Communicator's Commentary series. The letters from communicators on the firing line in pulpits, classes, study groups, and Bible fellowship clusters across the nation, as well as the reviews of scholars and publication analysts, have indicated that we have been on target in meeting a need for a distinctly different kind of commentary on the Scriptures, a commentary that is primarily aimed at helping interpreters of the Bible to equip the laity for ministry.

This positive response has led the publisher to press on with an additional twenty-one volumes covering the books of the Old Testament. These new volumes rest upon the same goals and guidelines that undergird the New Testament volumes. Scholar-preachers with facility in Hebrew as well as vivid contemporary exposition have been selected as authors. The purpose throughout is to aid the preacher and teacher in the challenge and adventure of Old Testament exposition in communication. In each volume you will meet Yahweh, the "I AM"" Lord who is Creator, Sustainer, and Redeemer in the unfolding drama of His call and care of Israel. He is the Lord who acts, intervenes, judges, and presses His people into the immense challenges and privileges of being a chosen people, a holy nation. And in the descriptive exposition of each passage, the implications of the ultimate revelation of Yahweh in Jesus Christ, His Son, our Lord, are carefully spelled out to maintain unity and oneness in the preaching and teaching of the Gospel.

In this volume on Job, you will discover the same scholarly acumen, practical wisdom, and pastoral insight so many readers have found in Dr. David McKenna's volume on Mark in the New Testament series.

One of the most helpful and unique aspects of Dr. McKenna's interpretation of the Book of Job is his use of the faith development theory as the means of understanding Job. This provides rich and fresh material for helping the communicator enable his or her listeners not only in appreciating Job, but in growing in primary faith in God and in advanced faith developed through living in the difficulties and distresses of life. Dr. McKenna uses the stages of faith development in order to clarify the conflicts between Job and his "friends." Then he shows how Job's suffering allows, even forces, him to grow in faith. This is clearly contrasted with the less mature faith of Job's simplistic "friends" who are unable to deal in depth with the problem of suffering or to grapple with the question "Why do the righteous suffer if God is both righteous and all-powerful?"

Dr. McKenna's basic theme of exposition is "Seeing through Suffering." He shows how Job sees through the façade of suffering to its deeper meaning and, because of his suffering, gains a greater vision of God. Job is able, therefore, to repent and to trust Him more profoundly.

David McKenna's great strength as an interpreter is that he takes the text as it stands, as a whole. Many critical scholars are so anxious to slice Job into its sources that they fail to deal with the canonical text as it is. Dr. McKenna takes seriously the dialogical structure of Job and communicates the drama of interaction in a way that makes the text come alive. In so doing, he assists the teacher and preacher in building a series of messages or classes to deal biblically, intellectually, and practically with people's aching questions about why God allows suffering, why bad things happen to good people, and why, if God cares, He permits problems.

This volume delivers rich rewards. It offers much-needed devotional meaning for Christians seeking to live their faith in our confusing times. I predict that it will stand the test of time to become a classic in the devotional literature. Because Dr. McKenna is a master teacher and preacher, no communicator can read this volume without having his or her own skills deepened and expanded magnificently. And finally, here is a guide for communicators to present the Book of Job in a life-transforming way.

David McKenna is one of the truly creative evangelical leaders of our time. His distinguished career as an educator, preacher, teacher, and leader of authentic renewal in the church has made him a prophet to the church as a whole and admired mentor of leaders. As president of Asbury Theological Seminary, he leads an academic family of faith with warmth and wisdom. He is actively involved as a denominational leader and visionary in developing and deploying dynamic leaders for our time. In this volume you will come to know him as a gifted writer who communicates with vivid clarity and gripping insight. As in his volume on Mark, you will meet a man immersed in the mind of the Master, and willing to share the discoveries of his own adventure in the exhilarating challenges of being a faithful disciple.

I am very thankful to claim David as a personal friend and covenant prayer partner. I have been deeply enriched by his writing, preaching, and teaching. Seeing him in action as a pace-setting leader has encouraged me in the quest of excellence. But most of all, I respect him as a man in Christ who lives the grace and hope he communicates so effectively.

It is my prayer that this volume of Job will be as stimulating and full for you as it has been for me.

LLOYD J. OGILVIE

Author's Preface

On the day I had to make a decision on which book I would write for the Old Testament series of the Communicator's Commentary, I visited with a lay person whose counsel I prize. In the course of our conversation, I posed this dilemma: "Today I must make a decision on whether to write a commentary on Genesis, Job, or Isaiah. From a lay person's perspective, on which book do you think I should write?" Always quick, but never glib, my friend answered, "Job. Let me tell you why.

"Last summer, my wife and I were using your commentary on Mark for our daily devotions. Then one morning, we got a telephone call reporting the accidental death of our grandbaby. We suffered, oh, how we suffered. And we kept asking the question: *Why?* After several weeks of grief, we returned to your commentary on Mark. The next lesson in the series was Jesus' words, 'Let the little children come to me and do not forbid them, for such is the kingdom of heaven' [10:14]. You ministered to us, David. Write on Job—we all suffer."

For the next year, I walked, jogged, soared, and stumbled on a journey of faith with Job. My research and writing fit into the early morning, late evening, weekend, and vacation "chinks" of an executive's time. The truth, however, is that Job is not just a book about which you can do research or writing. Job is a book to be experienced. So, for every waking moment in the past year, I have lived Job—not in physical suffering but in dealing with intellectual contradictions, emotional frustrations, and spiritual shortcomings. To some this may be a disadvantage.

Most writings on Job are either dispassionately clinical or intensely personal. It is hard to believe that some critical commentators can treat the book as a literary or theological specimen to be dissected. Something also seems to be lost when a person who has suffered tragic loss—usually of an innocent child—uses the book as a grief manual. Someplace in between, a communicator's commentary has a special contribution to make to the understanding of this inspired work. Balancing between criticism and comfort without ignoring either, the multiple dimensions of the book can be explored and experienced.

With this approach in mind, I have purposely chosen to concentrate on the character and faith development of Job, with an admitted bias toward the prophetic leanings of his journey toward the incarnate Christ. Most amazing of all is to discover the incomparable moments when the veil of truth is lifted and the image of Christ comes into view. Then, as quickly as the veil lifts, it falls again under the weight of excruciating pain. For this reason, I have chosen to give the book the theme, "Seeing through suffering."

Everyone is invited to join with me on this journey with Job. The path is tortuous for small minds and rocky for weak faith; but, if once we see through to God as Job does, our fears give way to trust and whatever righteousness we claim gives way to grace. In the end, we too can be remembered with Job as persons who return grace for grace because of the image and Spirit of Christ in us.

Like Job in his original prosperity and later restoration, my life is filled with family and friends who encouraged me to write and helped me with the manuscript. How grateful I am—to Janet, my wife, and Rob, our son, who never were jealous of Job when he took some of their time; to Sheila Lovell, English teacher extraordinaire, turned my executive assistant who wielded her red pencil as editor; to Bobbi Graves, my secretary turned mother, who typed volumes and volumes of pages and nagged me for more; to Lois Mulcahy, who stepped in to finish the copy while adjusting to the ways and workings of a seminary president's office; to Floyd Thatcher, Editor-in-Chief of Word, who first encouraged me to write; to Lloyd Ogilvie, general editor of the Communicator's Commentary and my covenant brother; and to the students of Asbury Theological Seminary, who let me test my thoughts with them in a chapel series on Job.

My prayer is that, together with Job, we may "see through suffering" in order to minister more effectively to those who ask: *Why?*

Introduction

Sooner or later, everyone identifies with Job. Suffering is part and parcel of the human condition. When that moment comes, whether innocent or guilty, we cry out in anguish, *Why?* Unless we are sadists obsessed with guilt, we feel that the pain of suffering is always more than we deserve. So, while few of us can match the uncontested innocence of Job, all of us in the time of suffering raise angry questions about God's justice, our righteousness, and religion's answer. Invariably, we also get down to the cosmic question "Why do the wicked prosper and the innocent suffer in an orderly universe created by a just God?" This is the question upon which scholars and skeptics stumble in their search for faith.

The Book of Job provides no ready answers to either the cosmic question or the sufferer's anguish. Only a perspective is given—the perspective of faith in which the question *why* gives way to the answer, *who.* Thus, the Book of Job is an impassioned experience in which the content of religious faith is explored and the process of spiritual growth is revealed. In this sense, the book cannot be studied, especially through the eyes of a Western Christian. Job can only be experienced as an adventure on the growing edge of the human spirit. Then, for all those who suffer and for all the rest who fear suffering, it is a book of hope.

How, then, do we approach the Book of Job? A scholarly critique leaves us wanting if our goal is communication. According to scholars, the author is unknown, the date of writing is uncertain, the locale is obscure, the historicity is doubted, and the literary integrity of the book is questioned. Even Job's place in the Canon of the Old Testament's Wisdom Literature is in dispute. To communicate the experience of Job, we must either bypass these questions or take some stated facts at face value. Choosing the latter, we believe that Job is a man of history from the land of Uz, whose journey to faith through suffering is essential to God's revelation in Scripture.

Still, Job does not lend itself to easy answers. The book refutes a stunted orthodoxy that cannot respond to new circumstances in human experience. Its extreme complexity is surpassed only by its multiple meanings. Like a gem of many facets, each time the Book of Job is turned, a new light shines. By letting Job speak for itself as the Word of God, every reading is a fresh experience. At one time, the literary value sparkles; at another time, the dramatic effect is overwhelming. Still another time, the psychological dynamics open a wealth of meaning and then give way to a challenging process in faith development.

But for a Christian who looks back upon the Book of Job from the perspective of Jesus Christ, every line leans forward into the promise of the Incarnation and the Resurrection. Admittedly, such a perspective is personal rather than critical, but is there any other way to communicate the truth that through suffering we see God? Søren Kierkegaard's invitation is for us to "read this Book as it were with our heart . . . You surely have read Job? Read him, read him, over and over again . . . because everything about him is so human."[1]

The Literary Value of Job

From a literary standpoint, Job is a monumental work—one of a kind. Scholars have tried to link it with Babylonian and Egyptian literature, in which there are stories of human suffering, but to no avail. Pessimism is the end of what is called the "Babylonian Job" and the "Egyptian Job." Other comparisons have been drawn with Plato's Dialogues, the Greek tragedy of Prometheus, and Homer's epic. All fall short. They cannot resolve the relationship between God's justice and man's suffering because they lack the Hebrew's intuitive sense of a transcendent, yet personal God who gives man hope. Prometheus, for instance, after his suffering at the hands of Zeus for giving man the secret of fire, slides from his rock and slips into the sea with one last cry of despair:

> Earth is convulsed; and the sound of thunder from the depths rolls past, and wreathing flames of lightning flash forth and whirlwinds roll

> up dust; and up leap blasts of all the winds declaring war one on another, blast against blast . . . O great my mother, O air that rollest light to all alike, thou seest me, how unjust are my sufferings.[2]

So, James Anthony Froude's prediction comes true. The Book of Job is seen "towering up alone, far above all the poetry of the world."[3] From that lofty literary position, Job's influence extends to other classics of world literature, such as Dante's *Divine Comedy,* Milton's *Paradise Regained,* and Goethe's *Faust.* Contemporary literature also reflects the book's impact. H. G. Wells's novel *Undying Fire* and Dostoevsky's *The Brothers Karamazov* have Jobian themes. No Biblical book has received greater literary praise. Tennyson acclaimed it as "the greatest poem of ancient and modern times." Thomas Carlyle's accolade, however, is unsurpassed: "A Noble book, All Men's book . . . there is nothing written, I think, in the Bible or out of it, of equal literary merit."[4]

Job is extolled as great literature for good reason. To qualify as a classic to critics, a writing must have *universal appeal, a timeless theme, matchless language,* and *a lasting moral.* Certainly, the subject of human suffering is universal in appeal and timeless in application. The Book of Job knows no boundary of culture, civilization, class, religion, or generation. It speaks with equal meaning to ancient, middle, or modern ages; "haves" or "have nots"; East and West; Jew or Gentile; and young, middle-aged, or old. Matchless language conveys its message. Where else can you find such passionate poetry, dialectical prose, soaring allegory, majestic songs, and quotable quotes? Even literary critics hail Job's unknown author as the "Shakespeare of the Bible."

Of course, its moral message has eternal value. Because there is no direct answer to Job's question of *why,* the moral is always just out of reach until faith takes hold. Even then, the meaning of the book is not disclosed to us. Job's faith through suffering opens his eyes to see what God is doing in the world and what He wants to do with those who trust Him. From a literary viewpoint, the Book of Job is worthy of Carlyle's exuberance, "one of the grandest things ever written."[5]

Job's place in the Wisdom Literature of the Old Testament is neither so exalted nor secure. In the company of Proverbs, Ecclesiastes, and Song of Solomon, Job almost stands alone. By definition, wisdom tends to be rational, objective, precise, and impersonal. Job is just the opposite—passionate, contentious, contradictory, and painful. Some scholars want to delete it from the Canon because the only obvious connection with the other books of Wisdom Literature is Job's hymn in praise of wisdom (chapter 28). Stepping back from the conflict for just a moment, Job reflects on man's ingenuity in the search for riches, but admits his futility in finding or buying wisdom. In a familiar refrain, he joins with all of the sages of the Wisdom School to conclude, "The fear of the Lord . . . *is* wisdom" (28:28).

My view is that the Book of Job deserves all of the accolades of the literary giants and all of the honor attributed to a book in the Canon of the Old Testament. Wisdom must be personal as well as proverbial, passionate as well as philosophical, especially where human suffering is involved. So, from a literary viewpoint, Job stirs in the crucible of inspiration—poetry and prose, emotion and thought, faith and reason, experience and tradition, form and content—to meet us where we are, to take us through the experience of suffering, and to give us the eyes of faith that see the God of grace.

Job as Drama

Job stands alone, not just as literature, but as drama. Neither the pattern of tragedy nor comedy applies to it. Job is a bit of both, perhaps a tragicomedy in which the hero struggles through the depths of human sufferings to the heights of human restoration. Dramatists are like philosophers—they find it hard to put a happy ending on a serious work. For this reason, there are those who want to end the Book of Job before his restoration cancels out the meaning of the book. They say that the restoration only proves that Job's friends were right all along—sin is the cause of suffering and prosperity is the reward for righteousness. Those who take this position do not see the drama of Job through the eyes of faith. Professing to be creative, they draw their own limits on creativity. Of course, Job is filled with mystery, contradiction, ambiguity, and open-endedness. Isn't that the context in which human beings live and faith comes to life?

Archibald MacLeish is criticized for exercising dramatic license in *J.B.,* his modern play on the life of Job. Yet, in his conclusion, J.B.'s restoration is symbolized by reconciliation with his wife. While hardly a Christian play, in it one can see that faith is rising as the curtain falls. *J.B.* is just another example of the universality and timelessness of God's message of hope through the suffering of Job.

Although oversimplified, the Book of Job takes on added power and meaning when read according to the pattern of dramatic movement. Classical drama always has a plot around which the action moves. Job has no obvious plot. The subject is human suffering; the critical question is *why;* and the contest is between God, man, and evil. But dare we give the story a plot? Individual perception now takes over.

After reading and rereading the book, I found Job becoming more and more a journey of faith in which "seeing through suffering" becomes the pivotal thought around which all the action turns. "Seeing through suffering" is an obvious play on words. If the emphasis is on "seeing *through* suffering," it addresses the personal question of suffering, giving hope to the individual who is in the midst of affliction. Then, just a minor shift in emphasis to "*seeing* through suffering" opens up the cosmic question of God, man, and evil from the perspective of faith. To live and relive the drama of Job with this theme in mind is to find meaning for both the process of spiritual growth and the perspective of religious faith.

Once the plot for the drama is identified, the action rises and falls in a common pattern:

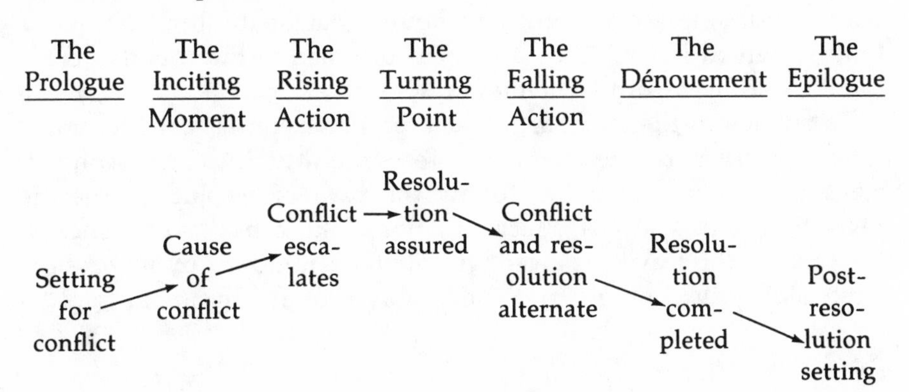

The drama of Job moves through this pattern. The prologue introduces Job as righteous, wise, prosperous, and a pious family man—the perfect setting for conflict. The inciting moment comes in heaven when Satan dares God to release Job from His protection in order to prove that Job's righteousness is dependent upon his prosperity and well-being—the cause of conflict. Rising action follows, in which the suffering Job cries, "Why?" His three friends try to comfort him, but instead move from the replies of sterile orthodoxy to personal attacks on the character of Job. The conflict escalates. At the peak of conflict and the depths of suffering, Job comes to the turning point when he leaps forward in faith to declare, "I know that my Redeemer lives, . . . That in my flesh I shall see God" (19:25–26). From here on, the resolution is assured. Yet, the conflict does not go away.

Job's friends continue their attacks, but the initiative now belongs to Job. He still despairs of his life and disputes with God, but the scales have tipped to the side of resolution. Praising wisdom, reflecting on past glory, objectifying his current misery, and reaffirming his innocence, Job confronts the contradictions out of which new faith can arise. Even Elihu's brash interruption and verbose speeches have edges of insight in them leading to resolution as he speaks "with the breath of the Almighty." More important, however, Elihu introduces the coming of God—the dénouement in which the mystery of creation closes Job's mouth and the mystery of grace opens his eyes.

In the revelation of God, resolution is complete. Still, the drama does not end without the epilogue in which Job is restored, not just with the doubling of wealth and family, but at the higher level of faith in which he responds as a man of grace to his friends, to his family, and even to his enemies.

To enter into the story of Job as a participant in a real-life drama is to identify with the characters, feel the intensity of the conflict, stand at the turning point, follow the path of resolution, see the revelation, and know the reconciliation. Like a peak experience in the theater, Job leaves us awed with its power, moved by its passion, stretched by its thought, and irrevocably changed by its message.

Job as Faith Development

The Book of Job may be read as a journey in faith. James Fowler, best known for his book *The Stages of Faith,* gives us a working definition of faith based upon seven assumptions, which can be paraphrased for our purpose:[6]

1. Faith is a way of moving in life.
2. Faith is based upon a comprehensive image of the conditions of existence.
3. Faith is trust in a center of value—an image of power.
4. Faith gives order, coherence, and meaning to the ultimate conditions of human existence.
5. Faith takes form and is sustained through community.
6. Faith is shaped by knowing, imagining, valuing, loving, and reasoning.
7. Faith transforms in the interaction of persons in changing events or circumstances, usually through doubt, darkness, contradiction, and despair.

Obviously, faith is not static. Compatible with other theories of human development, a person either grows, plateaus, or regresses in faith as the circumstances of age, experience, and events change. Fowler has also devised a helpful scale of faith development with six sequential stages:[7]

1. *Intuitive-projective faith* is associated with a child's faith, based upon fantasy and imagination.
2. *Mythical-literal faith* is the family faith of the early school years, which is sustained by moral rules and either/or thinking.
3. *Synthetic-conventional faith* is an adolescent faith that conforms to the tradition of the community and creates the "kind" of person of faith whom it models or rejects.
4. *Individuative-reflective faith* is the faith of the young adult who is capable of critical thinking, independent reflection, and dialectical reasoning.
5. *Conjunctive faith* is a mid-life and old-age faith that integrates self-identity with a comprehensive world view to see the order, coherence, and meaning of life in order to serve and be served.
6. *Universalizing faith* is the rare faith of a world citizen who incarnates a transcendent vision into a disciplined, active, and self-giving life.

Faith and its development, in this context, applies to the characters in the Book of Job. The Wisdom School of Israel stood between the priests and the prophets. Either by time or choice, their view of religion did not include the law under which the priests operated or the direct revelation from which the prophets spoke. Rather, their source of authority came from natural revelation and human reason. Their doctrine can be summed up in the axiom, "The fear of the Lord is the beginning of wisdom." Their piety can be understood in the practical proverbs of ethical behavior, which are intended to lead to righteousness and wisdom. Still, they offered regular sacrifices as precautions against secret sins and obvious omissions in their code of moral rectitude. For them, all of life fits into either/or categories, including the belief that the righteous are prosperous and the wicked are miserable.

Job, as characterized in the opening chapter of the book, personifies the righteous and prosperous man of wisdom. Eliphaz, Bildad, and Zophar are his peers, if not his equals. Together, they represent growth in faith to the synthetic-conventional stage. Remnants of the mythical-literal stage of faith still remain in their dependency upon moral rules and an either/or view of the world. Yet, they have advanced to the synthetic-conventional level of faith in which the traditional values of the community are espoused. At this level, they also go beyond moral rules to develop the picture of the "kind of person" who is honored as righteous and wise. Their faith at this level is strong and secure. It moves them through life with an image of an all-powerful and all-knowing God of justice who gives order, coherence, and meaning to their sheltered and comfortable existence. When Job suffers in silence, his friends can comfort him in the unspoken knowledge that he has sinned and will return to prosperity through patient submission and genuine repentance. Sad to say, their faith is not open to the challenge of change.

Each of the first five stages of faith as described by Fowler has the potential of "break-out" and transformation to the next higher stage. Circumstances or events that are outside the established system of faith are the catalysts for change. In the transition between stages, doubt, darkness, and despair are common. Yet, through the dark night of the soul, faith can leap to higher levels.

Both Job and his friends start out at the same level of faith in the Wisdom School. When the circumstances of Job's suffering do not fit their faith experience, however, they part ways. Job embarks on a tortuous journey toward higher levels of faith, while his friends suffer either arrested development or regression to a lower stage. Job's anguished cry "Why?" in chapter 3 defies the formula for faith upon which the Wisdom School depended. Then, when Job poses the contradiction between God's justice and his own innocence, the threat is more than his friends can bear.

Eliphaz, the oldest and presumably the wisest of the friends, actually retreats under threat to a mythical-intuitive faith when he invokes a personal vision as his authority to support the formula that sin is the cause of suffering. To Bildad's credit, he at least advances the argument upward to the level of synthetic-conventional faith when he appeals to the tradition of the community to defend the justice of God. Zophar, then, comes to the argument vacillating between these two levels of faith. From the mythical-intuitive level, he takes the simplistic answer of an either/or ethic; and, from the synthetic-conventional level, he translates his black-and-white world into the portrait of the "wicked man" who stands in sharp relief to the image of the "wise man."

In succeeding cycles, the three friends move back and forth, up and down between these stages of faith—defending and retreating, retreating and defending, but never daring to enter the realm of contradiction where Job suffers and where faith can be transformed. In the end, God condemns them for speaking the untruth of arrested and regressive faith.

Job, however, struggles through his suffering, not just of physical pain, social rejection, and spiritual isolation, but of faith development. At times, he stops at the adolescent level; at other times, he regresses all the way back to his child's faith based upon fantasy and imitation, but eventually he moves forward. Out of his question *why,* he confronts the new circumstances in life for which the orthodoxy of the Wisdom School has no answer. Stubborn independence and self-confident righteousness propel him into the individuative-reflective level of faith where he confronts the contradictions of paradoxical truth and dialectical reasoning. Then, at the turning point in his suffering when he makes his declaration of faith (19:25–26), Job foresees a conjunctive faith when he puts together identity and ideology, symbol and concept, to declare, "I know that my Redeemer lives, . . . That in my flesh I shall see God." Reverting, then, to the highest level of faith that he has learned from the Wisdom School, Job tries to put his world together in a hymn to wisdom (chapter 28) and in a summary of his case (chapters 29–31).

Elihu's interruption is a young man's claim to understanding faith at the conjunctive level. But he only touches the edges of higher truth before falling back into the formula of the Wisdom School, which has already failed. Only God can lead to the higher levels of faith. In His revelation of the mystery of Creation, God shows Job a world-view in which he finds his unique identity—the essence of conjunctive faith. Then, God honors Job by taking him into the mystery of grace—the only realm in which faith is universalized.

Although Job's restoration in the final chapter of the book specifies the doubling of his possessions, the most significant outcome of his reconciliation with God is his advancement in faith. Showing the qualities of universalizing faith, Job lives with paradox, loves life but holds it loosely, relates to the world community, and even has fellowship with persons at lower levels of faith. Although his struggle and growth are not ended, Job has climbed the mountain of faith and has seen the other side.

Job as Prophetic Leaning

A Christian cannot experience Job's journey of faith without seeing Christ. Ancients, such as Zeno, the Bishop of Verona, saw the parallels between Job and Jesus Christ. Both are righteous, tempted, impoverished, afflicted, rejected, faithful, and restored. In fact, I found myself identifying Job as the "Intermediate Adam." Adam, Job, and Christ—Pilate's words *Ecce Homo* apply to all of them. Adam is man in sin, Job is man in suffering, and Jesus is man in salvation. In between Adam and Christ, Job represents the acme of righteousness based upon natural revelation and human reason. In contrast with the first Adam, he does not sin, and yet he suffers the effects of sin and cries out of his innocence, "Why?"

Throughout the story, Job plummets into the depths of despair just short of hell itself and vaults upward to the heights of revelation just short of the Incarnation itself. To ride with him on this roller-coaster of spiritual emotion is to cry out for Christ at both the bottom and the top. In the dark depths of suffering, the question *why* breaks forth on the lips of humankind more plaintive than ever. Only Christ can answer the question. Through Christ's suffering, God comes to man from across the abyss that separates Him from Job. Never again can Job's charge be made that God is distant and unconcerned.

More than that, only in Christ do we see the meaning of suffering. When the righteous suffer, they are reunited with the sinner in a common experience through which they respond as persons and intercede as Christians. Finally, it is only in Christ that we see the end of suffering. Job's question *why* will remain unanswered because suffering can never be explained fully. But when Christ takes on the load of human suffering, we foresee the end in John's Revelation, "And God will wipe away every tear from their eyes" (7:17). Job reached the depths of human despair, but Christ touched the bottom of eternal hell. Because of Him, no suffering goes deeper and all suffering will end.

At the heights of Job's spiritual insight, we find ourselves leaning forward to Christ again. Who can ever forget Job's vow from excruciating pain, "Though He slay me, yet will I trust Him" (13:15). Echoes of Christ's commitment in the garden of suffering are heard as Christ vows, "Not My will, but Yours, be done" (Luke 22:24). Or listen to Job's early and repeated cry for an intercessor, which is not answered until Christ puts Himself between God's justice and our sins to plead for mercy.

Again, feel the frustration of Job's pioneering foray into the realm of miracles when he ventures to ask, "If a man dies, shall he live again?" (14:14). As quickly as he asks the question, he falls back into the futility of his limited understanding of God. Although the prophets foresaw the prospect of eternal life, only in Christ is Job's presumptuous question answered: "Whoever . . . believes in Me shall never die" (John 11:25).

Finally, enter into the prophetic movement when Job reaches up to an unsurpassed moment in Old Testament revelation and stakes his destiny on his Living Redeemer whom he shall see in person. No one comes closer to Christ's valediction, "I am the resurrection and the life. . . . He who . . . believes in Me shall never die" (John 11:25–26). Only a case-hardened skeptic can read Job without seeing the prophetic leanings that point toward Jesus Christ.

No apology is needed for a multifaceted approach to the Book of Job. To analyze only one facet of this spiritual gem is to miss the larger experience that God has for us in His Word. So, to communicate the meaning of the Book of Job, we will keep turning it around and around to the light. In the end, our goal is to see God's Truth across a broad spectrum of many colors—one or more of which will reflect in the face of our own experiences so that we with Job will be able to "see *through* suffering" and "*see* through suffering."

NOTES

1. Søren Kierkegaard, in *The Dimensions of Job,* ed. Nahum N. Glatzer (New York: Schocken Books, 1969), pp. 253ff.
2. Aeschylus, *The Prometheus Bound,* line 1080ff.
3. J. A. Froude, *The Book of Job* (London: n.p., 1854), p. 3.
4. Thomas Carlyle, quoted in Glatzer, *The Dimensions of Job,* p. ix.
5. Ibid.
6. James W. Fowler, *The Stages of Faith* (New York: Harper and Row, 1976), pp. 14–15.
7. Ibid., chap. 14.

An Outline of Job

SEEING THROUGH SUFFERING

I. Prologue: Job's Righteousness/God's Reward: 1:1–5
II. God's Risk/Job's Ruin: 1:6—2:13
    A. Satan's Challenge: 1:6–12
    B. Job Loses Fortune and Family: 1:13–22
    C. Satan's Challenge Extended: 2:1–6
    D. Job Loses Health and Home: 2:7–10
    E. Job Loses Fame and Friends: 2:11–13
III. Job's Rebellion/His Friends' Reaction: 3:1—14:22
    A. Job—A Cry for Mercy: 3:1–26
    B. Eliphaz—The Reaction of Experience: 4:1—5:27
    C. Job—A Cry for Justice: 6:1—7:21
    D. Bildad—The Reaction of Tradition: 8:1–22
    E. Job—A Cry for a Mediator: 9:1—10:22
    F. Zophar—The Reaction of Common Sense: 11:1–20
    G. Job—A Cry for God: 12:1—14:22
IV. His Friends' Rebuke/Job's Resolve: 15:1—21:34
    A. Eliphaz—The Rebuke of Experience: 15:1–35
    B. Job—The Resolution of Will: 16:1—17:16
    C. Bildad—The Rebuke of Tradition: 18:1–21
    D. Job—The Resolution of Trust: 19:1–29
    E. Zophar—The Rebuke of Common Sense: 20:1–29
    F. Job—The Resolution of History: 21:1–34
V. His Friends' Reproach/Job's Rebuttal: 22:1—27:23
    A. Eliphaz—The Reproach of Experience: 22:1–30
    B. Job—The Rebuttal of Innocence: 23:1—24:25

C. Bildad—The Reproach of Tradition: 25:1–6
D. Job—The Rebuttal of Dilemma: 26:1—27:23

VI. Job's Reflection/Review: 28:1—31:40
A. On the Source of Wisdom: 28:1–28
B. On the Glory of the Past: 29:1–25
C. On the Agony of the Present: 30:1–31
D. On the Oath of Innocence: 31:1–40

VII. Elihu's Remonstrance/Readiness: 32:1—37:24
A. On the Right to Speak: 32:1–22
B. On the Discipline of Suffering: 33:1–33
C. On the Price of Rebellion: 34:1–37
D. On the Question of Motive: 35:1–16
E. On the Purpose of Pain: 36:1–23
F. On the Goodness of God: 36:24—37:24

VIII. God's Revelation/Job's Repentance: 38:1—42:6
A. God—The Mystery of Creation: 38:1—39:30
B. Job—Submitting in Silence: 40:1–5
C. God—The Mystery of Grace: 40:6—41:34
D. Job—Seeing through Suffering: 42:1–6

IX. Epilogue: God's Redemption/Job's Restoration: 42:7–17

CHAPTER ONE

Prologue: Job's Righteousness/ God's Reward

Job 1:1–5

Two simple facts introduce our story. The locale is the land of Uz and the protagonist is a man named Job. These facts are relatively unimportant in comparison with the portrayal of Job's righteousness. He is "perfect" in meeting all of God's demands. Thus, Job is rewarded with a family that is "perfect" in numbers and with a prosperity that makes him the *"greatest of all the people of the East"* (1:3). His righteousness is further rewarded by a unified family that knows the value of celebration. Yet, Job takes no chances. He is priest as well as father for his family, making regular sacrifices for their salvation. The man is perfect, the setting is ideal, and the stage is set for challenge.

Every great civilization, nation, or institution is developed and sustained by the image of the person who exemplifies the values and aspirations of the culture. Job, the man of Uz, is the epitome of the Wisdom School of righteousness, the standard for prosperity in the East, and the patriarchal ideal of fatherhood. In simple terms, the word is *perfect*—in righteousness, riches, and relationships.

> 1 There was a man in the land of Uz, whose name was Job; and that man was blameless and upright, and one who feared God and shunned evil.
>
> 2 And seven sons and three daughters were born to him.
>
> 3 Also, his possessions were seven thousand sheep, three thousand camels, five hundred yoke of oxen, five hundred female donkeys, and a very large household, so that this man was the greatest of all the people of the East.
>
> 4 And his sons would go and feast in their houses,

each on his appointed day, and would send and invite their three sisters to eat and drink with them.

5 So it was, when the days of feasting had run their course, that Job would send and sanctify them, and he would rise early in the morning and offer burnt offerings according to the number of them all. For Job said, "It may be that my sons have sinned and cursed God in their hearts." Thus Job did regularly.

Job 1:1–5

Job the Wise Man

Some scholars see Job as a heathen who reaches the highest heights of righteousness that can be attained through natural revelation and human reason outside of the Law and the covenant of the Old Testament. This view is consistent with the view that he is the "Intermediate Adam"—cast out of the garden, suffering under sinful nature, but still seeing God through the wonders of creation and searching through human reason for the wisdom that Satan promised Eve in their encounter.

Job's character is presented as "perfect"—not in sinless perfection, because Job himself confessed that he shared in the sin of humankind, but as inner "blamelessness" and outer "straightness." In other words, his spiritual essence equaled his religious ethics. Because the Wisdom School had nothing more to go on than the rules of righteousness, Job's consistency is a commendation that escapes many Christians who claim the grace of Jesus Christ. One well-known financier has said, "On the weekend, my priorities are God, family, and business. When I arrive at the office on Monday morning, the order is reversed." Job does not suffer this contradiction. He has integrity—*being* equals *doing*.

With limited revelation, Job has to rely upon human intellect for his understanding of God. Awed by the power of God in creation, Job logically responds with fearful submission. So, we read that Job fears God—a negative response to be sure—but nevertheless the "beginning of wisdom." The moral motivation is enough to turn him away from the paths of evil. While an ethic based upon fear is at the most elementary level of moral development, one can only envy the discipline that guides Job's conduct without the motivation of love and the power of grace. Who would not want to be known as a complete and consistent person who fears God and shuns evil? According to the knowledge he has, Job lives a blameless life. As Christ challenges his enemies, "Which of you convicts Me of sin?" (John 8:46), Job challenges his friends to find the sin in his life. In both cases, the challenge goes unanswered. By discipline, Job does not sin; by nature, Christ knows no sin.

Job the Wealthy Man

"And [so] seven sons and three daughters were born to him" (1:2). The use of the conjunction *and* links Job's righteousness with his riches. Job, along with other disciples of the Wisdom School, fears God because he sees His justice at work in the order, rhythm, and meaning of natural creation. Transferring this understanding to human life, he reasons that a just God rewards the righteous with prosperity and punishes the wicked with suffering. Probably this idea of "cause-and-effect" or "cash-register justice" was first advanced as an intellectual observation, then taught as revealed truth, eventually used as a test of spirituality, and finally linked to the survival of the religious system that grew up around it.

Job's wealth in family and possessions serves as a case in point for the doctrine that God rewards righteousness with prosperity. His family and his herds were counted in "perfect" numbers, indicating the sufficiency of his wealth, confirming the totality of his blessing, and establishing Job's reputation as *"the greatest of all the people of the East"* (1:3).

Particular significance is attached to Job's standing as *"the greatest of all the people of the East."* The land of the east of Israel drew pioneers who were willing to take a risk in order to make a fortune. Some of the land was wild and inhabited by nomads who moved with their herds. Bandits preyed upon these tribes, rustling their herds, plundering their possessions, and killing their people. For the most part, however, fertile land in the east attracted ranchers and farmers, who settled near the cities and towns of the region. Job's assets in sheep, camels, oxen, and female donkeys, as well as unnumbered servants, tell us that he belongs to the "landed gentry" of the East, living in the city, with widespread holdings in ranch and farmland in the area. Caravans of camels carried his products to distant cities for sale and trade. By inference, then, Job fits the role of a self-made man who comes to greatness as an entrepreneur with impeccable ethics. For those who watched his rise to wealth, the direct connection between his righteousness and God's rewards has made him a living legend in his time.

Job the Worthy Man

Righteousness rewarded by riches does not guarantee a worthy person. Often the opposite is true. The righteous rich can develop an arrogance that causes them to forget their roots and the source of their blessings. Or righteousness can be separated from wealth in compartments of contradictory ethics. Wealth itself can stimulate an insatiable appetite which makes the love of money its own end. Perhaps this is why Jesus warns against the temptation of riches and its power to subvert entrance into the kingdom of God.

Job's relationship with his family witnesses to his ability to handle wealth without arrogance, complacency, or greed. Each of his seven sons has his own home, and, in keeping with the custom of the day, his daughters live at home with their father. Wealth does not spoil their relationship. "On appointed days"—perhaps birthdays, wedding days, harvest days, and sheep-shearing days—the family celebrates together. Job has set the tone for his family. Despite the moral regimen of his life that keeps him from sin, he does not communicate a joyless religion to his children.

Setting the tone for the family is the father's responsibility. Many years ago, *The Saturday Evening Post* featured a cover in four sections with a picture in each quarter-section. On top, at the left, a boss was shown bawling out an employee. At the top right, the employee took out his frustration by yelling at his wife at home. The bottom left showed the wife spanking their child and, in the last picture on the page, the child kicks the family dog. It all started at the office with the father!

In contrast, I remember the efforts we made to create a celebrating community at Seattle Pacific University. During a coffee orientation for new employees, I would ask, "What is your first impression of the university?" More than once, a new employee summed up the spirit of the place by saying, "It's fun to work here. There's always a reason for a party." He or she was not indicting the university as a place of perpetual partying. The work got done but we encouraged people to celebrate. Birthday cakes began to appear at coffee breaks, anniversary flowers appeared on desks, and administrators, faculty, staff, and students became a family over punch and cookies.

Bill Turner of Columbus, Georgia, is the chairman, president, and director of several corporations and foundations. A family inheritance plus effective executive leadership has made him wealthy. Yet, more than thirty-five years ago, when he married, he and his wife, Sue Marie, began sitting together in the front pew of St. Luke's United Methodist Church. Five children were born to them. One by one, they joined their parents in the pew. The children married and their spouses added to the family numbers. Then, at last count, there were thirteen grandchildren. Today, whenever the family is home, the Turners take up two or three pews on Sunday morning and by long tradition go out to eat together after church. When a parishioner was asked how she remembers Bill Turner, she answered, "You always see him with a child in his arms."

Job communicates that same love and leadership to his family. *Neither righteousness nor riches has torn his family apart.* Brothers invite brothers to each other's homes and, as an exception to the expectations of the day, they in turn invite their sisters to join them for the feast. Once together, in witness to the healthy religion of their father, they celebrate without sin.

Many modern youth from wealthy families fall victim to the dread disease "affluenza." Rather than finding happiness in affluence, they suffer the symptoms of being lost, lonely, and loveless. Often they resort to hard and expensive drugs, giving credence to the statement "Cocaine is God's way of telling you that you have too much money." When asked to explain their problems, children of the rich and famous wistfully recall the absence of their parents from the home and the attempt to fill in the vacuum of love with money and things.

Job gives his children more than parental love; he serves as their spiritual priest. In the ancient land of the East, the Israelites had no priest. The responsibility fell upon the father of the family. Job takes the initiative for this role and follows it faithfully. Even though his children do not sin overtly in their celebrations, Job calls them together regularly and offers burnt sacrifices for them if perchance they have sinned and cursed God *"in their hearts."* Job, the father-priest, serves as intercessor and mediator for the spiritual life of his children.

Fathers today have turned the priestly function of the spiritual responsibility over to the established church and the professional pastor. Something of high value is lost. Spiritual life in our homes does not match the spiritual expectations that we have for our children. We expect the church, Sunday school, youth camp, Bible club, and Christian school to do it for us. Yet, one of my most precious childhood memories is of our family devotions at home. Although I resented the intrusion into my playtime and often fell asleep on my knees, I cannot forget my father calling us to prayer, reading the Scripture, and being the first to pray. Later, when I responded to the public invitation to accept Christ, my father came from the opposite side of the church to meet me at the altar to intercede on my behalf. Job's children would share the same memory. They knew their father as their religious mentor and spiritual mediator.

How ideal! In the eyes of man, Job is "perfect" in righteousness and, therefore, rewarded by God with "perfect" riches and a "perfect" family. In the eyes of God, Job is more. In fulfillment of his righteousness, he is wise; in his gratitude for riches, he is wealthy; in his love for his family, he is worthy. Job has been introduced to us as God's best representative of His purpose for man on earth.

CHAPTER TWO

God's Risk/Job's Ruin

Job 1:6—2:13

Surprise is introduced early in the Book of Job when the ideal setting of earth is contrasted with conflict in heaven. God is presiding over heaven's council when Satan appears from his restless wandering on earth. God commends the goodness of His servant Job, only to provoke the cynicism of Satan. Contending that Job's piety is only for protection of his prosperity, Satan dares God to put Job in his power. With confidence in Job, God accepts the challenge but defines the limits. Satan is released to test Job's virtue.

Natural calamity follows. Job loses his wealth and his family. Yet, in proof that his faith is not dependent upon his fortune, he praises God.

Satan persists. Returning to the presence of God, he throws down the gauntlet once again. God is challenged to let Satan work his destructive power on Job's body. Permission is given but with the limitation that Satan cannot take Job's life. Plagued by boils, Job is urged by his wife to curse God and die. Despite the loss of physical health and support at home, Job does not sin.

Satan's Challenge

> 6 Now there was a day when the sons of God came to present themselves before the Lord, and Satan also came among them.
>
> 7 And the Lord said to Satan, "From where do you come?" So Satan answered the Lord and said, "From going to and fro on the earth, and from walking back and forth on it."

> 8 Then the LORD said to Satan, "Have you considered My servant Job, that there is none like him on the earth, a blameless and upright man, one who fears God and shuns evil?"
> 9 So Satan answered the LORD and said, "Does Job fear God for nothing?
> 10 "Have You not made a hedge around him, around his household, and around all that he has on every side? You have blessed the work of his hands, and his possessions have increased in the land.
> 11 "But now, stretch out Your hand and touch all that he has, and he will surely curse You to Your face!"
> 12 And the LORD said to Satan, "Behold, all that he has is in your power; only do not lay a hand on his person." So Satan went out from the presence of the LORD.
>
> *Job 1:6–12*

With ironic twist, the scene shifts from Job's ideal setting on earth to conflict between God and Satan in heaven. This portion of the story is a stumbling block to scholars and lay readers alike. What is Satan doing in heaven? Does God take bets on His people? Is He a party to human suffering? The questions are valid but any one of them can become as complex as the one that consumed theologians in the Middle Ages, How many angels can dance on the head of a pin? The best approach is to get on with the purpose of the story. Single and final answers may not come, but, at least, sticky questions may be understood in context.

Great literature is known for its artistry in character development. Job is no exception. While the author is giving us the dramatic details of the inciting moment that leads to Job's suffering, he is also showing us in depth the characters of God, Satan, and Job.

The Character of God

God is introduced to us as sovereign. In a glimpse of heaven, He is presiding over a council of the *"sons of God"* or "host of the universe" over which He alone reigns as Lord. Even Satan, the rebellious son, is one of His creations. There is no dualism.

Further, God governs the universe. In heaven's council, the agenda includes a "reporting" session in which the *"sons of God"* give an accounting for their delegated roles and designated responsibilities as "watchers" (Deut. 4:13, 17, 23) and "protectors" (Zech. 1:10ff., 6:5ff.) on earth. Deists, who contend that God created the universe, wound it like a watch, and left it running, are refuted. God pays infinite attention to His universe and guarantees its moral order. Later, this fact will become the subject of a bitter debate between Job and his friends. For now, it is a "given."

Even though God is sovereign as creator and governor of the universe, He is open to challenge. His creatures are endowed with the freedom to raise questions and even rebel. God is not threatened, then, when Satan appears among the *"sons of God"* at heaven's council. Rather than banishing him from heaven, God calls him to accountability: *"From where do you come?"* (1:7). Perhaps, there is a wistful note in God's voice as He welcomes home a prodigal "son." Satan's answer lets Him know that he comes as a restless and rebellious, not repentant, spirit. Still not threatened by the intruder, God shows another trait of His character when He asks Satan if he has noticed Job, whom God honors as His servant. He commends Job for the same qualities with which he was introduced to us in the opening verse: *"A blameless and upright man, one who fears God and shuns evil"* (v. 8). The message is clear. God rejoices in His creation. He has not given up on the world and will not, even though He may have only one person who exemplifies His purpose on earth. While the God of Job is sovereign over all the earth, He is not so distant that He does not govern, not so powerful that He does not allow freedom, and not so independent that He does not care. To the contrary, He rejoices in a man like Job.

The Character of Satan

God's goodness accentuates the evil traits of Satan. Without an invitation, he intrudes upon heaven's council meeting. Like the student rebel who appeared in my class in the late 1960s, Satan comes to disrupt, not to learn. Yet, by his presence before God, Satan admits his ultimate subjection to the "Lord of hosts."

In answer to God's inquiry about his whereabouts, Satan tips his hand on the nature of his character. *"From going to and fro on the earth, and walking back and forth on it"* (v. 7) is the confession of a vagabond spirit, pacing the earth with the frustration of a caged lion and preying upon unsuspecting victims "seeking whom he may devour" (1 Pet. 5:8). In stark contrast to the orderly and meaningful nature of God at work in heaven's council, Satan epitomizes the ultimate of evil, when alienation, aimlessness, and anxiety—the essence of hell—obsess the soul.

Cynicism is a natural result of Satan's inner character. In contrast to God's enthusiastic recommendation of Job, Satan scoffs, *"Does Job fear God for nothing?"* (1:9). Satan knows nothing about the intrinsic value of righteousness that springs from a good heart or genuine love. To him, every human act can be explained by a selfish motive. As an ancient exponent of what is now called the "equity theory," Satan puts Job's righteousness on one side of the scale and balances it out with God's prosperity on the other side. Take away the prosperity, Satan contends, and Job's righteousness will not only disappear but turn into bitterness. Both God's character and Job's character are called into question. Satan attacks Job's righteousness as false and God's integrity as flawed. By inference, God needs Job to love Him and so protects and prospers him to assure his love. If so, God is not sovereign.

Insolence adds poison to Satan's challenge of God. He sneers, *"But now, stretch out Your hand and touch all that he has, and he will surely curse You to Your face!"* (v. 11). The pronouns *your* and *you* that Satan chooses are words that are used to address an equal at best and an inferior at worst. Like a rebellious son who attacks a faithful father, Satan has no respect for authority or recognition of love.

God, however, has full confidence in His servant Job. He accepts Satan's challenge, not on a whimsical dare or because His character is threatened, but because He is once again willing to give man the freedom to choose good or evil and thereby love or reject Him. In Job, mankind will walk with Adam from the Garden of Eden toward the Garden of Gethsemane where Christ Himself will suffer. In each case, God's purpose is redemption.

A note of high truth rings through God's response to Satan's cynical challenge. God does not accept Satan's terms that He stretch His hand over Job and *"touch all that he has."* God does not do evil. Rather,

He draws the boundaries within which evil may work in the world. To some, this is a contradiction because it implies that God could eliminate evil if He chose. Does this make Him a partner in sin? Again, we are forced back to the fundamental fact that God has chosen to give man his freedom with the risk of a decision that brings sin and its consequences upon His creatures and His creation. To preserve that choice, God permits evil within limits, until the great and terrible day of judgment when the earth will forever be freed from its suffering. This is good news, even for those of us who live with the reality of sin and its consequences.

Not until I wrote the Communicator's Commentary on Mark did I fully understand the extent of Christ's mental suffering in the garden and His physical suffering on the cross. In the garden when "His sweat became like great drops of blood" (Luke 22:44), Christ realized for the first time that all the dread forces of evil would be unleashed upon Him. Then on the cross, when He called, "My God, My God, why have You forsaken Me?" (Mark 15:34), Christ entered hell where God lifts all the limits on evil. We know nothing about such suffering. Even for those who experience "hell on earth," their suffering is only the intimation of evil. God is still drawing those limits, so that each new day brings evidence of His "hedge" against evil in our lives as well as the possibility of suffering. God puts all that Job has in Satan's hands, but with the caveat that he cannot touch the person.

Job Loses Fortune and Family

13 Now there was a day when his sons and daughters were eating and drinking wine in their oldest brother's house;

14 and a messenger came to Job and said, "The oxen were plowing and the donkeys feeding beside them,

15 "when the Sabeans raided them and took them away—indeed they have killed the servants with the edge of the sword; and I alone have escaped to tell you!"

16 While he was still speaking, another also came

and said, "The fire of God fell from heaven and burned up the sheep and the servants, and consumed them; and I alone have escaped to tell you!"

17 While he was still speaking, another also came and said, "The Chaldeans formed three bands, raided the camels and took them away, yes, and killed the servants with the edge of the sword; and I alone have escaped to tell you!"

18 While he was still speaking, another also came and said, "Your sons and daughters were eating and drinking wine in their oldest brother's house,

19 "and suddenly a great wind came from across the wilderness and struck the four corners of the house, and it fell on the young people, and they are dead; and I alone have escaped to tell you!"

20 Then Job arose, tore his robe, and shaved his head; and he fell to the ground and worshiped.

21 And he said:

"Naked I came from my mother's womb,
And naked shall I return there.
The LORD gave, and the LORD has taken away;
Blessed be the name of the LORD."

22 In all this Job did not sin nor charge God with wrong.

Job 1:13–22

From the calamities that befall Job, we learn something about the sources of evil. Nature, which groans under the weight of sin and operates within the impartial laws of chance, can bring tragedy to us in the form of accidents. Such is the case for Job when he loses his sheep to lightning and his children to a tornado. With God's protective hedge against accidents lifted, Satan can direct the hazards of the region under the pretext of letting nature take its course. Evil men give Satan his other weapons. This time using the hatred and violence in the wild land of the East, he brings down marauding bands of Sabeans and Chaldeans to destroy Job's oxen, asses, and camels, as well as his servants. Noteworthy is the fact that Satan has no source of evil within Job with which to act. More often than not, our suffering is self-inflicted by our own sin. If Satan had found sin in Job as a weapon to be used, there would have been no Book of Job.

The Character of Job

Everything new that we learn about Job in this section is consistent with the prologue, which identified him as "blameless and upright, and one who feared God and shunned evil." Now we see that quality of character in the crucible of calamity. Attention is usually drawn to Job's worshipful recognition that all of human existence—calm and calamity, prosperity and poverty, life and death—are within God's providence and order:

> *Naked I came from my mother's womb,*
> *And naked shall I return there.*
> *The LORD gave, and the LORD has taken away;*
> *Blessed be the name of the LORD* (v. 21).

These are the words with which we associate graveside services. In the final commitment of the body to the earth, Job gives us a ritual of resignation that needs to be balanced by the promise of the resurrection: "I AM He who lives, and was dead, and behold, I am alive forevermore. Amen. And I have the keys of Hades and of Death" (Rev. 1:18).

To isolate Job's words for a funeral is to miss the spirit with which he spoke. On a day of calamity when Satan has wiped out all that he has on earth, beginning with his prized oxen and ending with his beloved children, Job *"worshiped"* God and thanked Him for his blessings. Tragedy reveals the inner spirit of the man.

Somerset Maugham, the novelist, kept a cracked earthen cup on the mantel in his plush London home. When asked about this ugly, broken centerpiece among all his exquisite *objets d'art,* Maugham explained, "During the First World War, on a troop ship crossing the ocean, our rations of water were reduced to just one cup a day. I drank my ration of water from that cup and keep it on the mantel as a reminder that I can never take my blessings for granted."

Job worships in the same spirit. In his prosperity, he does not forget to praise God for his blessings. Thus, when the temporary is taken away, the permanent still remains. Someone has said that we are more prone to sin in prosperity than in poverty. If so, Job stands taller than ever as a "perfect" man. In prosperity, he cultivated a spirit of praise that revealed the true nature of the inner man in calamity. Satan meets his match. Sure that Job would curse God, he must have gone into devilish rage when he heard the words of praise.

SATAN'S CHALLENGE EXTENDED

> 1 Again there was a day when the sons of God came to present themselves before the LORD, and Satan came also among them to present himself before the LORD.
>
> 2 And the LORD said to Satan, "From where do you come?" So Satan answered the LORD and said, "From going to and fro on the earth, and from walking back and forth on it."
>
> 3 Then the LORD said to Satan, "Have you considered My servant Job, that there is none like him on the earth, a blameless and upright man, one who fears God and shuns evil? And still he holds fast to his integrity, although you incited Me against him, to destroy him without cause."
>
> 4 So Satan answered the LORD and said, "Skin for skin! Yes, all that a man has he will give for his life.
>
> 5 "But stretch out Your hand now, and touch his bone and his flesh, and he will surely curse You to Your face!"
>
> 6 And the LORD said to Satan, "Behold, he is in your hand, but spare his life."
>
> *Job 2:1–6*

In the second round of controversy between God and Satan, the sequence is the same—heaven's council, Satan's appearance, God's inquiry, Satan's challenge, God's acceptance, Job's calamity and response. Now, however, Satan attacks Job's health and a new person comes onto the scene—Job's wife. We get a glimpse at her character as well as another in-depth look at the characters of Satan, God, and Job.

Satan's Persistence

If Satan has one virtue, it is persistence. Intruding into a meeting of heaven's council once again, he acts as if nothing has happened. When God commends his servant Job for holding his integrity under test, Satan spits through his teeth, *"Skin for skin"* (2:4). Rather than admitting failure, he casts the blame on God for refusing to let him put Job to the acid test—an attack upon his person. *"Skin for skin"* is a proverb of the east that has been variously interpreted. Most likely it means that Job has been tested at only the superficial level and, therefore, has given a superficial response. But if God releases Satan to attack the man in bone and flesh, he is sure that Job will curse God. Self-centeredness dominates all of Satan's thinking. He cannot believe that the loss of possessions and family really matters if the person himself is untouched. Therefore, he uses self-centeredness, the only motive he knows, as an excuse for his failure and as a way to advance his next challenge to God.

Satan's tactic is to probe and probe until he finds the fatal flaw in a person's character that leads to sin. In Jesus' temptation, Satan comes at Him three times, probing for the point of vulnerability. The natural drives of body, mind, and spirit—passion, pride, and power—were all projected from legitimate to sinful desires. Of course, Satan personalized his probe to appeal to Jesus' specific needs at that time and place. So it is always. Most people are selectively strong or weak in character.

The conundrum of the Mafia godfather illustrates the point. In business, the godfather engages in crimes that range from mayhem to murder, but with his family he holds a strict code of conservative ethics. There is a bit of the godfather in each of us. We would never steal a railroad but we might cheat on our income tax. We would never get drunk but we might become hooked on drugs. In Harold Begbie's *Twice-Born Men,* he tells the story of "O.B.D."—"Old Born Drunk"—who comes to Christ from the gutters of London through the ministry of the Salvation Army. He gets his name "O.B.D." because no one ever remembers seeing him sober. After his conversion he never drinks again. When someone asks if alcohol remained as his "thorn in the flesh," he answers that he had no desire to drink but the miracle was that "God had to deliver him from his pipe."[1] The Word warns us, "Let Him who thinks he stands take heed lest he fall" (1 Cor. 10:12). Satan has nothing else to do but wander the earth, preying upon our souls and probing for our weaknesses.

God's Pain

One short phrase in God's response to Satan's first attack on Job takes us deeper into His character. He says, *"You incited Me against him, to destroy him without cause"* (2:3). Even though God refuses to be the agent whose hand touches Job, He takes full and personal responsibility for the tragedies that befell him. Of course, this opens up the imponderable question, Does God's permission equal responsibility? Fathers will understand the problem. My sixteen-year-old son has just earned his driver's license. Until he gets more experience on the road, limits are drawn around the obvious hazards, such as Saturday night driving on a certain road that has the highest alcohol-related accident rate in the state. Sooner or later, the limits will be lifted, even though the danger remains. If he should be the innocent victim of an accident on that road, how would I respond? Like God, would I not speak with pain, "I am responsible and all for naught"? All of the parts of this argument may not hold together theologically, but, as a father, I find it makes sense of God's response. While His permissive will balances intention against His personal responsibility, there is no paradox in the nature of His love.

Job Loses Health and Home

7 So Satan went out from the presence of the LORD, and struck Job with painful boils from the sole of his foot to the crown of his head.

8 And he took for himself a potsherd with which to scrape himself while he sat in the midst of the ashes.

9 Then his wife said to him, "Do you still hold fast to your integrity? Curse God and die!"

10 But he said to her, "You speak as one of the foolish women speaks. Shall we indeed accept good from God, and shall we not accept adversity?" In all this Job did not sin with his lips.

Job 2:7–10

God has unswerving confidence in Job's integrity. Therefore, despite the pain that he suffers and will suffer, God puts Job in Satan's hands for the crucial test. Still the limits are drawn. Satan cannot take Job's life, but, knowing his nature, we can expect he will invoke the worst of human suffering short of death upon his victim.

Job's Patience

Job's disease has been diagnosed as boils or leprosy, but most likely, it is elephantiasis. Throughout the book, the symptoms are described: itching and open sores (2:7–8); feelings of terror (6:4); maggots bred in ulcers (7:5); sleeplessness (7:4); nightmares (7:14); depression (7:16); fetid breath (19:17); failing vision (16:16); rotting teeth (19:20); weeping (16:16); emaciation (19:20); fever (30:30); corrosion of bones (30:17); and then blackening and falling off of skin (30:30).

In total, these symptoms create a physical monster, not unlike the pitiful creature in the book and film, *Elephant Man.* The message is powerful. Because we continue to indulge in the sin of judging a person by appearance, we dehumanize a victim of elephantiasis by exploitation and ostracism. For the victim, however, the pain is so great that there is no alternative to suffering in silence. Everyone connects the name Job with the virtue of patience. In his Epistle, James commends Job as a man of patience (James 5:11). In truth, Job will lose patience with his suffering, break his silence with the question *why* and provoke his friends to rage. Only in the first stages of his illness does he submit in silence to the shock, pain, and disgrace that comes with a fall from the picture of health in the prime of life down, down, down to the caricature of an elephant man.

At the risk of endless repetition, it should be noted that Satan still has no avenue of attack in the character of Job. His point of entry is physical. Most likely, Job carried in his body the weakness for the disease elephantiasis. A healthy immune system protected him, but, if the immune system broke down, he immediately became a candidate for the disease.

During my clinical training in counseling at a university hospital, we were told the story about medical interns who worked in the TB ward during the war. A severe shortage of help required that they work to exhaustion on double and triple shifts. Soon, one after another of the interns contracted tuberculosis themselves. Our lecturer explained that most of us carry TB germs in our lungs, but they are encased in a calcium sac that prevents them from breaking out. Exhaustion can break down the calcium, release the germs, and make a person vulnerable to the disease.

Satan might have used the same technique of attack. When God lifts the protective hedge around Job's life, Satan strikes at his weakness. Disease and pain take over, but the psychological, social, and spiritual suffering are worse than death itself.

A Wife's Pride

Job's wife plays only a cameo role in the story of her husband's suffering. She has been maligned through the ages as a second Eve who tempts her husband to curse God and die. St. Augustine labeled her as *diaboli adjutrix*—"devil's advocate." St. Chrysostom called her "the devil's best scourge," and Calvin condemned her as *organum satani*—the embodiment of Satan. She deserves a fairer judgment.

Long ago, an Ann Landers column taught me the lesson of identification between a husband and wife. A reader wrote in to ask Ann if a new Ph.D. should be addressed as "doctor" in public. Wisdom filled Ann's short answer, "Ask his wife." In other words, her ego was his ego. In a day when husbands and wives pursue independent careers, the identification may not be quite as strong. Still, even when couples are separated and fighting, caution warns against criticizing one in front of the other.

Job's wife suffers with her husband. To see her dream decimated by disease and her hero ridiculed by rowdies is more than she can take. Her reaction witnesses to the intensity of Job's near-fatal suffering. Who has not sat at the bedside of a loved one who has endured intense suffering and not prayed for the mercy of death? Job's wife speaks the words that we have felt. Cursing God means a sure, but merciful, death. Of course, Job's wife gives the wrong advice and inadvertently serves Satan's purpose. With her husband, we may call her foolish, but not evil.

Job Loses Fame and Friends

Job is now the repulsive symbol of rejection by God and man. On an ash heap outside the city, he represents the evidence of the prevailing belief that suffering is caused by sin. Three friends—Eliphaz, Bildad, and Zophar—who are wise men of the East, come to comfort him. The sight of Job, however, throws them into mourning. Seven days of silence speak their belief—Job is as good as dead.

> 11 Now when Job's three friends heard of all this adversity that had come upon him, each one came from his own place—Eliphaz the Temanite, Bildad the Shuhite, and Zophar the Naamathite. For they had made an appointment together to come and mourn with him, and to comfort him.
>
> 12 And when they raised their eyes from afar, and did not recognize him, they lifted their voices and wept; and each one tore his robe and sprinkled dust on his head toward heaven.
>
> 13 So they sat down with him on the ground seven days and seven nights, and no one spoke a word to him, for they saw that his grief was very great.
>
> *Job 2:11–13*

Job is on the ash heap. Each ancient town in the Middle East had a waste site outside the protective gates where garbage and dung were dumped. Periodically, the rotting, smelly mess was burned as a primitive method of sanitation. The fire left ashes which hardened into a mound that rose higher with each burning. On top of the ash heap sat lepers and other victims of contagious or unexplained diseases in medical quarantine and social isolation. For Job, the ash heap represents ultimate humiliation. He who has enjoyed the reputation as the "greatest of all the people of the East" now sits highest on the ash heap—his cross—just beyond the spit of the wretches who ridicule him. Job is all alone—without children, wife, or friends.

Three distant friends hear of his plight. Eliphaz, Bildad, and Zophar, from three different cities, covenant together to meet and comfort their friend Job. They too have a reputation for wisdom and wealth, even though they do not match Job for greatness. Some scholars also make them kings who prefigure the three kings who came from the East to worship the baby Jesus. In any case, they are loyal friends who come with good intentions to comfort a brother in need.

The Shock of Recognition

News of Job's perch on the ash heap must have spread far and wide. From a distance, his three visitors peer at him but see nothing that resembles the Job they know. Coming closer, then, they are so shocked at Job's appearance that they tear their royal robes, throw dust into the air in distress, and fall to the ground in mourning. They had not expected the sight of "walking death" that greets them. No words pass between the friends. Job's sunken eyes, blackened skin, running sores, and swollen lips speak with silent horror.

Job's friends come to the same conclusion as Job's wife—the man might as well be dead. Furthermore, their doctrine of "cash-register justice" can only lead them to the conclusion that Job's terrible suffering is punishment for some terrible sin. As with a terminally ill patient for whom the doctor leaves the order, "Make him as comfortable as possible," Job's friends conclude that the compassion of mourning is the greatest comfort they can give. To their credit, they do not turn away from their repulsive friend as others have done.

The Sacrament of Silence

For seven days, Job's friends sit with him in the traditional ritual of mourning. If death is imminent, no one speaks until the mourner speaks. William E. Hulme, in his book *Dialogue in Despair,* sees a deeper value in the silence.[2] As a counselor who deals with grief, Hulme commends Job's friends for not speaking when words are useless. Each of us knows the awkward moment when we enter the room of a person who is fighting for life. "How are you?" is the most inappropriate greeting and yet this is what we invariably say. The unspoken communication of eyes that meet and hands that touch may well convey the compassion that we want to share and the communication that our friend needs. Hulme calls such a moment "the sacrament of silence," when kindred spirits meet and share the meaning of life in the midst of death.

My father-in-law was a preacher who loved people. He had a gift for words in and out of the pulpit. Even after his retirement, he ministered to people with his across-the-street greetings and side-walk conversation. Anyone who asked, "How are you?" got the cheery answer, "Finer than a frog's hair." One day, he went on an automobile trip with a college president who was known for his deep thoughts and limited words. As they rode along, my father-in-law tried in vain to engage his friend in conversation. Frustrated, he lapsed into a silence that lasted many miles. Finally, he could stand it no more. Turning to his driver, he said, "Leroy, do you know that we have ridden together now for almost fifty miles without a word?" Not turning his head or breaking his train of thought, the college president answered, "Good friends don't need to talk." Obviously, they rode all the rest of the way in silence.

Job's friends did not have to talk either. Any words would have been wrong. In the long nights of terror, Job knew that they were there. During the burning days of insufferable pain, Job sensed their compassion. Today, "Job's comforters" is a disparaging term. We forget that until Job spoke his anguish, they were truly his comforters.

NOTES

1. Harold Begbie, *Twice-Born Men* (New York: Grosset & Dunlap, 1909), p. 107.

2. William E. Hulme, *Dialogue in Despair* (Nashville: Abingdon, 1968).

CHAPTER THREE

Job's Rebellion/His Friends' Reaction

Job 3:1—14:22

Out of the depth of his suffering, Job cries out in anguish. Cursing his birth, he attests that life has lost its meaning and God has forsaken him. With words that border on blasphemy, Job spits out his bitterness, shouts his doubts, and sobs his wish for death.

Job—A Cry for Mercy

1 After this Job opened his mouth and cursed the
day of his birth.
2 And Job spoke, and said:
3 "May the day perish on which I was born,
And the night in which it was said,
'A male child is conceived.'
4 May that day be darkness;
May God above not seek it,
Nor the light shine upon it.
5 May darkness and the shadow of death claim
it;
May a cloud settle on it;
May the blackness of the day terrify it.
6 As for that night, may darkness seize it;
May it not rejoice among the days of the year,
May it not come into the number of the months.
7 Oh, may that night be barren!
May no joyful shout come into it!
8 May those curse it who curse the day,
Those who are ready to arouse Leviathan.

9 May the stars of its morning be dark;
May it look for light, but have none,
And not see the dawning of the day;
10 Because it did not shut up the doors of my mother's womb,
Nor hide sorrow from my eyes.
11 "Why did I not die at birth?
Why did I not perish when I came from the womb?
12 Why did the knees receive me?
Or why the breasts, that I should nurse?
13 For now I would have lain still and been quiet,
I would have been asleep;
Then I would have been at rest
14 With kings and counselors of the earth,
Who built ruins for themselves,
15 Or with princes who had gold,
Who filled their houses with silver;
16 Or why was I not hidden like a stillborn child,
Like infants who never saw light?
17 There the wicked cease from troubling,
And there the weary are at rest.
18 There the prisoners rest together;
They do not hear the voice of the oppressor.
19 The small and great are there,
And the servant is free from his master.
20 "Why is light given to him who is in misery,
And life to the bitter of soul,
21 Who long for death, but it does not come,
And search for it more than hidden treasures;
22 Who rejoice exceedingly,
And are glad when they can find the grave?
23 Why is light given to a man whose way is hidden,
And whom God has hedged in?
24 For my sighing comes before I eat,
And my groanings pour out like water.
25 For the thing I greatly feared has come upon me,
And what I dreaded has happened to me.
26 I am not at ease, nor am I quiet;
I have no rest, for trouble comes."

Job 3:1–26

Who knows what went through Job's mind during his weeks, if not months, of suffering on the ash heap? Job must have tried to praise God for the privilege of suffering, to submit to His sovereign will, and even to exercise the stoicism of a resolute will in which he tries to "tough it out." Nothing makes a difference. Then the arrival of his friends brings him new hope. They represent religious wisdom and spiritual maturity. Surely they will answer Job's doubt and feel his despair. For seven days, they sit with him and share his suffering in sacramental silence. Job respects their silence, but he is not prepared for the surprise at the end of seven days. One commentator envisions them getting up without a word and walking away. For the first time, Job realizes that they came not to help him but to bury him! This is when all the doubt and despair that have been building up in Job explode in a torrent of anguish and anger.

The Curse of *May*

Job's outburst is rational only to the extent that it is guided by two words—*may* and *why*. *May* is a curse spit through gritted teeth as Job pounds the ground:

> ***May*** *the day perish on which I was born,*
>
> . . . .
>
> *Oh,* ***may*** *that night be barren!*
>
> . . . .
>
> ***May*** *the stars of its morning be dark;*
> ***May*** *it look for light, but have none*
> (vv. 3–9, emphasis mine).

Job is venting his spleen. Deep within him, bitterness has been building. Pain has taken its toll. Patience has worn thin. Philosophy has failed. Only one conclusion remains: he is the innocent victim of unwarranted suffering. Only one emotion remains: he shouts his anger against the unjust universe that brought him into being. Curses fly against the night of his conception, the day of his birth, the dawn of his existence. C. S. Lewis confesses, in *A Grief Observed,* that his prayer is more a "yell" than a thought after he and his dying wife had come to the end of all their hopes and found them false.[1]

There is a time for anger even when it is not particularly righteous. In his book *Creative Suffering,* Paul Tournier describes anger as a necessary response in the healthy person. He repeats the story of a research student who visited an old man whose happy life had been crushed in a series of tragic blows. A language barrier stopped him from expressing his grief and despair until the research student heard his story and responded by pounding his fist on the table and shouting, "It's not fair! It's not fair!" The old man got the message. For the first time, his sad eyes lighted up because someone understood his plight.[2]

Anger is close to acceptance, according to Tournier. Although contrary in theory, in practice, he says, "They hold hands like dancers in a folk dance."[3] One goes with the other.

At the start of my career, I served as a college dean of men. My most difficult task was to dismiss an unrepentant student for flagrant violations of the community code. I surprised Larry one day by calling him into my office and presenting incontrovertible evidence of a violation that meant automatic dismissal. He flew into a rage that sprayed the office air with curses and threats. Shaking his fist and spinning on his heel, he headed for the door. Just as he started to open it, I asked with unusual calm, "You can leave, Larry, but where will you go?" The words stopped him like a hollow-point slug. Anger drained from his face as he turned and looked back at me. His defiant shoulders slumped and he burst into tears, sobbing over and over again, "I don't know. I don't know." An hour later, he left the office a redeemed man. At the end of the year, his English professor showed me a copy of the daily journal that Larry had turned in. On the day of our meeting, he wrote, "When I left the dean's office, every tree looked different for miles around." For Larry, anger and acceptance danced as partners.

Job's curses come out of deeper despair than we have known. His prolonged suffering on the borders of death intensifies because of depression and loneliness. More than that, he has no guilt to moderate the pain. Under no circumstances will he curse God. So, righteous anger, at once the hottest and the coldest of human emotions, consumes him. Directly, he curses the day of his birth; indirectly, he protests injustice; and, inferentially, he accuses God, his last friend.

The Protest of *Why*

Once his rage is vented with his curses, Job gains enough perspective to raise the protest:

> ***Why*** *did I not die at birth?*
>
> . . . .
>
> *Or* ***why*** *was I not hidden like a stillborn child,*
>
> . . . .
>
> ***Why*** *is light given to him who is in misery,*
>
> . . . .
>
> ***Why*** *is light given to a man . . . whom God has hedged in?*
> (vv. 11–23, emphasis mine).

Why is the human question—universal as well as individual, essential as well as existential. Sometimes it is the question of curiosity, as when a child or a scientist asks *why.* Sometimes it is the question of doubt, as when Satan tempts Eve or the cynic refuses to believe. At other times, as in Job's case, *why* is a cry of despair arising from an unexplainable contradiction.

Before his affliction, Job embraced with utter confidence a worldview that centered in an all-powerful and all-knowing God who governed justly in the affairs of men with the same order, coherence, and meaning with which He ruled the universe. Out of this belief came the logical conclusion: God rewards the righteous with prosperity and punishes the wicked with suffering. Yet, Job's faith went beyond this formula. In the joy of righteousness, he and God became friends. God does not hesitate to recommend Job as "My servant," and Job speaks praise as naturally as breathing, "Blessed be the name of the LORD" (1:21).

Is there any wonder that Job cries, "Why?" All the ground on which he has stood gave way under his feet and the fulcrum of faith with which he had moved the world broke in his hands. Worst of all, the only friend on whom he could really count appeared to abandon him. *Why* is far more than an intellectual inquiry about the nature of God and His ways in the world. It is a protest against injustice and a plea for help. Job is caught between two worlds, in Matthew Arnold's phrase, "one dead, the other powerless to be born." The contradiction between his innocence and his suffering is more than he can bear. Job needs a friend to help him from the pit of total despair to the heights of new faith. Otherwise, the sign of his suffering will continue to read, "No Exit."

> *I am not at ease, nor am I quiet;*
> *I have no rest, for trouble comes* (3:26).

Kierkegaard senses the depth of Job's despair when he speaks of the suffering that makes you want to die but you cannot. Job must realize that the curse of *may* and the question of *why* are resolved by living, not by dying.

Eliphaz—The Reaction of Experience

Job's cry of anguish prompts Eliphaz to reply. His words are gentle, but filled with subtle inferences that Job's suffering is caused by sin. In fact, he begins by reminding Job that he himself invoked this principle when counseling others in distress. To support his position, Eliphaz tells of a private vision of God's holiness and man's sinfulness. Suffering, therefore, is justified because the root of suffering is in man himself. Yet there is hope. God uses suffering as a correcting and purifying process. If Job will submit to suffering and trust God with patience, his repentance will return him to prosperity.

4:1 Then Eliphaz the Temanite answered and said:
2 "If one attempts a word with you, will you
become weary?
But who can withhold himself from speaking?
3 Surely you have instructed many,
And you have strengthened weak hands.
4 Your words have upheld him who was
stumbling,
And you have strengthened the feeble knees;
5 But now it comes upon you, and you are weary;
It touches you, and you are troubled.
6 Is not your reverence your confidence?
And the integrity of your ways your hope?
7 "Remember now, who ever perished being
innocent?
Or where were the upright ever cut off?
8 Even as I have seen,
those who plow iniquity
And sow trouble reap the same.
9 By the blast of God they perish,
And by the breath of His anger they are
consumed.
10 The roaring of the lion,

The voice of the fierce lion,
And the teeth of the young lions are broken.
11 The old lion perishes for lack of prey,
And the cubs of the lioness are scattered.
12 "Now a word was secretly brought to me,
And my ear received a whisper of it.
13 In disquieting thoughts from the visions of the night,
When deep sleep falls on men,
14 Fear came upon me, and trembling,
Which made all my bones shake.
15 Then a spirit passed before my face;
The hair on my body stood up.
16 It stood still,
But I could not discern its appearance.
A form was before my eyes;
There was silence;
Then I heard a voice saying:
17 'Can a mortal be more righteous than God?
Can a man be more pure than his Maker?
18 If He puts no trust in His servants,
If He charges His angels with error,
19 How much more those who dwell in houses of clay,
Whose foundation is in the dust,
Who are crushed before a moth?
20 They are broken in pieces from morning till evening;
They perish forever, with no one regarding.
21 Does not their own excellence go away?
They die, even without wisdom.'
5:1 "Call out now;
Is there anyone who will answer you?
And to which of the holy ones will you turn?
2 For wrath kills a foolish man,
And envy slays a simple one.
3 I have seen the foolish taking root,
But suddenly I cursed his dwelling place.
4 His sons are far from safety,
They are crushed in the gate,
And there is no deliverer.
5 Because the hungry eat up his harvest,

Taking it even from the thorns,
And a snare snatches their substance.
6 For affliction does not come from the dust,
Nor does trouble spring from the ground;
7 Yet man is born to trouble,
As the sparks fly upward.
8 "But as for me, I would seek God,
And to God I would commit my cause—
9 Who does great things, and unsearchable,
Marvelous things without number.
10 He gives rain on the earth,
And sends waters on the fields.
11 He sets on high those who are lowly,
And those who mourn are lifted to safety.
12 He frustrates the devices of the crafty,
So that their hands cannot carry out their plans.
13 He catches the wise in their own craftiness,
And the counsel of the cunning comes quickly
upon them.
14 They meet with darkness in the daytime,
And grope at noontime as in the night.
15 But He saves the needy from the sword,
From the mouth of the mighty,
And from their hand.
16 So the poor have hope,
And injustice shuts her mouth.
17 "Behold, happy is the man whom God corrects;
Therefore do not despise the chastening of the
Almighty.
18 For He bruises, but He binds up;
He wounds, but His hands make whole.
19 He shall deliver you in six troubles,
Yes, in seven no evil shall touch you.
20 In famine He shall redeem you from death,
And in war from the power of the sword.
21 You shall be hidden from the scourge of the
tongue,
And you shall not be afraid of destruction when
it comes.
22 You shall laugh at destruction and famine,
And you shall not be afraid of the beasts of the
earth.

23 For you shall have a covenant with the stones
of the field,
And the beasts of the field shall be at peace with
you.
24 You shall know that your tent is in peace;
You shall visit your dwelling and find nothing
amiss.
25 You shall also know that your descendants shall
be many,
And your offspring like the grass of the earth.
26 You shall come to the grave at a full age,
As a sheaf of grain ripens in its season.
27 Behold, this we have searched out;
It is true.
Hear it, and know for yourself."

Job 4:1—5:27

Eliphaz is the senior member and, therefore, the first spokesman for Job's three friends. Some interpreters see him as a courteous statesman of the Wisdom School. He is criticized for answering Job's cry for help with general principles that bypass Job's specific situation and need. But, at the same time, doesn't he deserve credit for handling Job's outburst of rage with a calm and collected response that puts the issue into perspective? Each of us knows what Hulme means when he says that anger threatens us because we are not sure that we can handle its momentum.[4]

Eliphaz gets no sympathy from me. The more I read his first speech the greater my rage. Job's curses and questions may have bordered on blasphemy by impugning the character of God, but he does not deserve the deceptive insult that Eliphaz throws at him under the pretext of a compassionate friend and authoritative teacher. Because he has health and wisdom, Eliphaz has the responsibility to walk the bridge over to his needy friend whose thoughts as well as feelings have been affected by prolonged and intensive suffering. Instead, he insults Job with the outline of a lecture that he must have given hundreds of times. In stark contrast with Job's irrational but relevant outburst of anger and anguish, Eliphaz follows the lock-step pattern of extending his apology, giving his analysis, invoking his authority, making his application, and offering his advice. The truth is that Eliphaz sees Job's anger as a threat to the religious system in which he has a personal investment. Therefore, he has the audacity to assume the voice of God in a battle for spiritual survival. His goal is to shame Job into submission. On the way to that goal, he demonstrates that he is the master of manipulation.

Extending His Apology

Eliphaz's apology can be read two ways. Either he wants to encourage Job by recalling his past ministry to those in suffering, or he uses the past as a weapon to shame his complaining friend. The word *"weary"* (4:2, 5) is the clue. Better translated "impatient" or "vexed in spirit," it reveals Eliphaz's true attitude and tips his hand toward the analysis he will make and the advice he will give. Job's "vexation" to him is a symptom of sin. Therefore, in a veiled apology, Eliphaz puts down Job with the tight-lipped suggestion that his counsel will not be just wasted but will actually turn Job's anger upon him. Eliphaz treats Job like the professor whose class stood up in the middle of his last sentence when the bell rang. "Just a moment," he beckoned them, "I have one more pearl to cast!" Eliphaz shows the same attitude toward Job. He hopes to shame him into submission by the "pearls-before-swine" technique of manipulation. Reminding Job of his past role as an effective teacher, counselor, and comforter in similar situations with other people, Eliphaz says in effect, "Physician, heal thyself." Then, with one more fling of disdain, Eliphaz plays upon Job's reputation for reverence and integrity as his confidence and his hope. Sarcasm hurts most when it comes under the guise of a compliment. As we shall see, Eliphaz has no doubt that Job suffers because he has sinned. Therefore, to commend his reverence and his integrity is the "dirtiest" of dirty tricks.

Giving His Analysis

Eliphaz changes his tactics again as he takes on the role of an authoritative lecturer rather than an offended friend. Only his attitude does not change. In a condescending tone, he admonishes Job to remember the quintessential doctrine of their faith where they stand on common ground. Eliphaz challenges Job with the questions:

> *Who ever perished being innocent?*
> *Or where were the upright ever cut off?* (4:7).

The impact of these questions is to permit no exceptions, including Job. Then, exercising his seniority, Eliphaz cites his own experience to present the proposition:

Those who plow inquity
And sow trouble reap the same (v. 8).

There is no alternative; there is no exception. Eliphaz claims to speak absolute truth that is the standard for orthodoxy and the test for spirituality. Then, in an oath of confirmation, Eliphaz vows that this truth is as automatic as the invariable life cycle of the lion—from the first roar to the last whimper, when the cycle starts all over again.

Religion that can be summed up in an equation requires more faith in the formula than it does in God. Eliphaz's primary equation reads, "Sin equals suffering," and its corollary is just the opposite, "Righteousness equals prosperity." Once a proposition such as this is stated and adopted, all human behavior can be analyzed accordingly.

Invoking His Authority

Arrogance rises in Eliphaz when he takes the occasion to reveal a secret vision in which a voice whispered to him,

"Can a mortal be more righteous than God?
Can a man be more pure than his Maker?" (v. 17).

Once God has spoken, who can argue? Eliphaz has defended his formula and asserted his authority as the bearer of truth. No matter that his revelation is not new; he is so presumptuous as to assume that God's righteousness and purity need to be defended in order to prove Job's sin. In so doing, he walks on the edge of deism, which puts such distance between a holy God and sinful man that the two can never come close enough to communicate or develop a relationship.

Any time a letter or conversation begins with the sentence, "God has spoken to me," there is no room for discussion. At one time in my career as a college president, a trustee who disagreed with a decision I had made wrote me a letter that began, "While in prayer last night, God told me to write you." He then went on to contest my administrative decision on spiritual grounds. Before he finished, inference and innuendo also cast doubt on the spirituality of my character as well as my decision-making. At the time, his letter awed me. With a little more experience in such matters, I would have answered, "We pray to the same God. Why hasn't He said the same thing to me?" Secret visions and whispered voices that bring private messages attributed to God are immediately suspect. Especially for those of us who have the full and final revelation of His Word in Jesus Christ, we believe that God has spoken "all things necessary for salvation, life, and conduct."

Making His Application

Eliphaz is a dangerous man because he speaks the truth at the wrong time and in the wrong spirit. His demeaning of Job continues in the fifth chapter as he directly dares him to cry out again but then indirectly condemns him as foolish and *"simple."* From this same oblique and cowardly angle, Eliphaz lets Job make his own application when he describes the punishment that God brings down in the wicked man through his sons who are *"crushed in the gate"* (5:4). Salt is poured into the open wounds of Job's soul. His words, "The LORD gave and the LORD has taken away; Blessed be the name of the LORD" (1:21), have returned to haunt him. Nothing hurts worse than to think that we are responsible for our children's suffering. Parenthood is to say, "Let me suffer but spare my children."

Eliphaz's strategy for shaming Job into submission comes to its conclusion in the familiar quotation:

Yet man is born to trouble [as sure]
As the sparks fly upward (5:7).

No longer is there any doubt about what Eliphaz means. Even though he still does not name Job, he locates the cause of his trouble in the man himself. Inherited depravity is a sound doctrine but also a vicious weapon when used arbitrarily and automatically with a suffering soul on the edge of death. In hospital work with dying patients, we pastors can find ourselves caught between our urgency to save the soul and our responsibility to respect the person. Only the most insensitive counselor would take advantage of a helpless patient by saying, "You are sick because you are a sinner," with a note of poetic glee.

Offering His Advice

Everything that Eliphaz says revolves around his own authority as the oldest and wisest of Job's friends. Thus, he presents his words of advice with the personalized counsel,

> *"But as for me, I would seek God,*
> *And to God I would commit my cause"* (v. 8).

His prescription is submission. Job is urged to follow the formula of confessing his sinfulness before God, who is majestic, holy, and just. According to Eliphaz, his need is his hope.

Eliphaz has one more technique of manipulation left in his bag of tricks. Sarcasm is gone; singing takes its place, *"Behold, happy is the man whom God corrects"* (v. 17). A beautiful psalm of hope follows. Again, the truth is not in question. In fact, Hebrews quotes Eliphaz as the only direct New Testament reference to the Book of Job with the words, "Whom the LORD loves He chastens" (12:6). It is the timing that is wrong.

During the most violent days of student protest in the early 1970s, a beleaguered college president opened an educational conference with the prayer, "Lord, your word says that those whom you love you chasten. If it would please you, we could get along with a little less love." Job must have felt the same way when he heard Eliphaz's promises about healing, deliverance, peace, prosperity, and a ripe old age. He needed relief, not promises.

Eliphaz's song of hope at the end of his speech puts the top slice on what is called the "praise-criticism-praise" sandwich. Communication theory for executives warns against conferences with employees in which the intention is reprimand, but the executive tries to soften the blow by putting it between slices of praise at the beginning and the end. For one thing, the employee hears only the reprimand. For another, he or she ends up in the confusion of asking, "If I'm so good, how can I be so bad?"

As we shall see in Job's response to Eliphaz, he hears nothing of the praise at the beginning of the speech or the promises at the conclusion. Job hears only the condemnation of his character. Eliphaz fails to follow the simple advice of *The One-Minute Manager.* Praise is to be separated from reprimand and when you must give a reprimand, "change the behavior but save the person."[5]

Eliphaz's formula of faith gives him no alternative. To defend his small God and save his narrow orthodoxy, he has to sacrifice Job's character. When faith is fixed in a Procrustean bed, the legs of growing people must be cut off to make them fit. Perhaps Eliphaz has his own hidden doubts about his rigid adherence to the equations that sin equals suffering and righteousness insures prosperity. Why does he have to bolster his own seniority in age and wisdom by concluding his speech with *"we"?* Why does he find it necessary to claim the empirical evidence of "examination" to reinforce revealed truth? Why does he have to hammer in one final nail in Job's suffering by reciting the obvious, *"It **is** true"* (5:27)? Eliphaz's final words insult Job's intelligence and betray the speaker's insecurity. Truly, he "doth protest too much."

Job—A Cry for Justice

Eliphaz's call for patience enrages Job. Admitting that his words are rash, he contends that they are equal to his suffering. Eliphaz's advice to seek God adds to Job's rage. God is his antagonist who has stung him with poisonous arrows. Therefore, Eliphaz's words of comfort are like dry streams for thirsty travelers. Turning again to God, Job bewails his unbearable agony and his hopeless future. Death in the land of shadows is no answer, because communication with God is broken off. In utter despair, Job contends that he has no future, now or ever. Only irony is left. If I am insignificant, why does God torture me? Even if I am a sinner, what is it to God? Why should I, even if I am a sinner, suffer when I am not the master of my will? Finally, in ultimate irony, Job dares to tell God that when he is gone, God will miss him.

> 6:1 Then Job answered and said:
> 2 "Oh, that my grief were fully weighed,
> And my calamity laid with it on the scales!

3 For then it would be heavier than the sand of the sea—
Therefore my words have been rash.
4 For the arrows of the Almighty are within me;
My spirit drinks in their poison;
The terrors of God are arrayed against me.
5 Does the wild donkey bray when it has grass,
Or does the ox low over its fodder?
6 Can flavorless food be eaten without salt?
Or is there any taste in the white of an egg?
7 My soul refuses to touch them;
They are as loathsome food to me.
8 "Oh, that I might have my request,
That God would grant me the thing that I long for!
9 That it would please God to crush me,
That He would loose His hand and cut me off!
10 Then I would still have comfort;
Though in anguish I would exult,
He will not spare;
For I have not concealed the words of the Holy One.
11 "What strength do I have, that I should hope?
And what is my end, that I should prolong my life?
12 Is my strength the strength of stones?
Or is my flesh bronze?
13 Is my help not within me?
And is success driven from me?
14 "To him who is afflicted, kindness should be shown by his friend,
Even though he forsakes the fear of the Almighty.
15 My brothers have dealt deceitfully like a brook,
Like the streams of the brooks that pass away,
16 Which are dark because of the ice,
And into which the snow vanishes.
17 When it is warm, they cease to flow;
When it is hot, they vanish from their place.
18 The paths of their way turn aside,
They go nowhere and perish.

19 The caravans of Tema look,
The travelers of Sheba hope for them.
20 They are disappointed because they were confident;
They come there and are confused.
21 For now you are nothing,
You see terror and are afraid.
22 Did I ever say, 'Bring something to me'?
Or, 'Offer a bribe for me from your wealth'?
23 Or, 'Deliver me from the enemy's hand'?
Or, 'Redeem me from the hand of oppressors'?
24 "Teach me, and I will hold my tongue;
Cause me to understand wherein I have erred.
25 How forceful are right words!
But what does your arguing prove?
26 Do you intend to rebuke my words,
And the speeches of a desperate one, which are as wind?
27 Yes, you overwhelm the fatherless,
And you undermine your friend.
28 Now therefore, be pleased to look at me;
For I would never lie to your face.
29 Yield now, let there be no injustice!
Yes, concede, my righteousness still stands!
30 Is there injustice on my tongue?
Cannot my taste discern the unsavory?
7:1 "Is there not a time of hard service for man on earth?
Are not his days also like the days of a hired man?
2 Like a servant who earnestly desires the shade,
And like a hired man who eagerly looks for his wages,
3 So I have been allotted months of futility,
And wearisome nights have been appointed to me.
4 When I lie down, I say, 'When shall I arise,
And the night be ended?'
For I have had my fill of tossing till dawn.
5 My flesh is caked with worms and dust,
My skin is cracked and breaks out afresh.

6 "My days are swifter than a weaver's shuttle,
And are spent without hope.
7 Oh, remember that my life is a breath!
My eye will never again see good.
8 The eye of him who sees me will see me no more;
While your eyes are upon me, I shall no longer be.
9 As the cloud disappears and vanishes away,
So he who goes down to the grave does not come up.
10 He shall never return to his house,
Nor shall his place know him anymore.
11 "Therefore I will not restrain my mouth;
I will speak in the anguish of my spirit;
I will complain in the bitterness of my soul.
12 Am I a sea, or a sea serpent,
That You set a guard over me?
13 When I say, 'My bed will comfort me,
My couch will ease my complaint,'
14 Then You scare me with dreams
And terrify me with visions,
15 So that my soul chooses strangling
and death rather than my body.
16 I loathe my life;
I would not live forever.
Let me alone,
For my days are but a breath.
17 "What is man, that You should exalt him,
That You should set Your heart on him,
18 That You should visit him every morning,
and test him every moment?
19 How long?
Will You not look away from me,
And let me alone till I swallow my saliva?
20 Have I sinned?
What have I done to You, O watcher of men?
Why have You set me as Your target,
So that I am a burden to myself?
21 Why then do You not pardon my transgression,
And take away my iniquity?

For now I will lie down in the dust,
And You will seek me diligently,
But I will no longer be."

Job 6:1—7:21

Eliphaz's veiled attack ignites an explosion of emotions in Job. His friends have failed him. To whom can he turn? With one desperate gasp, he tries to justify his rash and angry cry (6:1–7), but the words ricochet off stone faces and a silent heaven to sting him even more deeply. He turns against himself, praying for a quick and merciful death (vv. 8–13). He lashes out with bitter sarcasm against his friends (vv. 14–30); and then, on the borders of blasphemy, he accuses God of injustice (7:1–21). Because of his innocence, Job can put into words the feelings that every sufferer knows but dares not speak.

Anger That Is Justified

One word deliberately dropped by Eliphaz drives Job to fury. In the course of his speech, Eliphaz says, "For wrath kills a foolish man" (5:2). After this utterance, Job hears nothing else. *"Wrath"* has a meaning that Eliphaz and Job both know. Like poison in the stomach, it acted, reacted, and rumbled inside Job until he had to explode it in his own retching words.

The Hebrew word for *wrath* is variously interpreted as "vexation," "impatience," or "grief." In our text, it is interpreted as "wrath" in Eliphaz's words (5:2) and *"grief"* in Job's opening words of response (6:2). To understand the point of interaction between Eliphaz and Job, it would be better to translate the word in both speeches as "wrath" or "vexation." In the Wisdom School to which both Eliphaz and Job belonged, the reason for a show of wrath or vexation of spirit separated a wise man from a fool. Because the Wisdom School taught reasoned moderation in all things, a wise man would only show wrath in the face of gross injustice. A fool, however, is a person who becomes vexed in spirit and wrathful in words after being rightfully rebuked. A "fool of fools," then, is the person who gets mad when chastened by God, whose rebuke is always right.

With one stroke of a scalpel dipped in disdain, Eliphaz cuts Job from the company of the wise and condemns him as the "fool of fools" along with those who say in their hearts, "there is no God." As if that is not enough, he proceeds to pronounce the punishment for Job's foolishness by making him responsible for his children's death:

> His sons are far from safety,
> They are crushed in the gate,
> And there is no deliverer (5:4).

Throughout his speech, Eliphaz continues to invoke the formula that Job's sin is the cause of his suffering. At first, Job seems to be more hurt than stung by Eliphaz's indictment. Picking up on the word *wrath,* he pleads for an understanding of his reaction. In effect, he asks that his friends of the Wisdom School consider his case as justification for wrath in the face of gross injustice. On the fulcrum of his innocence, Job puts his wrath on the scale with his suffering. As suffering weighs him down, heavy as the sands of the sea (6:3), his wrath rises on the other side of the scale.

Sound psychology backs up Job's analogy. He is arguing that his reaction of wrath is proportionate to his suffering and therefore appropriate. Healthy emotional reactions are always appropriate to the stimulus. Grief, for instance, is the appropriate response to death. If a person shows no grief at the death of a loved one, something is wrong. Yet, if a person continues to grieve for years after a loved one dies, something else is wrong. In either case, the reaction of grief on one side of the scale does not balance with the weight of death on the other side of the scale.

Job admits that his reaction is *"rash,"* but argues that it is in balance with his suffering because of his innocence. Vivid pictures come to his mind as he pleads for understanding. Like a wild ass, he would not *"bray"* if he had his grass. Life for him is just the opposite—as tasteless as the white of an egg, or even worse, as repulsive as the "slime of purslane," which gags you until you have to spit it out.

For all of us who want to share the pain of those who suffer, we must begin with an understanding that their reactions will be "rash" and even "wrathful." If they threaten us, we cannot comfort them. But if their reactions are appropriate to their suffering and we accept them, we will understand what Job means when he weeps, *"Is there any taste in the white of an egg?"* (6:6).

Prayer That Is Unanswered

The fire of wrath smoldered in Job's heart and mind ever since Eliphaz castigated him as a fool and dared to link the death of his children with the sin of their father. Once he begins to speak, Job cannot contain himself. The fire breaks out and spews white-hot flames in every direction. They begin by burning within Job himself. He prays that God will crush him and cut him off from life (v. 9).

Two conflicting motives reside in our human nature. We have a *will to live,* and, at the same time, a *wish to die.* A tenacious *will to live* dominates the healthy personality. John Hersey has written a book entitled *Here to Stay,* in which he tells the true stories of persons who mustered superhuman power to survive in circumstances where death appeared to be inevitable.[6] A World War II commander of a torpedoed PT boat, for instance, swam in circles around islands in the Pacific Ocean throughout the night in a semiconscious state. Humanly speaking, he should have been exhausted and swept out to sea by the changing tide. Instead, the indomitable *will to live* in John F. Kennedy kept him swimming until searchers, working against all odds, found him after more than twenty-four hours in the ocean.

On the other extreme, who has not said at one time or another, "I wish I could die"? As age and illness overtake us and we confront our own mortality, the wish to die gains its place among our motives. No one faults an aged parent or a terminally ill patient who openly and honestly speaks of a desire to "go home to be with my Lord."

Suicides are special cases for whom life has lost its meaning. For any number of reasons, their will to live is weakened and their wish to die becomes an obsession. Christians share Shakespeare's implied answer to suicide,

> Then is it sin
> To rush into the secret house of death
> Ere death dare come to us?[7]

Aquinas specifically answered that question by reasoning that life and death are God's will. Therefore, to take either life or death in human hands is the sin of flaunting God's will. Artists, poets, and philosophers throughout the centuries have tried to justify and romanticize suicide. A. Alvarez, a literary critic, has traced that history in a book called *The Savage God: A Study of Suicide.*[8] An infamous honor roll of suicides, called the "aristocrats of death," includes Socrates, Seneca, Cleopatra, Van Gogh, Virginia Woolf, and Ernest Hemingway. In our time, we can add Will Durant and Paul Tillich, among others. Presumably, these are creative souls for whom suicide, according to Camus, becomes their last "great work of art." In truth, it is what Dostoevsky called "tomorrow's zero," when life has lost its meaning and immortality is no longer a hope.

Job loses the will to live and prays for death. When the will to live has been drained by the agony of his suffering, at the bottom of the well he finds the bedrock belief in the existence of God and the unshakeable conviction of his innocence. Even though his limited revelation of the nature of God does not include the prospect of immortality, he refuses to take his own life. Yet, Job dares God to *"crush"* him because he will die with the comfort and even the triumph of his innocence.

Job knows that his prayer for death will go unanswered. He sinks down into his deepest despair and he realizes that more than his strength is gone. He has no hope within himself and his end is futile. Suicide seems an option as he asks,

> *And what is my end,*
> *that I should prolong my life?* (6:11).

The question itself is absurd. As C. S. Lewis has written, Job knows that "death ends the dialogue."[9]

Friends Who Fail Us

After turning upon himself and plunging to the depths of despair where the *wish to die* dominates his thoughts, Job finds that his belief in God and in his own innocence becomes the fan that flames the smoldering ashes of his *will to live.* Turning outwardly with the same fire of emotion, he attacks his friends for their failure to comfort him. Not unlike all those who suffer, one minute Job gives up on life, the next minute he is more alive than ever with the power of a sharpened mind, the beauty of a poetic tongue, and the strength of an indomitable will.

Job's intellect has been honed by suffering to a needle point. Couching his disappointment in a principle of survival in the ancient East, he says,

> *To him who is afflicted, kindness should be shown by his friend,*
> *Even though he forsakes the fear of the Almighty* (v. 14).

The worm has turned! Even if his friends expel Job from the company of the Wise because he forsakes the fear of God, they cannot cancel the simple act of *"kindness,"* which is a covenant between brothers. In the code of conduct to which they ascribe, *"kindness"* represents the most elementary evidence of spirituality. Thus, with the barbed tongue of satire, Job stings Eliphaz as deeply with the word *"kindness"* as his antagonist has stung him with the word "wrath." As if this were not enough, Job adds mimicry to his satirical weapons. Eliphaz had sealed his indictment with a magnificent doxology extolling the majesty of God (5:8–16), Job chooses the metaphor of desert streams to seal his friends' failure. As the Old Testament commentator Francis Andersen notes, Job's poetry reaches "Homeric proportions."[10] He likens the response of his friends to desert streams that run dry when parched travelers expect them to be full and find nothing but sand.

Job's sharpened intellect is matched by uncanny insight into the reason for his friends' failure. In a diagnosis that would be the envy of the most skilled psychiatrist, Job says, *"You see terror and are afraid"* (v. 21). The truth is out. Eliphaz and his friends are terror stricken at the sight of Job's suffering and the sound of his "wrath." Perhaps with some sympathy, Job softens his satire by pleading once again, *"Teach me, and I will hold my tongue"* (v. 24). More rational now, he offers to put aside his windy words if they will put aside their futile sophistry to get a fair hearing on the issue between them. Boldly on the offensive, Job challenges them to *"look at me;/For I would never lie to your face"* (v. 28).

Arab businessmen are known for wearing sunglasses during their transactions. Neither are their eyes weak nor is the light strong. In the Middle East, business transactions are conducted at close quarters. Honesty or dishonesty is read by "eye language." Therefore, to keep a competitor from knowing when they are lying, waffling, or afraid, Arabs wear sunglasses as part of their business dress. To attest his innocence, Job challenges his friends to a duel between the eyes as well as a debate over the facts. Once and for all, he wants these questions settled,

> *Is there injustice on my tongue?*
> *Cannot my taste discern the unsavory?* (v. 30).

God Who Confounds Us

Without waiting for his friends to answer his questions, Job's flaming tongue strikes again. This time the object of his wrath is God. His first cry of anguish (chapter 3) was an impersonal shout to the winds. But now, his bitterness has become focused—first, upon himself; next, upon his friends; and, now, upon God. With direct inference to the character of God, Job asks in anger, "Why me?" This is every sufferer's question, saint or sinner, in the angry stage of suffering. Job's retort is repeated,

> *What have I done to You,*
> *O watcher of men?*
> *Why have You set me as Your target?* (7:20).

Why Me? God's Target for Indignity

Even though Job is consumed with anger, he is learning from his suffering. Perhaps for the first time, he identifies with the common lot of people on earth—hirelings and servants—for whom life is hard (7:1–2). Later, we learn that Job always listened to his hired hands and treated the poor with generosity and justice. Still, there is a difference. As long as he held his wealth and enjoyed his health, Job could not feel the plight of the poor and the diseased.

Philip Yancey, in his book *Where Is God When It Hurts?,* quotes Helmut Thielicke's answer to the question "What is the greatest defect among American Christians?" Thielicke said, "They have an inadequate view of suffering."[11]

Job prefigures Jesus in being "emptied" of his glory and identified with suffering people on the lowest rung of the human ladder. Jesus humbled Himself to become a man, take the form of a servant, and die the death of a criminal (Phil. 2:7–8) to identify with the suffering and sin of mankind. Although not of his own accord, Job's physical and social suffering lets him see, for the first time, life from the "bottom up."

Although he now understands the solidarity of suffering with all humankind, Job still believes that he is God's special target for gross indignity. At least the hireling and the servant anticipate relief from hardship and reward for labor (7:2)—not Job. He has been victimized by months of futile suffering, eternal nights of tossing, and tortuous days of pain from open, infected, and dirty sores aggravated by cracked and bleeding skin. "Why me?" Job asks. He holds God responsible for singling him out for the destruction of his dignity.

Why Me? God's Target for Alienation

Job's suffering brings him another insight into human nature that he might have missed during his prosperity. As he later admits, Job fully expected to die in his "nest," multiply his days as the "sand," and then perpetuate his heritage like a root spread out to the waters (29:18–19). Suffering short-circuits long-range planning. Now, Job sees that life goes by with the swiftness of *"a weaver's shuttle,"* the passing wind, the glancing eye, and the vanishing cloud (7:6–10).

Perhaps, for the first time, Job identifies with people whose destiny is squeezed into the time span of the radical *now.* In a book called *The Unheavenly City,*[12] Edward Banfield writes that the ghetto dweller is buffeted between the promises of affluence and the reality that there is no "escape hatch" through which he or she can rise above poverty. Without a future, time perspective is limited to the present moment and its emergencies of food, clothing, shelter, and medicine as well as its indulgences of alcohol, drugs, sex, and gambling. We who have a long-range, optimistic, and realistic time perspective fail to realize that the ghetto dweller has nothing to lose in rumbles, riots, and ruin. When Job says, *"My days are swifter than a weaver's shuttle,/And are spent without hope"* (v. 6), he identifies with the wretched of the earth for whom the present is the only reality because the future is a dead end.

Having climbed the peak of prosperity and fallen into the pit of poverty, Job believes that he is a targeted victim of God. "Why me?" he asks again. This time, Job cannot understand why God, his friend, has broken their relationship. By His silence, God seems content to let him die. But Job reminds God that if he dies, he will *"never again see good,"* never again be seen, never again be alive, and never again return (vv. 7–10).

Appealing to the beauty of their past relationship, Job assumes that God needs him as much as he needs God. Utterly confused by a sense of unprovoked alienation, Job asks God, "Why me?"

Why Me? God's Target for Injustice

Like a ghetto dweller who has nothing to lose by rioting, Job now feels as if he has nothing to lose by rebelling against God. Belligerently, he says:

> *I will not restrain my mouth;*
> *I will speak in the anguish of my spirit;*
> *I will complain in the bitterness of my soul* (v. 11).

From that poisonous well, Job launches out his most violent attack on God. "Why me?" is still the question, but now Job dares to doubt the justice of God. In so doing, he reflects upon the character of God and risks his soul, as well as his life. God is not threatened; God does not retaliate. He knows that Job speaks from intolerable suffering, cries from an unshakeable faith, and tests the limits of honest doubt.

Three pointed questions carry Job's complaint against God. By asking, *"Am I a sea, or a sea serpent,/That You set a guard over me?"* (v. 12), he chides God for acting as if he were a threat to Him. Job contends that he is harmless, and yet God scares him with dreams and terrifies him with visions (v. 14). *"Let me alone"* (v. 16) is his cry of utter frustration.

Job's second question is even more pointed. Reaching back down into the well of bitterness from which he attacked his friends, he turns the edge of his sarcastic tongue against God. Borrowing the profound question of the psalmist, he asks, *"What is man?"* (v. 17). To this common question, the psalmist and Job come to opposite answers:

What is man
that You are mindful of him,
And the son of man
that You visit him?
For You have made him a little
lower than the angels,
And You have crowned him
with glory and honor (Ps. 8:4,5).

What is man,
that You should magnify him,
That You should set Your heart on him,
That You should visit him every morning,
And test him every moment? (Job 7:17,18).

Job has made a parody of the psalm. Rather than seeing man exalted as God's cherished creation, he digs at God for magnifying the insignificance of man by constantly watching him, visiting him, and testing him. By claiming "I am little," Job is pointing out what seems to him at this time to be a contradiction in the character of God. His argument is this: If God is so great and man is so small, why does God set His heart on man, visit him, and test him? Unwittingly, Job is setting the paradoxical stage for the incarnation of Christ and the redemption of man. But for himself in this moment, Job can only see God's way with man as a contradiction. Breaking forth with frustration he can only sob, *"How long?"* and plead for the mighty God to turn away His face and leave him alone so that he can strangle on his spit.

Dangerously close to cursing God, taking his wife's advice, and justifying Satan, Job knows that he has gone too far. In another quick reversal, he leaves sarcasm behind and returns to the only solid ground he knows—his innocence. *"Have I sinned?"* he asks God.

What have I done to You?
. . . .
Why then do You not pardon my transgression,
And take away my iniquity? (vv. 20–21).

Who dares to speak to God this way? Only a man of faith who knows God personally. On the surface, Job's questions sound skeptical. But, if you scratch under the skin of these same questions, you discover an unshakeable faith in the character of Job and an unbroken relationship between two friends. How else could Job say, *"Why then do You not pardon my transgression, / And take away my iniquity?"* Despite the contradiction between his suffering and his innocence, despite his quandary over God's justice, Job is confident that the essence of God's character is love and His desire is to forgive. How else could Job finish his second speech like a love letter between estranged friends?

> *For now I will lie down in the dust,*
> *And You will seek me diligently,*
> *But I will no longer be* (v. 21).

Two different interpretations come to mind. One is that Job is teasing God into a response. When our children don't get their way, they often say, "You'll be sorry when I'm gone." Knowing that they are kidding, we usually answer, "Where are you going?" with the full assurance that they will not run away. Job may have been trying the same childish tactic with God to test their relationship and get his way.

The other interpretation is more sublime. Job views God as one who comes to man as He did in the Garden of Eden, seeks him diligently with the call "Where are you?" and misses him if there is no answer. What started out in anger and built into borderline blasphemy has now turned into one of the most touching and intimate pictures of the relationship between God and man in holy Scriptures. It is said that Charles Spurgeon lived so close to God that he began his prayers with the salutation, "Ah, my Beloved." Nothing more need be said. Job anticipated the hymn written by George Matheson in 1882, centuries after his experience:

> O Love that will not let me go,
> I rest my weary soul in Thee;
> I give Thee back the life I owe,
> That in Thine ocean depths its flow
> May richer, fuller be.

Job is also foreseeing Paul's faith in his letter to the Romans: "For I am persuaded that neither death nor life, nor angels nor principalities nor powers, nor things present nor things to come, nor height nor depth, nor any other created thing, shall be able to separate us from the love of God which is in Christ Jesus our Lord" (Rom. 8:38–39).

What an end to a lover's quarrel! After venting his spleen, Job says to God, "Ah, my Beloved . . . You will miss me when I am gone."

BILDAD—THE REACTION OF TRADITION

Heat is rising in the debate. Job's friends are now his opponents. Job has contested the justice of God. Bildad comes to God's defense by appealing to the authority of the past. He repeats the formula that righteousness and prosperity, sin and suffering are in a mechanical, cause-and-effect relationship. Using the analogies of the water's reed, the spider's web, and the plant on rocky ground, Bildad repeats the advice of Eliphaz—confess your sin, submit to God, and wait patiently for His reward.

1 Then Bildad the Shuhite answered and said:
2 "How long will you speak these things,
And the words of your mouth be like a strong wind?
3 Does God subvert judgment?
Or does the Almighty pervert justice?
4 If your sons have sinned against Him,
He has cast them away for their transgression.
5 If you would earnestly seek God
And make your supplication to the Almighty,
6 If you were pure and upright,
Surely now He would awake for you,
And prosper your rightful dwelling place.
7 Though your beginning was small,
Yet your latter end would increase abundantly.
8 "For inquire, please, of the former age,
And consider the things discovered by their fathers;
9 For we were born yesterday, and know nothing,
Because our days on earth are a shadow.
10 Will they not teach you and tell you,
And utter words from their heart?
11 "Can the papyrus grow up without a marsh?
Can the reeds flourish without water?
12 While it is yet green and not cut down,
It withers before any other plant.

13 So are the paths of all who forget God;
And the hope of the hypocrite shall perish,
14 Whose confidence shall be cut off,
And whose trust is a spider's web.
15 He leans on his house, but it does not stand.
He holds it fast, but it does not endure.
16 He grows green in the sun,
And his branches spread out in his garden.
17 His roots wrap around the rock heap,
And look for a place in the stones.
18 If he is destroyed from his place,
Then it will deny him, saying, 'I have not seen you.'
19 "Behold, this is the joy of His way,
And out of the earth others will grow.
20 Behold, God will not cast away the blameless,
Nor will He uphold the evildoers.
21 He will yet fill your mouth with laughing,
And your lips with rejoicing.
22 Those who hate you will be clothed with shame,
And the dwelling place of the wicked will come to nothing."

Job 8:1–22

What started out as a debate is rapidly turning into a diatribe. Bildad brushes aside Job's despair that took him to the brink of suicide. Equally ignored is the anger that provoked Job to alienate his friends on the charge of breaking their covenant vows as brothers. Bildad even refuses to dignify Job's accusation that Eliphaz, Zophar, and he failed to pass the most elementary test of spirituality, showing "kindness" to a person in need. All of this is dismissed in Bildad's denunciation of Job, "You are a windbag" ("wild and whirling words"—Moffatt).

With Job's anguish and anger swept out of the way, Bildad proceeds to defend the character of God. His tactic is to invoke mechanically and mercilessly the formula doctrine that *sin is the cause of suffering* and its corollary, *prosperity is the reward for righteousness.*

Eliphaz has already articulated this doctrine of "cash-register justice." He contended that it is consistent with the majestic and moral character of God. Furthermore, he claimed that God revealed this truth to him personally in a midnight vision.

Bildad implements this same doctrine by personal application and ancient parable. His role is to be the "simplifier" for this perceived truth—the Adolf Eichmann who acts in blind obedience to bring about the "final resolution of the Jobian question." Taking each doubt that Job raises about the justice of God, Bildad rings down the changes of counter-condemnation without so much as a tear in his eye. At least, the crafty Eliphaz couched his attack in courtesy. Bildad is like the grand inquisitor of Dostoevsky's novels who sends Christians to the stake under the pretext of purging their sin and saving their souls. He confuses cruelty with righteousness under the pretext that manifest destiny has chosen him to defend the character of God.

Does God Twist Judgment?

Out of the seething cup of suffering, Job came close to cursing God. Only the difference between a question mark and an exclamation point kept him from blasphemy as he baited God,

> What have I done to You,
> O watcher of men?
> Why have You set me as Your target,
> So that I am a burden to myself?
> Why then do You not pardon my transgression,
> And take away my iniquity? (7:20–21).

Bildad cannot believe his ears. After denouncing Job as a "windbag," he takes up the challenge for God with a shout of the same intensity:

> *Does God subvert judgment?*
> *Or does the Almighty pervert justice?* (8:3).

Even though the answer is rhetorical, it is not enough for Bildad. In the unkindest cut of all, he stabs at the heart of Job by citing the death of his children as indisputable evidence of their sin and incontrovertible proof of God's justice. Feelings do not count with Bildad. While ignoring Job's suffering, he does not hesitate to play upon his guilt.

Even if Job's children had died because of their sin, Bildad's vengeance on behalf of God is inexcusable. He knows that Job's children are his point of vulnerability. In the prologue, we learned that Job himself was "blameless," but he made regular sacrifices for his children, who enjoyed the luxury of his wealth, just in case they "sinned and cursed God in their hearts" (1:5). By coincidence, Job's children were partying together when they were killed by a tornado. Had they sinned or were they sinning when the wild wind struck them? Job does not know and it is too late to offer a sacrifice for them.

Bildad has no doubt. Rubbing fresh salt in a raw wound, he pronounces the verdict that Job's children died for their sins as proof that God's justice operates on a straight line and without a twist.

An employee whom I recommended for dismissal refused to shake my hand or speak to me. His actions hurt, but I reasoned that the broken relationship was part of the price for executive responsibility. Then, my daughter, who knew nothing about the incident, met the man on the street. A cheery "hello" received a stony stare of disdain. When my daughter asked me, "What's wrong with him?" my smoldering hurt flamed into white-hot rage. In that moment, I could have wiped him from the face of the earth and taken my chances in hell. Only distance kept me from a face-to-face encounter in which I would demand an apology from him for letting his hate for me spill over onto my innocent children. Only Job's proverbial patience, his weakened condition, or his own self-doubts must have kept him from stopping Bildad in his verbal tracks and screaming, "Attack me if you will, but leave my children out of this."

Gratuitously, Bildad speeds on to the flip side of the formula. If Job *would* earnestly seek God and if Job *were* pure and upright, God would restore him to a prosperity that would make his past wealth and reputation look like a "small beginning" (8:7). The use of the conditional term "if" reveals Bildad's basic assumption. Job has not *"earnestly"* sought God and Job is not *"pure and upright."* Bildad has no alternative for these assumptions. If God's justice works according to His formula, Job must repent of his sins.

Does God Refuse to Speak to Man?

Job's plaintive cry, "How long?" echoes back across the chasm that separates him from a silent God. His plea is the heart cry of those who suffer in every generation. There comes a time when any answer from God—whether healing or death—is good. God's will can be handled more easily than His silence.

Of course, Bildad has the ready answer. God has spoken through the wisdom of the ages as discovered by the fathers (v. 8). Whereas Eliphaz invoked the authority of personal revelation through a midnight vision to attest the doctrine of "cash-register" justice, Bildad rests his case on tradition. If *Fiddler On the Roof* had been written four thousand years ago, Bildad might have asked Job to sing Tevye's famous song "Tradition," about the papa and his never-ending struggle to make a living, feed a wife and children, and say his daily prayers—the reward for which gives him the right as master of the house to have the *final word* at home. The papa, the papa—*tradition! tradition!*

Bildad also believes that God's "final word" has been given to the fathers through tradition.

His position is not to be despised. God does speak through tradition. Without tradition, a society lacks continuity and stability. Education, for example, has the responsibility to transmit the cultural heritage from generation to generation. Yet, today the knowledge and values of the past are despised or confused so that educators cannot agree on a "common core" of learning which every student should experience. Like the Athenians whom the apostle Paul chided from Mars Hill, we are "intellectual seedpickers" who spend our time "in nothing else but either to tell or to hear some new thing" (Acts 17:21).

Fads and crazes are now moving through our society in shorter and shorter cycles because of the mass media. The hula hoop, for instance, lasted nine months in the early 1950s. Today, the fad would be gone in six or eight weeks! If our fads and crazes were limited to hula hoops, we could laugh them off. Sad to say, the same faddish cycle affects ideas as well as issues, values as well as tastes, and people as well as things in our society. Tradition deserves a modern hearing.

Bildad misuses tradition. Not only does he make it the weapon to bludgeon Job, but he sets it in concrete to harden in order to prove his case. Picking up on Job's poetic despair, "My days are swifter than a weaver's shuttle" (7:6), Bildad leaps to the conclusion that *"we were born yesterday,/and know nothing"* (8:9). Therefore, he says, let tradition teach us.

For Bildad himself, the retreat into tradition is a backward step in faith development. Job's questions dare him to critical thinking and personal reflection. They also threaten him with new information that does not fit into his formula of faith. Yet, there is no other way to grow in faith development. Bildad has the opportunity to move to the advanced level of *individuative-reflective faith* as a person who is capable of critical thinking, independent reflection, and dialectical reasoning. Even the next level of *conjunctive faith* opens before him if he could have moved with Job to a faith position that "integrates self-identity with a comprehensive world view in order to see the order, coherence, and meaning of life in order to serve and be served."[13] Alas, Bildad rejects these options and regresses back to *synthetic-conventional faith,* which Fowler defines as an "adolescent faith which conforms to the tradition of the community."[14] Bildad is a puppet through whom the fathers speak and tradition pulls the strings. A person with a borrowed faith can only mouth platitudes when the Jordan rises in the land of peace to test one's faith and when horses replace footmen in the race of life (Jer. 12:5).

Does God Make the Innocent Suffer?

Job dared to ask God, "Have I sinned?" (7:20). If he is innocent and still suffers, Bildad's case is lost. Bildad is not dumb. He knows that Job has the reputation for being "blameless." Therefore, he employs the tactic of admitting that his protagonist appears to be innocent. From that position, Bildad lets the wisdom of the fathers speak through three ancient parables. The first is the Parable of the Papyrus. If the reed grows up overnight without water, it has the appearance of a fresh and lively green shoot. But before the day is out, its lack of water is revealed when it withers and dies under the rays of the scorching sun. Bildad points a finger at Job and says, *"So are the paths of all who forget God"* (8:13). In a vivid picture, Bildad indicts Job for letting his righteousness go to his head and losing contact with his spiritual source. Job's innocence is "style without substance."

Tradition speaks again through the Parable of the Spider's Web. Bildad compares Job's self-confidence in claiming his innocence with the frailty of the spider's web. In its own dimensions, it appears to be strong and secure. But if a man leans on it, it does not stand, and if a man depends on it, it does not endure (vv. 14–15).

Charlie Brown, the lovable, round-headed, round-eyed, and round-mouthed character of the *Peanuts* comic strip, invariably snags his kite in a tree. It symbolizes the scandal of the cross of Christ which foils our human ambitions. Then, Charlie Brown has a flash of insight. While the tree continues to snarl his kite, he remembers that it also serves as a shade from the sun, a covering from the rain, and, when life is most disappointing, Charlie says, "It is very good to lean against."

In contrast with that strong tree of faith, Bildad likens Job's faith to the spider's web. If you lean on it, it will fall, and if you count on it, it will fail. At best, according to Bildad, Job's claim of innocence is "self-confidence without security."

Bildad draws a third word picture from the wisdom of the ages in the Parable of the Gourd. Although the New King James Version simply says, *"He grows green in the sun,"* other translations, such as the New International Version, add the qualifier "He is like *a well-watered plant* in the sunshine" (8:16). Biologists will identify the plant of the parable as a gourd whose roots snake along the ground in search of nooks in the rocks and crannies in the stone (v. 17). Although described as "green," "well-watered," and "luscious" in its prime, the gourd leaves no permanent roots in the ground when it dies. Thus, through the parable, Bildad refutes Job's belief that God will miss him when he is gone (7:21). Like the gourd that prospers in its season and then dies without leaving a trace of its existence, Bildad envisions Job's end when God will deny that He ever saw him (8:18). This indictment foreshadows the final judgment when God will pronounce the sentence on religious pretenders, "I never knew you; depart from Me" (Matt. 7:23). Daring to put similar words into God's mouth, Bildad concludes his parable with the warning to Job,

If he is destroyed from his place,
Then it will deny him, saying,
"I have not seen you" (8:18).

According to Bildad, Job has "prosperity without permanence."

Bildad the simplifier has an answer for everything. Admitting that he cannot refute Job's claim of innocence, he uses three parables to press home the only other conclusion that his doctrine of God's justice will permit: *Job is guilty of secret sins!* On the surface, he says, Job appears to be innocent because of his reputation, his self-confidence, and his prosperity. Now, the moment of truth has come. Job's suffering is positive proof that he has been living behind a facade. Like the Pharisees of Jesus' time, his life is a whited sepulcher, spotless on the outside, but inside it is full of dead men's bones. With his faith cemented in place by tradition, Bildad can come to no other conclusion.

Does God Leave Us without Hope?

Job has declared that his days are not only "swifter than a weaver's shuttle," but they are also "spent without hope" (7:6). In response to this voice of despair, Bildad finishes his speech on what appears to be a high note of hope,

> *He will yet fill your mouth with laughing,*
> *And your lips with rejoicing* (8:21).

His doctrine of "cash-register justice" has its side of joy as well as its side of doom. A dilemma is created by the fact that Bildad speaks the truth. God does reward the righteous with joy and punish the wicked with death. The way in which Bildad applies the truth, however, makes all the difference in the world.

One of the signs of the *synthetic-conventional faith* into which Bildad retreated is the tendency to pigeonhole people into one of two categories—those in whom the community rejoices as "models" of tradition and those whom the community rejects as "mavericks" against tradition. Everyone fits into one category or another. Bildad reveals this mindset in applying the formula of "cash-register justice" to human behavior. Job has his choice. If he is "blameless," his mouth will laugh and his lips will rejoice again. If he is an *"evildoer,"* God will destroy his tents and leave no trace of his existence (8:22).

Bildad's logic has its own deceit. Under the guise of offering Job hope, he twists a word and condemns his character. There is a world of difference between *"evildoers"* (v. 20) and *"the wicked"* (v. 22). Semantics teach us the meaning of our words. If a schoolteacher catches Johnny stealing a pencil, she may accuse him of the act by saying, "Johnny, you stole a pencil." Or, she may jump to judgment about his character by the condemnation, "Johnny, you are a thief." Her first words condemn the act of stealing; her next words indict the character of the person. Bildad chooses the second tactic when he sets Job's reputation for being "blameless" on one side of the ledger, and then advances his judgment of Job as one of *"the wicked"* on the other side of the ledger. By pushing his doctrine to its logical extreme, Bildad has hardened the categories and reversed the character of Job from being "blameless" to being "evil" through and through.

Bildad must have closed his speech with the confidence that he has brought the final resolution of the Jobian question. God's justice has been successfully defended, truth has been graphically pictured, tradition is intact, secret sins have been exposed, and Job has no recourse except to repent or be wiped from the face of the earth. Thus speaks Bildad, the grand inquisitor of religious tradition.

Job—A Cry for a Mediator

Job continues to be obsessed with Eliphaz's praise of the power of God. Citing the destructive side of God's power, Job contends that man is so insignificant that he has no hope of contending with Him. In fact, he goes on to say that God uses His destructive power indiscriminately upon the innocent as well as the wicked. More than that, God has given the world over to the wicked and even mocks the suffering of the innocent. Job has reached the bottom of his bitterness. Still, he reaches up to call for a mediator who can stand equal between him and God as he pleads his case. Knowing that he has none, he can only turn on God again to scream, "Do you delight in what you are doing?" "Is your vision short?" "Is your life brief?" "Do you need to take out vengeance on me?"

Regaining some reason, Job points out the contradiction that he sees in God. If he is God's creation, why does God want to destroy him? When God does not answer, Job sinks back in the pit of despair, crying out for a moment's peace before death in the land of shadows where even light is darkness.

9:1 Then Job answered and said:
2 "Truly I know it is so,
But how can a man be righteous before God?

3 If one wished to contend with Him,
He could not answer Him one time out of a thousand.
4 God is wise in heart and mighty in strength.
Who has hardened himself against Him and prospered?
5 He removes the mountains, and they do not know
When He overturns them in His anger;
6 He shakes the earth out of its place,
And its pillars tremble;
7 He commands the sun, and it does not rise;
He seals off the stars;
8 He alone spreads out the heavens,
And treads on the waves of the sea;
9 He made the Bear, Orion, and the Pleiades,
And the chambers of the south;
10 He does great things past finding out,
Yes, wonders without number.
11 If He goes by me, I do not see Him;
If He moves past, I do not perceive Him;
12 If He takes away, who can hinder Him?
Who can say to Him, 'What are You doing?'
13 God will not withdraw His anger,
The allies of the proud lie prostrate beneath Him.
14 "How then can I answer Him,
And choose my words to reason with Him?
15 For though I were righteous, I could not answer Him;
I would beg mercy of my Judge.
16 If I called and He answered me,
I would not believe that He was listening to my voice.
17 For He crushes me with a tempest,
And multiplies my wounds without cause.
18 He will not allow me to catch my breath,
But fills me with bitterness.
19 If it is a matter of strength, indeed He is strong;
And if of justice, who will appoint my day in court?
20 Though I were righteous, my own mouth would condemn me;

Though I were blameless, it would prove me
perverse.
21 "I am blameless, yet I do not know myself;
I despise my life.
22 It is all one thing;
Therefore I say, 'He destroys the blameless and
the wicked.'
23 If the scourge slays suddenly,
He laughs at the plight of the innocent.
24 The earth is given into the hand of the wicked.
He covers the faces of its judges.
If it is not He, who else could it be?
25 "Now my days are swifter than a runner;
They flee away, they see no good.
26 They pass by like swift ships,
Like an eagle swooping on its prey.
27 If I say, 'I will forget my complaint,
I will put off my sad face and wear a smile,'
28 I am afraid of all my sufferings;
I know that You will not hold me innocent.
29 If I am condemned,
Why then do I labor in vain?
30 If I wash myself with snow water,
And cleanse my hands with soap,
31 Yet You will plunge me into the pit,
And my own clothes will abhor me.
32 "For He is not a man, as I am,
That I may answer Him,
And that we should go to court together.
33 Nor is there any mediator between us,
Who may lay his hand on us both.
34 Let Him take His rod away from me,
And do not let dread of Him terrify me.
35 Then I would speak and not fear Him,
But it is not so with me.
10:1 "My soul loathes my life;
I will give free course to my complaint,
I will speak in the bitterness of my soul.
2 I will say to God, 'Do not condemn me;
Show me why You contend with me.
3 Does it seem good to You that You should
oppress,

That You should despise the work of Your hands,
And smile on the counsel of the wicked?
4 Do You have eyes of flesh?
Or do You see as man sees?
5 Are Your days like the days of a mortal man?
Are Your years like the days of a mighty man,
6 That You should seek for my iniquity
And search out my sin,
7 Although You know that I am not wicked,
And there is no one who can deliver from Your hand?
8 'Your hands have made me and fashioned me,
An intricate unity;
Yet You would destroy me.
9 Remember, I pray, that You have made me like clay.
And will You turn me into dust again?
10 Did You not pour me out like milk,
And curdle me like cheese,
11 Clothe me with skin and flesh,
And knit me together with bones and sinews?
12 You have granted me life and favor,
And Your care has preserved my spirit.
13 'And these things You have hidden in Your heart;
I know that this was with You:
14 If I sin, then You mark me,
And will not acquit me of my iniquity.
15 If I am wicked, woe to me;
Even if I am righteous, I cannot lift up my head.
I am full of disgrace;
See my misery!
16 If my head is exalted,
You hunt me like a fierce lion,
And again You show Yourself awesome against me.
17 You renew Your witnesses against me,
And increase Your indignation toward me;
Changes and war are ever with me.
18 'Why then have You brought me out of the womb?
Oh, that I had perished and no eye had seen me!

19 I would have been as though I had not been.
I would have been carried from the womb to the grave.
20 Are not my days few?
Cease! Leave me alone, that I may take a little comfort,
21 Before I go to the place from which I shall not return,
To the land of darkness and the shadow of death,
22 A land as dark as darkness itself,
As the shadow of death, without any order,
where even the light is like darkness.' "

Job 9:1—10:22

A sudden reversal in tone is detected in Job's response to Bildad. The bitter sarcasm with which he answered Eliphaz is gone. In its place is a concession that Bildad speaks the truth, followed by a tightly woven argument surrounding the question, *"How can a man be righteous before God?"* (9:2). Job gives us the impression of a man who has stepped back from his inner anguish and outer anger to take a reasoned look at the doctrines of God's justice and man's righteousness.

Job's Rational Answer to Bildad

How do we account for the reversal in tone? Perhaps it is the fact that Bildad concluded his speech on the positive note:

He will yet fill your mouth with laughing,
And your lips with rejoicing.
Those who hate you will be clothed with shame,
And the dwelling place of the wicked will come to nothing (8:21–22).

Or perhaps the traditional answers of Bildad put Job back on the familiar ground of his past knowledge from which he can speak with confidence.

Suffering itself may have had a bearing on Job's response. Perhaps, at this moment, the pain lifts so that Job can think clearly once again. Or perhaps his pain reaches that unexplainable stage when the mind is honed to a razor's edge of incisive and insightful thinking. Whatever the reason, Job enters into the danger zone where cold and steely skepticism can take over hot and malleable anguish.

During the days of student protest in the late 1960s, we shuddered under the curses of radical students who marched on our streets, trashed our offices, and threatened to blow up our buildings. Perspective came back only when we recognized that Marx, Engels, and Lenin were more dangerous than Jerry Rubin on the streets crying, "Do it!" How true. The fiery hate of the radical students has burned out, leaving only the ashes of their rebellion. But Marx's theory of class struggle, which was refined by Lenin's call for violent revolution, which in turn gave rise to the Communist dictatorship, continues to feed tension, hatred, and upheaval across the world.

Job survived the raving of his emotions. Can he survive the logic of his despair? Cutting cynicism is detected in his question, *"How can a man be righteous before God?"* Both Eliphaz and Bildad advised him to repent and return to righteousness. In response to them, Job has already come to the conclusion that even a righteous man cannot stand before the sovereign God.

> *If one wished to contend with Him,*
> *He could not answer Him one time out of a thousand* (9:3).

To prove his point, Job employs a simple syllogism:

Major premise: God's power is so great.
Minor premise: Man's righteousness is so weak.
Conclusion: God and man cannot be reconciled.

Job refutes the advice of Eliphaz and Bildad by cold logic. But, in so doing, he compounds his own futility by arriving at another dead end in his search for hope.

The Overwhelming Nature of God's Power

For Job, man has no righteousness of his own. It must always be found in relationship to the character of God. Therefore, to answer the question, *"How can a man be righteous before God?"* Job begins with a doxology or "Hymn of God" that matches similar songs sung by Eliphaz and Bildad. Majestic poetry and profound truth flow through the lines as Job proclaims, *"God is wise of heart and mighty in strength"* (v. 4). But then Job goes on to declare that the way in which God exercises His wisdom and strength puts Him far beyond the understanding and control of man. In staccato sentences, Job recounts the power of God at work in creation: removes mountains, shakes the earth, commands the sun, seals off the stars, spreads out the heavens, treads on the seas, and made the constellations (vv. 5–9).

Thus, man can only infer the nature of God from the tracings of His power at work in the "great things" and the *"wonders"* (v. 10) of creation. Human eyes cannot *"see"* Him, human minds cannot *"perceive"* Him (v. 11), human will cannot *"hinder"* Him, and human reason cannot question Him (v. 12). Before the power and wisdom of God who is so far removed from man, the only posture is to fall prostrate at His feet (v. 13).

Those of us who are privileged to know the love and grace of God as shown in Jesus Christ may jump to judgment on Job's primitive theology. We forget that he had only the natural revelation of the created world and human conscience to guide him.

Without the revelation of God's Word or God's Son, Job has to draw his image of God from the limited perspective of the two attributes that are clearly seen in the created order: *power* and *wisdom.* Both of these attributes are impersonal, unreachable, and overwhelming. Therefore, man's relationship to God is limited to submitting to His power and searching for His wisdom. Conscience, the divine spark given in the creation of man, is the only guide for righteousness. Rather than judging Job's theology as primitive and his faith as small, we should be amazed at his spiritual maturity that reached to the boundaries of his limited knowledge of God and even pressed by faith into a redemptive future.

The Indefensible Nature of Man's Righteousness

To draw the striking contrast between God's power and man's righteousness, Job envisions a courtroom scene in which he pleads the case for his righteousness. The problem is that God is prosecuting attorney, judge, and jury. Whatever Job says and however eloquently he speaks, his ignorance and impotence will condemn him before the all-wise and all-powerful God (9:20).

What difference is there, then, between blameless and wicked people? Using his own case, in which he continues to contend for his innocence and yet confesses that he does not know himself, Job reasons that God is so distant that He wields His power of destruction upon the blameless and the wicked without discrimination (v. 22). Turning Eliphaz's and Bildad's arguments back upon them, Job lays down the gauntlet by denying the doctrine of "cash-register justice" upon which their faith is built. The price of this position, however, almost costs Job his own faith. His logic leads him from a *deistic God* who does not care to a *devil God* who *"laughs at the plight of the innocent"* (v. 23). Job will live to regret his words, *"If it is not He, who else could it be?"* (v. 24).

Human attempts to explain suffering and still believe in God always fall into the same trap. If a person denies the existence of God, suffering is no problem because it can be explained as the "luck of the draw" in a universe of random chances. C. S. Lewis, in *A Grief Observed,* wrote: "Not that I am (I think) in much danger of ceasing to believe in God. The real danger is of coming to believe such dreadful things about Him. The conclusion I dread is not 'So there's no God after all,' but 'So this is what God's really like. Deceive yourself no longer.' "[15]

Following the path of human reason, Job comes to that dreadful intellectual conclusion. Only the confidence of his past relationship with God will keep him from relinquishing his faith and succumbing to the explanation that a devil God delights in his suffering. Yet, because he raised the question and inferred the answer, his words will come back to haunt him time and time again as his friends personalize their attacks.

Human reason can never explain suffering. If God exists, He is either distant or devilish. Another alternative is that God is limited in power. Edgar Brightman, the philosopher, dealt with the problem of human suffering when his wife died. He reasoned that if God cared, He would heal her. Healing did not come, so Brightman could only maintain his concept of a personal God by concluding that His power was limited. A distant God who does not care, a devil God who laughs at suffering, a limited God who cares but cannot heal— is there any alternative other than atheism? With all Christians who suffer, Job finds himself suspended in the paradox of a loving God who permits suffering among the innocent and the righteous as well as among the wicked. To try to escape the paradox by human reason is to run down a dead-end street.

Like a rat in a maze, Job's mind turns back from one end of reason and runs down other alleys. Taking the advice of his comforters, he thinks about putting on a happy face. Invariably, a person who suffers is told, "Look on the bright side of things."

Charlie Brown, the *Peanuts* character, goes to Dr. Lucy's psychiatric stand because no one likes him. Lucy counsels him to look on the bright side of life by saying, "Cheer up, Charlie Brown; you have lots of friends." With widened eyes, Charlie responds with bright surprise, "I do?" "Of course you do, Charlie Brown," Lucy assures him. "I do, I do," Charlie tells himself. "I have lots of friends." As he walks away with his head in the air repeating those words, Lucy taunts after him, "Name one."

Job feels as if God will treat him the same way. If he puts on the smile of a happy face, God will condemn him for gladness (9:27–28); if he washes himself with the purest of water and the strongest of soap, God will dunk him in a slime pit (vv. 30–31). Neither reason, righteousness, nor repentance will make a difference. God, the prosecutor, condemns him; God, the jury, pronounces him guilty; and God, the judge, sentences him to punishment without appeal.

The Only Hope for Irreconcilable Differences

Human reason has driven Job to the edge of a chasm over which he cannot see. On the far and unseeable side is the transcendent God—all-wise and all-powerful. On the near and seeable side, Job stands with all humankind—ignorant and impotent. Even if he is innocent, there is no chance that he can contend with God in the court of the universe. Futility is ready to flood his soul once again except for a flash of prophetic insight that sends a shudder through his being. *A mediator!* Job sees the only way across the chasm between God and man. Reason is not a dead end after all. Job's vision of a courtroom scene opens up one last hope. If only he had a mediator who would stand with one hand on God and one hand on him, he could plead his case. In one of the most indelible images and insightful moments of Old Testament Scriptures, Job foresees Christ through the eyes of faith. This is the truth that shakes the earth. Job's hope is not in reason; it is in reconciliation!

Who can ever forget the image of a mediator standing in the gap of irreconcilable differences with a hand on each of the contending parties? This is the scene on the cross where Jesus dies while reaching out with one hand touching the holy God and the other hand touching sinful man. This is also the scene that is being repeated each time that a soul is redeemed, a prayer of intercession is prayed, a biblical sermon is preached, a human relationship is healed, or a cup of cold water is given in Jesus' name. In every case, Christ or "Christ in us" stands in the gap of irreconcilable differences, reaches out to touch contending parties, and brings healing through personal sacrifice. All other avenues to reconciliation between God and man or person and person are blind alleys. Although Job's plea for a mediator will temporarily fall on deaf ears, he teaches us that the answer to human suffering is found in reconciliation, not reason. With this insight, Job dismisses the rational question *what* and returns to ask God directly the relational question *why*.

Job's Relational Questions to God

Reason has taken Job to a dead end where he knows that he cannot contend with God or count upon a mediator to plead his case for him. His only hope is to fall back upon the relationship that he had with God before his suffering. He honored God with a "blameless" life (1:1) and God honored him with the commendation to Satan, "Have you considered My servant Job?" (1:8 and 2:3). Even though Job did not hear God's words spoken in heaven's council, he has the same sense of assurance that we have when "the Spirit Himself bears witness with our spirit that we are children of God" (Rom. 8:16). With the same boldness that lets us come before the throne of God and cry, "Abba, Father," Job is willing to put that relationship to the test. The question *why* returns to his lips, but it is no longer a shout to the winds. Directly and freely, he confronts God with the question, "Why does your current behavior contradict our past relationship?" Like a wounded lover, Job wants to know, "Who has changed, you or I?" In his boldest words to date, Job challenges God to account for the apparent contradictions in His behavior.

Throwing down the gauntlet, again he speaks brashly, *"Show me why You contend with me"* (10:2).

Why Do You Behave Like a Man?

In a series of stinging questions, Job pulls God down from His transcendent perch and accuses Him of acting like a man—enjoying oppression, despising creation, and exalting the wicked (v. 3). To add insult to injury, Job even accuses God of being a man, seeing through eyes of flesh (v. 4), living out brevity of life (v. 5), and playing games with temporal power (v. 6).

If Job's accusations are true, God is nothing more than a man-god who deserves a niche in the pantheon of the Greeks. Although Job knows better, at least he would understand why God tries to ferret out his sin and refuses to deliver him.

Why Do You Destroy Your Own Creation?

In a beautiful sequence of creation pictures, Job further reveals his personal relationship to God. Inspiration leads him to say, *"Your hands have made me and fashioned me, / An intricate unity"* (v. 8). Then, almost scolding God, Job reminds Him that He is like the potter who shaped him out of clay, the dairyman who poured him out like milk and curdled him like cheese, or the tailor who clothed him with skin and flesh and knit him with bones and sinews (vv. 9–11). More than that, Job asks God to remember that He granted him life, showed him favor, and preserved his spirit with His loving care. Centuries later, Job would have stopped to sing John Greenleaf Whittier's hymn:

> I know not where His islands lift
> Their fronded palms in air,
> I only know I cannot drift
> Beyond His love and care.

But while singing the last note, Job would break into tears and cry, "Why, O why, God, do You now destroy Your creation?"

Why Do You Hide Your Purpose from Me?

Once again, we are utterly amazed by the evidence of Job's mature faith when his knowledge of God is limited to natural revelation in physical creation and human conscience. Now we learn that personal communication characterized his relationship with God. Job might well sing another well-known hymn ("In the Garden," C. Austin Miles) as he recalls his communion with God:

And He walks with me,
And He talks with me,
And He tells me I am His own,
And the joy we share as we tarry there,
None other has ever known.

Such singing only aggravates the pain of broken communion. Job seems to say that if God would talk to him again, he would understand why He is marking him, making him miserable, hunting him like an animal, bringing witness after witness against him, and piling up anger upon anger toward him (10:14–17). But God hides His purpose in His heart and refuses to speak to him, so Job moans, *"Changes and war are ever with me"* (v. 17). He would now sing the dirge: "Things fall apart; the centre cannot hold."[16]

Job's suffering is more than physical. Without telling him why, God has broken off communication with him. In a limited way, Job is experiencing the hell through which Jesus went when He cried, "My God, My God, why have You forsaken Me?" (Mark 15:34).

Why Do You Let Me Live?

A full cycle has turned when Job repeats his first cry of anguish, "Why did I not die at birth?" (3:11). This time, however, he is charging God with contradiction. Having once known the care of God, Job cannot accept the fact that he is now the target for destruction. Therefore, he calls God to one last show of consistency with the plea,

Leave me alone,
that I may take a little comfort,
Before I go to the place from which
I shall not return (10:20–21).

All of those who suffer will identify with his final plea. More often than not, there is a moment of relief from pain, a memorable word to the family and a smile of peace just before death. I hang onto my last words to my father, "Dad, I love you," the last meal with my mother, and the last prayer of my father-in-law. All of life gets wrapped up in those moments when God gives His grace and shows us the hope of eternity.

Job's suffering is intensified because he has neither that grace nor that hope. God gives him no relief, and death means compounded darkness. Job's attitude shames those of us who live righteously because of the hope of heaven. Job has only the land of darkness awaiting him after death,

> *as dark as darkness itself,*
> *As the shadow of death, . . .*
> *Where even the light is like darkness"* (v. 22).

In the New Testament, such eternal darkness belongs to the vilest of those who deliberately turn their backs upon Jesus Christ and become "wandering stars for whom is reserved the blackness of darkness forever" (Jude 13).

If only Job knew how God really felt about him! If only he knew how God anticipated his companionship in heaven! Even without this knowledge, Job refuses to give up his belief in the God of wisdom and might who created him, cares for him, speaks to him, and sustains him. His past relationship with his God must hold him because the present relationship of suffering is a contradiction.

Zophar—The Reaction of Common Sense

Job's daring attack on the justice of God drives Zophar to fury. Living in a simplistic black-and-white world of absolute righteousness, Zophar lets Job know that he is getting less than he deserves for his sins, many of which are secret. Extolling God's limitless wisdom and power once again, he places any human attempt at understanding in the category of utter folly. Zophar also counters Job's charge that God uses His power indiscriminately by saying that God does not ignore iniquity. Finally, he counters Job's futility with a declaration of hope, but within the context of submission, which is the only way to happiness. Not content to stop on a positive note, Zophar ends with the warning that unless Job repents, he is in the company of the wicked for whom there is no hope.

1 Then Zophar the Naamathite answered and said:
2 "Should not the multitude of words be answered?
And should a man full of talk be vindicated?
3 Should your empty talk make men hold their peace?
And when you mock, should no one rebuke you?
4 For you have said,
'My doctrine is pure,
And I am clean in your eyes.'
5 But oh, that God would speak,
And open His lips against you,
6 That He would show you the secrets of wisdom!
For they would double your prudence.
Know therefore that God exacts from you
Less than your iniquity deserves.
7 "Can you search out the deep things of God?
Can you find out the limits of the Almighty?
8 They are higher than heaven—what can you do?
Deeper than Sheol—what can you know?
9 Their measure is longer than the earth
And broader than the sea.
10 "If He passes by, imprisons, and gathers to judgment,
Then who can hinder Him?
11 For He knows deceitful men;
He sees wickedness also.
Will He not then consider it?
12 For an empty-headed man will be wise,
When a wild donkey's colt is born a man.
13 "If you would prepare your heart,
And stretch out your hands toward Him;
14 If iniquity were in your hand, and you put it far away,
And would not let wickedness dwell in your tents;

15 Then surely you could lift up your face without spot;
Yes, you could be steadfast, and not fear;
16 Because you would forget your misery,
And remember it as waters that have passed away,
17 And your life would be brighter than noonday.
Though you were dark, you would be like the morning.
18 And you would be secure, because there is hope;
Yes, you would dig around you, and take your rest in safety.
19 You would also lie down, and no one would make you afraid;
yes, many would court your favor.
20 But the eyes of the wicked will fail,
And they shall not escape,
And their hope—loss of life!"

Job 11:1–20

Like a leopard springing from ambush upon its unsuspecting prey, Zophar enters the debate clawing and scratching for Job's jugular vein. As the youngest of the three friends, he has been biding his time and building his rage. Lacking the courtesy of Eliphaz, which prompted him to apologize before speaking, or the cowardice of Bildad, which led him to hide behind tradition, Zophar minces no words and spares no feelings in his vehement attacks on Job. Whereas Eliphaz and Bildad tried to make their suffering friend feel guilty by reciting the formula that sin equals suffering, Zophar tries to bludgeon Job with verbal violence that will reduce him to shame.

The stage is set in Zophar's opening words. As if mimicking Job's description of the four shades of darkness that engulf the soul after death, Zophar counts four sounds of verbiage that he hears from Job's lips—unnecessary words, empty words, false words, mocking words (11:2–3).

It is one thing to call Job a "windbag" as Bildad does. The term, although derogatory, suggests that Job's words are unnecessary and *"empty."* Therefore, they should not be taken seriously. It is quite another thing for Zophar to make moral judgment on Job's words by pronouncing him "false" and "mocking." According to Zophar, Job is far more than a "windbag"; he is a heretic and a blasphemer. Youthful anger has pushed Zophar to an extreme position, which he must now defend. His tactic is to exaggerate the truth and exploit Job's suffering to shame him into repentance.

Far back in my memory is a scene at a sawhorse altar in the tabernacle of an outdoor camp meeting. As a teenage boy, I responded to the evangelist's call for total surrender. Despite confessing with tears and pleading with sweat, God did not come to me, at least not with the emotional gusher that was promised to purge my soul. When the evangelist saw my plight, he laid his hands upon my head and stormed the gates of heaven on my behalf. Eventually, he lapsed into prolonged moaning when nothing happened. Suddenly, his moans were broken by the shout, "I know what's wrong! His sin is pride. He is proud of his curly hair!" Ten calloused fingers roughed up my scalp and messed up my hair presumably to expose my secret sin and cancel my pride. Although only a teenager, I might have become a skeptic. The evangelist did not know that I had begged my mother all week to let me get a "burr cut" like the other guys on the football team. Perspective lets me laugh at the incident now, but it also helps me understand how Job must have felt under the lashing of Zophar. Anyone who claims to know God's "secret" reason for sin or suffering is a brutal "comforter."

Exaggerating God's Justice

Zophar has already violated one of the cardinal rules of debate, negotiation, or counseling. He lets anger drive him into the corner of overcommitment. In political debate, for instance, the rule is "never say never." Candidates who win elections on such a promise usually live to regret their words. Zophar's four-fold denunciation of Job's words as "unnecessary," "empty," "false," and "mocking" fit the same category of verbal overcommitment. To prove his point, Zophar must continue to exaggerate the truth and jump to judgment on his former friend.

True to form, Zophar breaks another rule of good communication when he puts words into Job's mouth. Communication breaks down, hope for reconciliation fades when an opponent declares, "You said," rather than saying, "I think I heard you say." Very seldom is the quotation consistent with the words of the speaker and if the words are repeated verbatim, the inflection of the voice and the language of the body can change the meaning. Zophar uses the ploy of saying, "You said," to misquote Job's testimony before God:

> *"My doctrine is pure,*
> *And I am clean in your eyes"* (11:4).

While Job believes that his reasoning is right and his heart is righteous, he does not use the words *pure* or *clean* with the connotation of being equal with God. Zophar hears what he wants to hear and quotes what he wants to quote.

His next ploy is no surprise. Zophar wishes that God would answer Job's prayer and speak to him. If God did speak as Zophar says, Job would learn the truth—the secrets of wisdom—about himself. But God does not have to speak. Young Zophar has the answer. Job would learn that God exacts from him *"less than his inquity deserves"* (v. 6). Beware of anyone who claims to know the secrets of God's mind. Privileged information is a vicious weapon when used to protect our own self-interest. Worse yet, if privileged information is turned into an offensive weapon to press a personal advantage, truth becomes one of its victims.

In Job's case, Zophar defends God's justice by putting the weight of Job's "secret" sins on a scale to overbalance his suffering. From the viewpoint of Christ's redemption, this is true. We deserve death for our sins. But from the viewpoint of the doctrine of God's justice as taught by Job's friends, Zophar's conclusion is illogical. In fact, he comes close to destroying the doctrine that he is trying to defend. Eliphaz and Bildad argued for the balanced equation that sin equals suffering and righteousness equals prosperity. If, however, Job's suffering is less than his sin, his sin may also be less than his suffering! In his zeal to shame Job, Zophar has fallen into the trap of "situational ethics" by opening up an exception to a truth he held to be absolute. Unwittingly, he lends credence to Job's argument that suffering or prosperity may be independent of a person's righteousness or wickedness. Anger that fuels exaggeration to shame an enemy or defend a doctrine is a force that turns upon itself in self-destruction.

Exaggerating God's Wisdom

The sheer beauty of Zophar's hymn of praise to the wisdom of God is baffling. Taken by itself and out of context, this hymn soars on the wings of divine inspiration. All four dimensions of the created universe are seen in God's domain, and yet they cannot contain His wisdom. Beyond the boundaries of creation is the mystery of God,

> *They are higher than heaven . . .*
> *Deeper than Sheol . . .*
> *longer than the earth*
> *And broader than the sea* (vv. 8–9).

Too bad that Zophar has to turn inspired truth into another weapon against Job. Ironically, he says the same thing that God will say to Job later. The difference is in Zophar's assumption and attitude. With a sneer, he scoffs at Job's attempts to probe the mystery of God's wisdom beyond the created order:

> *Can you search out the deep things of God?*
> *Can you find out the limits of the Almighty?*
> . . . .
> *what can you know?* (vv. 7–8).

Assuming that he has put Job in his place, Zophar mars the beauty of his hymn of praise by making himself privy to God's mind in order to defend his own doctrine. With an Olympic leap of logic, he springs from the "mystery" of God's wisdom to the "certainty" of God's judgment:

> *Then who can hinder Him? . . .*
> . . . .
> *Will He not then consider it [wickedness]?"* (vv. 10–11).

The formula works once again. Job suffers for his sins. Anger and arrogance then combine in Zophar's exaggerated oath,

> *For an empty-headed man will be wise,*
> *When a wild donkey's colt is born a man* (v. 12).

Zophar falls victim to his own verbiage. His agitation ignites verbal violence that flares up and becomes a careless curse. Not only does he denounce Job as an "empty-headed ass," but in contemporary language he declares that wisdom will elude Job "till hell freezes over."

Somewhere in the process, Job's pitiful condition has been forgotten and his anguished cry has been ignored. Zophar is consumed by his own anger and personifies the quip, "With friends like you, who needs enemies?" Pity the sufferer who is comforted by the likes of Zophar.

Exaggerating God's Promises

Zophar is a form player. Everything he says is predictable. After likening Job to an empty-headed donkey, he bends down to redeem him. Four spiritual steps are required, he says: *"Prepare your heart,"* pray to God, put away iniquity, and repudiate wickedness (vv. 13–14).

Zophar's religion is right but ritualistic. Righteousness for him is a lockstep system of religious discipline. Little provision is made for a personal relationship between God and man. Instead, justice rules the relationship. Zophar deserves credit for being consistent at this point. *If God's justice rules righteousness, does it not also rule His rewards?* Zophar follows through by holding out God's rewards for righteousness like carrots on a stick. If Job will follow the four-step path to righteousness, Zophar assures him:

> *You could lift up your face without spot;*
> *Yes, you could be steadfast, and not fear;*
> *Because you would forget your misery, . . .*
> *And Your life would be brighter than noonday. . . .*
> *you would be like the morning.*
> *And you would be secure, . . .*
> *Yes, you would . . . take your rest in safety. . . .*
> *no one would make you afraid;*
> *Yes, many would court your favor* (vv. 15–19).

For twentieth-century Christians, these promises have a familiar ring. "Prosperity" religion is being marketed through the media and over the pulpit as the evidence of faith. Success, status, and security are promoted as automatic results of dependence upon God. Healing for those who suffer is guaranteed as the will of God. How unrealistic! How unfair to God! Faith in Christ is not weighed on one side of the scale with prosperity, success, status, security, and healing on the other. Just the opposite. Christ identifies Himself with the last, the least, and the lost in His age. We, in turn, can only identify with Him as we share His compassion and His suffering. To weigh our faith on a scale with our rewards is nothing more than a spiritual application of the "equity theory" that was noted earlier.

According to this theory, human relationships are put on the scale of self-interest so that every issue of life becomes a question, "What's in it for me?" Zophar's brand of righteousness was based upon the same scale: righteousness is weighed against prosperity. Such a rigid system of justice stands in radical contradiction to the love of God as revealed in Jesus Christ. A mature faith is a growing relationship, not a reward system. As mutual trust develops between God and us, He permits us to be tested and we remain true. Keep in mind that Job is suffering because of God's confidence in him, not because of his sin. Under Zophar's religious system, he would have cursed God and died when the first wild wind wiped out his family.

Sweetness easily turns to bitterness in Zophar's shallow faith. To conclude his strange speech of exaggerated truth, blemished beauty, and unrealistic promises, he pulls back the carrot and wields the stick. With curled lip, Zophar sarcastically answers Job's prayer for a sign of hope with the warning, *"And* [your] *hope—loss of life!"* (v. 20).

May all who suffer be spared the comfort of Zophar. To feel no compassion for pain, to pretend to know the "secret" of suffering, to claim the inside knowledge of the mystery of God, to reduce the relationship between God and man into a ritual, and to hold out glossy and unrealistic hopes for righteousness—Zophar will either destroy the final shreds of Job's faith or deepen the pain of his suffering.

Job—A Cry for God

Sarcasm replaces skepticism in Job's reply to Zophar. Lashing out at his friends, he claims equal if not superior knowledge of God's power in natural creation, human experience, and the social order.

Then, adding injury to insult, Job denounces the worthless wisdom of his friends and turns again to God with the astounding affirmation, *"Though He slay me, / yet will I trust Him"* (13:15). This confidence gives Job the boldness to repeat his demand for an audience with God to present his case. He only asks that God speak to him and specify his sins. When God does not answer, Job lapses back into the despair of seeing human life as short, unclean, and futile. In one desperate thrust of thought, Job asks if there is life after death, but it becomes a precipice from which he falls into the deeper despair of believing that death is universal, final, and hopeless.

12:1 Then Job answered and said:
2 "No doubt you are the people,
And wisdom will die with you!
3 But I have understanding as well as you;
I am not inferior to you.
Indeed, who does not know such things as these?
4 "I am one mocked by his friends,
Who called on God, and He answered him,
The just and blameless who is ridiculed.
5 A lamp is despised in the thought of one who is at ease;
It is made ready for those whose feet slip.
6 The tents of robbers prosper,
And those who provoke God are secure—
In what God provides by His hand.
7 "But now ask the beasts, and they will teach you;
And the birds of the air, and they will tell you;
8 Or speak to the earth, and it will teach you;
And the fish of the sea will explain to you.
9 Who among all these does not know
That the hand of the LORD has done this,
10 In whose hand is the life of every living thing,
And the breath of all mankind?
11 Does not the ear test words
And the mouth taste its food?
12 Wisdom is with aged men,
And with length of days, understanding.
13 "With Him are wisdom and strength,
He has counsel and understanding.

14 If He breaks a thing down, it cannot be rebuilt;
If He imprisons a man, there can be no release.
15 If He withholds the waters, they dry up;
If He sends them out, they overwhelm the earth.
16 With Him are strength and prudence.
The deceived and the deceiver are His.
17 He leads counselors away plundered,
And makes fools of the judges.
18 He loosens the bonds of kings,
And binds their waist with a belt.
19 He leads princes away plundered,
And overthrows the mighty.
20 He deprives the trusted ones of speech,
And takes away the discernment of the elders.
21 He pours contempt on princes,
And disarms the mighty.
22 He uncovers deep things out of darkness,
And brings the shadow of death to light.
23 He makes nations great, and destroys them;
He enlarges nations, and guides them.
24 He takes away the understanding of the chiefs
of the people of the earth,
And makes them wander in a pathless wilderness.
25 They grope in the dark without light,
And He makes them stagger like a drunken man.
13:1 "Behold, my eye has seen all this,
My ear has heard and understood it.
2 What you know, I also know;
I am not inferior to you.
3 But I would speak to the Almighty,
And I desire to reason with God.
4 But you forgers of lies,
You are all worthless physicians.
5 Oh, that you would be silent,
And it would be your wisdom!
6 Now hear my reasoning,
And heed the pleadings of my lips.
7 Will you speak wickedly for God,
And talk deceitfully for Him?
8 Will you show partiality for Him?
Will you contend for God?

9 Will it be well when He searches you out?
Or can you mock Him as one mocks a man?
10 He will surely rebuke you
If you secretly show partiality.
11 Will not His excellence make you afraid,
And the dread of Him fall upon you?
12 Your platitudes are proverbs of ashes,
Your defenses are defenses of clay.
13 "Hold your peace with me, and let me speak,
Then let come on me what may!
14 Why do I take my flesh in my teeth,
And put my life in my hands?
15 Though He slay me, yet will I trust Him.
Even so, I will defend my own ways before Him.
16 He also shall be my salvation,
For a hypocrite could not come before Him.
17 Listen carefully to my speech,
And to my declaration with your ears.
18 See now, I have prepared my case,
I know that I shall be vindicated.
19 Who is he who will contend with me?
If now I hold my tongue, I perish.
20 "Only two things do not do to me,
Then I will not hide myself from You:
21 Withdraw Your hand far from me,
And let not the dread of You make me afraid.
22 Then call, and I will answer;
Or let me speak, then You respond to me.
23 How many are my iniquities and sins?
Make me know my transgression and my sin.
24 Why do You hide Your face,
And regard me as Your enemy?
25 Will You frighten a leaf driven to and fro?
And will You pursue dry stubble?
26 For You write bitter things against me,
And make me inherit the iniquities of my youth.
27 You put my feet in the stocks,
And watch closely all my paths.
You set a limit for the soles of my feet.
28 "Man decays like a rotten thing,
Like a garment that is moth-eaten.

14:1 "Man who is born of woman
Is of few days and full of trouble.
2 He comes forth like a flower and fades away;
He flees like a shadow and does not continue.
3 And do You open Your eyes on such a one,
And bring me to judgment with Yourself?
4 Who can bring a clean thing out of an unclean?
No one!
5 Since his days are determined,
The number of his months is with You;
You have appointed his limits, so that he cannot pass.
6 Look away from him that he may rest,
Till like a hired man he finishes his day.
7 "For there is hope for a tree,
If it is cut down, that it will sprout again,
And that its tender shoots will not cease.
8 Though its root may grow old in the earth,
And its stump may die in the ground,
9 Yet at the scent of water it will bud
And bring forth branches like a plant.
10 But man dies and is laid away;
Indeed he breathes his last
And where is he?
11 As water disappears from the sea,
And a river becomes parched and dries up,
12 So man lies down and does not rise.
Till the heavens are no more,
They will not awake
Nor be roused from their sleep.
13 "Oh, that You would hide me in the grave,
That You would conceal me until Your wrath is past,
That You would appoint me a set time, and remember me!
14 If a man dies, shall he live again?
All the days of my hard service I will wait,
Till my change comes.
15 You shall call, and I will answer You;
You shall desire the work of Your hands.
16 For now You number my steps,
But do not watch over my sin.

17 My transgression is sealed up in a bag,
And You cover my iniquity.
18 "But as a mountain falls and crumbles away,
And as a rock is moved from its place;
19 As water wears away stones,
And as torrents wash away the soil of the earth;
So You destroy the hope of man.
20 You prevail forever against him, and he passes on;
You change his countenance and send him away.
21 His sons come to honor, and he does not know it;
They are brought low, and he does not perceive it.
22 But his flesh will be in pain over it,
And his soul will mourn over it."

Job 12:1—14:22

No one calls another person an "empty-headed donkey" without a reaction. In Zophar's case, he got just the opposite of what he expected. Rather than shaming Job into repentence, he stabbed him wide awake at the point where his self-esteem had not been shattered by suffering. In his knowledge of God and his ability to think, Job was inferior to no one.

When Dr. Robert Fine, senior pastor of the First Free Methodist Church in Seattle, Washington, lay dying of cancer, he told a friend, "I am so thankful I learned to live in the world of ideas. Despite a weak body and a hospital bed, in the world of ideas, I am strong and free."

Zophar's humiliating insult makes Job strong and free in the world of ideas. Suddenly, he stops speaking with the anguish of self-pity because of his suffering. Suddenly, the momentum of the debate turns as he takes the offensive against his friends-turned-tormentors. Suddenly, his thoughts quit rambling and his tongue stops stuttering as he answers Zophar's smear with the wit of sarcasm,

No doubt you are the people,
And wisdom will die with you! (12:2).

Then, rising from the ash heap and sticking out his jaw without a trace of shame, Job shouts his defiance:

I am not inferior to you.
Indeed, who does not know such things as these? (v. 3).

A new Job is speaking. His tongue still bites with sarcasm as he proves that he is not inferior in knowledge to his friends (12:4—13:2). Anger mixed with pity takes over as he warns his friends who failed him of the dangers of trying to defend God (13:3–12). Sarcasm and anger are quickly spent, but Job's strength remains in mellow tones as he pleads for his friends to understand why he turns to God in blind trust (13:13–19). At the risk of his life, he has no alternative.

Proving His Equality

Job resents the grounds on which Zophar has made him an inferior. First, he says that he is mocked and made a "laughing-stock" by his friends because he dares to ask God why he suffers when he is just and blameless.

A certain ghoulish glee always attends the downfall of the high and the mighty. Jealous tongues cluck with juicy gossip whenever a great person shows signs of weakness, makes a false move, or experiences a failure. Americans, in particular, cannot countenance human weakness in their leaders. The slightest physical flaw in a president sends the stock market spinning downward and starts the cartoonists' pencils doodling caricatures that make the person a laughingstock. Job pays the price of greatness when he protests his innocence from an ash heap. Perverting their own sense of justice, his friends pronounce him guilty until proven innocent and laugh with scorn at his pleas for a hearing with God.

Second, Job resents the attitude of his friends toward his misfortune. An old proverb is cited, "*A* [disaster] *is despised in the thought of one who is at ease*" (12:5). Until we suffer, we can never share the pain of all those who suffer, nor understand the attitude of disdain with which healthy and comfortable people treat the sufferer. Handicapped people are doubly afflicted by this attitude. "Normal" people avoid them, talk down to them, and assume their handicap cripples the total personality. War heroes who lose their limbs are honored briefly, pitied for a period, and then cast into the permanent lot of cripples whom we ignore and despise. Job, for the first time, learns what it means to be on the receiving end of that attitude when Zophar dehumanizes him as an "empty-headed donkey." Despised or not, Job refuses to accept his suffering as the result of sin. In contradiction to Bildad's guarantee that "the dwelling place of the wicked will come to nothing" (8:22), Job observes peevishly:

> *The tents of* [the wicked] *prosper,*
> *And those who provoke God are secure"* (12:6).

In response to his call upon God for an answer to his personal questions, "Why does an innocent man suffer?" and "Why do the wicked prosper?" Job chides his friends for reciting the obvious. "Who's an empty-headed donkey?" he asks by reminding them that dumb animals and the mindless earth know that the Lord is the source of life and breath (vv. 9–10). To all creation, this comes as natural as words to the ear and food to the mouth (v. 11). Wisdom and understanding, however, belong to men of age and experience (v. 12). Equally obvious is the knowledge of God's wisdom and strength in world history. Mocking the narrow and negative view of God that his friends have invoked upon him, Job recites one-sided facts from the history of nature (vv. 14–15), men (vv. 16–22), and nations (vv. 23–25). In each case, Job demonstrates his knowledge of God's power and prudence, equaling if not surpassing his friends by poetic images and factual overkill. Coming full cycle, then, he rests his case by repeating his contention:

> *What you know, I also know;*
> *I am not inferior to you* (13:2).

Pitying His Friends

A sad commentary follows. From his position of strength, Job strikes out at the friends who have failed him. White-hot anger is felt when he indicts them as *"forgers of lies,"* but sadness mingles with bitterness in the follow-up charge that they are *"worthless physicians"* (v. 4).

Job lets us know how much he hopes for healing from his friends. Even when they didn't have ready answers for his questions, he still needed their loyalty, not their advice. In fact, he remembers the comfort of their silence during their first seven days together and wishes that they would let silence be their wisdom again as they hear him out (vv. 5–6).

"Healing silence" has been rediscovered by physicians and psychologists as therapy for "burned-out" people. In a period of silence, all the symptoms of stress are reduced and brain waves begin to show the patterns for creative thinking and problem solving. Usually a person is alone in such moments, but in extreme suffering there is no substitute for friends whose silent presence is stronger than words.

While Eliphaz, Bildad, and Zophar had no ready theological prescriptions for the suffering of a righteous man, they still had the chance to be physicians of the soul by their silent presence. Instead, to use a current expression that is true to the Hebrew meaning of "worthless physicians," they tried to put "a Band-Aid on a cancer" by applying their simplistic theory of God's justice to Job's complex and contradictory condition.

A theology that treats only symptoms is dangerous for its practitioners as well as its patients. In order to defend its inadequacy, its advocates must promise more than they can deliver. Job exposes the weakness in the advice of his friends when he charges them with being *"forgers of lies"* under the pretense of defending God. A severe warning falls from his lips when he accuses them of *"speak[ing] wickedly, . . . talk[ing] deceitfully, . . . show[ing] partiality"* (vv. 7–8).

In contending for God, they mock Job for empty-headed ignorance. He, in turn, accuses them of malicious intent. Their motive for self-defense is wicked, their method of manipulating the person is deceitful, and their mode of presenting one-sided truth is prejudicial. Job has gone for the jugular. If what he says is true, his friends have put themselves under the judgment of God according to their own doctrine. They, not Job, should fear the refining fire of God's holiness that will turn their platitudes into ashes and crush their defenses like walls of clay (13:10–12).

Preferring His God

Job bids his friends to return to silence and listen to him plead his case with God. Just as Elijah dared to call down the fire of God upon the true sacrifice on the altar at Mt. Carmel, Job is willing to let God reveal whether or not he is innocent or guilty. *"Why do I take my flesh in my teeth?"* he asks (v. 14). Because of a confidence in God that rises like three shining mountain peaks out of the dark clouds that cover his existence, Job can say:

> *Though he slay me, yet will I trust Him. . . .*
> *He also shall be my salvation,*
> . . . .
> *I know that I shall be vindicated* (vv. 15–18).

Most of us easily quote Job 13:15 when we need a proof-text to declare our unswerving faith in God. Few of us, however, speak from the depths of physical pain, psychological despair, social rejection, and spiritual condemnation that make Job's utterance so meaningful. For him, this is a turning point. Having given up hope for healing from the counsel of his friends, he can only turn to God, with nothing to lose but his life. As black slaves, who were hopelessly trapped in human misery, used to sing:

> Where could I go,
> O' where could I go,
> Seeking a refuge for my soul,
> Needing a friend
> To help me to the end,
> Where could I go but to the Lord?

Pioneering in Faith

Turning his back upon his stunned and silent friends, Job raises his head toward heaven and speaks to God with new-found strength and confidence. As if he is talking man to man, he lays down two conditions for their confrontation. If God will take His hands off from him and lift the dread from his heart, Job is willing to be either plaintiff or defendant (vv. 20–22). Even more boldly, he sets the docket for his hearing before God with the questions:

> *How many are my iniquities and sins? . . .*
> *Why do You hide Your face,*

And regard me as Your enemy?
Will You frighten a leaf driven to and fro?
And will You pursue dry stubble? (vv. 23–25).

Recalling Human Futility

Assuming that God accepts his conditions and his agenda, Job rushes to his carefully outlined case. First, he probes into his past, blaming God for writing bitter things about him because of the *"iniquities of my youth"* (13:26). How unfair it is, Job complains, to penalize me now for the errors, failures, and rebellion of my youth. *"You put my feet in the stocks"* so that I cannot move, *"and watch closely all my paths"* like a hound dog sniffing out the footprints for the *"soles of my feet"* (v. 27). Second, he pauses in the present to repeat his charge that God is unfair to make man the target of His wrath when life is so brief and so troubled (13:28–14:6). Likening man's lot in life to the treadmill existence of a hired hand, Job pleads that even the hireling can look forward to rest at the end of the day. Why can't he?

Third, from the pessimistic present, Job moves to the future. Comparing a tree to a man, he rightly contends that a tree that is cut down can sprout again (14:7–9). But when a man dies, *"where is he?"* (v. 10). Water is the common symbol of life for both trees and men. What a difference it would have made if Job could have heard Jesus' promise to the woman at the well, "The water that I shall give him will become in him a fountain of water springing up into everlasting life" (John 4:14). Such hope is far into the future. Job can only envision dry oceans and parched rivers (14:11), leaving man with an unquenched thirst for eternal life (v. 12).

For Seeing Eternal Life

Perhaps, like a man crawling in the desert, with sand in his throat, Job sees the mirage of a green oasis fed by an everflowing spring of water. Something prompts him to foresee life beyond the grave in the character of God. We who have the promise of Christ, "I am the resurrection and the life" (John 11:25), still find it hard to accept death at a graveside. Imagine, then, how much faith it takes for Job to ask the question of his day, *"If a man dies, shall he live again?"*

(14:14). Everything that theologues knew about God at that time militated against an affirmative answer. Yet, without the slightest sign of hope, Job says that he will endure his suffering and wait in the grave if he knows that God will remember him, seek him out, and reveal his transgressions (vv. 14–17). True faith is always more practical than visionary. Job does not yearn for a Shangri-La existence in eternal life. Rather, he envisions conversation with God (v. 15), a mutual relationship between Creator and the created being (v. 15), and a time when the veil of mystery over God's purpose will be lifted (v. 17).

At the end of his life, E. Stanley Jones anticipated his appearance before the presence of God by asking the Lord for twenty-four hours to greet his friends; "I shall go up to Him and say, 'Haven't you a world somewhere which has fallen people who need an evangelist like me? Please send me there.' For I know no heaven beyond preaching the gospel to people."[17] He and Job share the same functional faith for a heaven of stimulating conversation, growing relationships, unfolding revelation, and satisfying work.

Lapsing into Loneliness

The thought of eternal life works against all the odds of reason or revelation that Job knows. As quickly as his vision of heaven opens up, it closes again with a slam. Punishing himself for indulging in fantasy, Job slumps before the only evidence he has. As surely as the laws of nature crumble mountains, move stones, and wash away the soil, God will *"destroy the hope of man . . . prevail forever against him, . . . change his countenance and send him away"* (vv. 19–20).

The thought is more than Job can handle. In succession, he has lost his family, his friends, and now it appears that he has lost his God. Wistfully casting backward for a point of hope, he remembers only that he will never see his sons come to maturity, whether in success or failure (v. 21). Utter loneliness envelopes Job's soul, the kind of loneliness that T. S. Eliot describes as hell itself. Excruciating pain returns to Job with a scream and the unspeakable burden of despair crushes his soul (v. 22). The first round in debate ends with Job crumbling to the ground and writhing again in the ashes—not beaten down with words, but languishing in his loneliness.

NOTES

1. C. S. Lewis, *A Grief Observed* (New York: Bantam Books, 1961).
2. Paul Tournier, *Creative Suffering* (New York: Harper and Row, 1981), p. 84.
3. Ibid., p. 82.
4. Hulme, *Dialogue in Despair,* p. 22.
5. Kenneth Blanchard and Spencer Johnson, *The One-Minute Manager* (New York: Wm. Morrow & Co., Inc., 1982).
6. John Hersey, *Here to Stay: Studies on Human Tenacity* (Hamish-Hamilton, 1962).
7. *Antony and Cleopatra,* act 4, sc. 15, line 80.
8. A. Alvarez, *The Savage God: A Study of Suicide* (New York: Random House, 1971).
9. Lewis, *A Grief Observed.*
10. Francis I. Andersen, *Job: An Introduction and Commentary* (Downers Grove, Ill.: InterVarsity, 1976), p. 37.
11. Philip Yancey, *Where Is God When It Hurts?* (Grand Rapids, Mich.: Zondervan, 1977), p. 15.
12. Edward C. Banfield, *The Unheavenly City* (Boston: Little, Brown & Co., 1968).
13. Fowler, *The Stages of Faith,* p. 182.
14. Ibid., p. 172.
15. Lewis, *A Grief Observed,* pp. 9–10.
16. William Butler Yeats, "The Second Coming."
17. E. Stanley Jones, *The Divine Yes* (Nashville: Abingdon, 1975), p. 148.

CHAPTER FOUR

His Friends' Rebuke/Job's Resolve

Job 15:1—21:34

Intensity and hostility continue to build as the second round of debate begins. Because of the barbs of insult that have been thrown back and forth between Job and his friends, the attack now becomes personalized. No longer are the arguments inferential. Fingers are pointed directly at Job as a sinner who deserves his suffering. Job's emotions, however, are spent, and he falls back upon the only resources he has left—his integrity, his trust, and his view of reality. Thus, Job comes to the turning point in the drama of his suffering. After he declares, *"For I know that my Redeemer lives, . . . That in my flesh I shall see God,"* he has a perspective from which he responds rather than reacts. Even though emotional and intellectual conflict continues, Job now takes the initiative in the debate.

ELIPHAZ—THE REBUKE OF EXPERIENCE

1 Then Eliphaz the Temanite answered and said:
2 "Should a wise man answer with empty
    knowledge,
  And fill himself with the east wind?
3 Should he reason with unprofitable talk,
  Or by speeches with which he can do no good?
4 Yes, you cast off fear,
  And restrain prayer before God.
5 For your iniquity teaches your mouth,
  And you choose the tongue of the crafty.
6 Your own mouth condemns you, and not I;
  Yes, your own lips testify against you.

7 "Are you the first man who was born?
Or were you made before the hills?
8 Have you heard the counsel of God?
Do you limit wisdom to yourself?
9 What do you know that we do not know?
What do you understand that is not in us?
10 Both the gray-haired and the aged are among us,
Much older than your father.
11 Are the consolations of God too small for you,
And the word spoken gently with you?
12 Why does your heart carry you away,
And what do your eyes wink at,
13 That you turn your spirit against God,
And let such words go out of your mouth?
14 "What is man, that he could be pure?
And he who is born of a woman, that he could be righteous?
15 If God puts no trust in His saints,
And the heavens are not pure in His sight,
16 How much less man, who is abominable and filthy,
Who drinks iniquity like water!
17 "I will tell you, hear me;
What I have seen I will declare,
18 What wise men have told,
Not hiding anything received from their fathers,
19 To whom alone the land was given,
And no alien passed among them:
20 The wicked man writhes with pain all his days,
And the number of years is hidden from the oppressor.
21 Dreadful sounds are in his ears;
In prosperity the destroyer comes upon him.
22 He does not believe that he will return from darkness,
For a sword is waiting for him.
23 He wanders about for bread, saying, 'Where is it?'
He knows that a day of darkness is ready at his hand.
24 Trouble and anguish make him afraid;
They overpower him, like a king ready for battle.

25 For he stretches out his hand against God,
And acts defiantly against the Almighty,
26 Running stubbornly against Him
With his strong, embossed shield.
27 "Though he has covered his face with his fatness,
And made his waist heavy with fat,
28 He dwells in desolate cities,
In houses which no one inhabits,
Which are destined to become ruins.
29 He will not be rich,
Nor will his wealth continue,
Nor will his possessions overspread the earth.
30 He will not depart from darkness;
The flame will dry out his branches,
And by the breath of His mouth he will go away.
31 Let him not trust in futile things, deceiving himself,
For futility will be his reward.
32 It will be accomplished before his time,
And his branch will not be green.
33 He will shake off his unripe grape like a vine,
And cast off his blossom like an olive tree.
34 For the company of hypocrites will be barren,
And fire will consume the tents of bribery.
35 They conceive trouble and bring forth futility;
Their womb prepares deceit."

Job 15:1–35

In his first speech, Eliphaz spoke with courtesy. Now his language turns violent as he calls Job a fool betrayed by his mouth. Matching satire for satire, he asks Job, "Who do you think you are?" rejecting the wisdom of age and refuting the majesty of God. Assuming the unquestioned authority of his own vision of truth, he repeats the principle that the wicked live in fear of God's retribution, their prosperity is temporary, and their end is suffering. With one last vicious cut, Eliphaz tells Job that the final proof of this revelation is the wicked man who loses his children. Eliphaz knows how to hurt Job.

A Fatherly Scolding

As the oldest and presumably the wisest of the three friends, Eliphaz has a special role to play. Age gives him the right and responsibility to speak first. Experience gives him the added authority of what he has seen, heard, and learned in his lifetime. The Wisdom School put a premium on the perspective of age and experience.

We remember Eliphaz's first speech. From his position of seniority and authority, he spoke with confidence—calm, gentle, reflective, and methodical. My image of Eliphaz is mirrored in my first appearance as a new graduate student before a Nobel prize-winning professor, scholar, and author. Leaning back in his desk chair against a bookcase that prominently displayed his writings, the personification of wisdom sat before me—white hair, waiting eyes, and folded hands. Quivering in his presence, I introduced myself and presented my case. Without a word, he listened intently, studied me with his eyes, and waited me out between pauses. Then, when I finished, he swiveled sideways in his chair, leaned back, looked up, and sucked deeply on his ever-present pipe. Intellectual awe filled the room as I shifted my feet and anticipated his words. Later, I would learn that two sets of perfectly formed smoke rings meant the answer had arrived. The first time I saw them, however, I could only marvel at their perfection as they lazed their way upward toward the ceiling. Just as perfectly, the professor made a smooth turn of the chair, glided toward me, eased the pipe out of his mouth, and spoke measured and resonant words of counsel that I still treasure as truth.

Try as he might, Eliphaz has difficulty maintaining his image as a calm, cool, and collected leader of the wise. Whereas he gave a lengthy apology for having spoken the first time, now he almost loses control of himself as he takes on the responsibility to rebuke the rebellious young man, as well as refute his heretical ideas. Still, his speech comes off as a fatherly scolding, quite in contrast with Zophar's biting tirade. Mustering all his accumulated seniority and collected knowledge to keep himself from spilling his spleen in sarcasm, Eliphaz forcefully and categorically pronounces his judgment on Job—you are not wise (15:1–13), you are not innocent (vv. 14–16), and you are not right (vv. 17–35).

Rejecting Job's Knowledge

Eliphaz takes personal offense at Job's contention that he is not inferior to him in knowledge and wisdom. His position and prestige are threatened. Therefore, rather than dealing with the factual deficiencies in Job's knowledge, he works on his words and the way he speaks. Eliphaz gives us a classic example of deteriorating orthodoxy:

> First, you defend *what* you believe.
> Then, you defend *why* you believe.
> Finally, you defend *how* you believe.

Or, perhaps, Eliphaz demonstrates the advice given to young preachers, "If your facts are strong, hammer on the facts; if your facts are weak, hammer on the pulpit." With tacit admission that his facts are weak, Eliphaz hammers on the four standards of wisdom, which Job violates both in his ranting and his reasoning.

First, if Job were wise he would speak with *moderation.* Like my professor blowing smoke rings, a wise man always follows the "golden mean" in speaking, never too strong, never too weak. Job's incoherent ramblings and emotional outbursts, then, are symptomatic of his foolishness. Never mind that he is a man who has plummeted from greatness to groveling, from prosperity to poverty, from the pink of health to unrelenting pain, and from righteousness to rejection—all without known cause. Eliphaz is so consumed with the threat to his own self-esteem that he misses Job's feelings and needs completely. In fact, he breaks his own standard of moderation in speech when he picks up on Bildad's image of Job as a "windbag." His analogy, however, is so gross it is almost unmentionable. To say that Job is "filled with the east wind" is to compare his speech to the expulsion of hot belly gas. If moderation of speech is the standard of wisdom, Eliphaz fails to measure up to it himself.

Second, Eliphaz charges that Job cannot be wise because his godless talk is a poor *model* for the young. As a father wishing to control or change a son's behavior, I have often used this argument. Both my sons have excelled in sports. More than once, I have seen younger boys imitating them. Later, at an opportune moment, I have said, "Whether you know it or not, son, younger people are watching you. Make sure that you are a good model."

Wise men, particularly in the oral tradition of the ancient East, prided themselves in their protégés. Only as the young learned from the master could wisdom be passed on from generation to generation. To fail as a model, then, betrayed the civilization as well as the student. Socrates, we remember, drank the hemlock after being sentenced to die for corrupting the young with heretical ideas. Eliphaz charges that Job's godless talk will also corrupt the young. By challenging the wisdom of the past, he is tearing at the roots of civilization. A wise man would never do that.

Third, Eliphaz blasts Job for breaking the rule of wisdom that lets the unknown remain a *mystery.* Evidently, a wise man put new facts and exceptions to old laws into the category of a mystery rather than enlarging the scope of knowledge or stretching the boundaries of faith. Job's unwillingness to let his suffering remain a mystery and his demand for an answer from God represent an arrogant precedent that Eliphaz cannot tolerate. Closed world views in theology or other fields are like propaganda. If one element of counter-truth is admitted, the whole system breaks down. Aldous Huxley's book *Brave New World* is the story of one man's defiance against a closed world system. As long as he lives, the system is in danger; so to save the system, the man must be destroyed.

Job's refusal to accept the assumption that sin caused his suffering put the whole system of the wisdom school in danger. As senior protector of the system, Eliphaz has no choice but to destroy or at least neutralize Job's credibility. To make him appear arrogant is one sure way to cancel those credentials among the wise for whom the air of humility is a virtue.

Eliphaz finally gets to his most important point. As the fourth standard for wisdom, he reminds Job that he is much older than his father and, therefore, should be revered as his *mentor.* In a patriarchal society, age is synonymous with wisdom and fatherhood is the role through which God gives His revelation. A mark of wisdom, then, is to respect age and believe a father. Job himself, we remember, assumed that role when he served as the priest of his family. Eliphaz takes advantage of this standard of wisdom when he reminds Job of his first speech in which he spoke gently of the consolations of God (15:11). The inference is that Job rejects the counsel of age and rebels against God by questioning Eliphaz. At last, Eliphaz has a specific sin of which he can accuse Job. Having failed to find blame in Job's life during his prosperity, knowing that he did not curse God during his calamity, and seeing no secret sins behind his suffering, Eliphaz becomes the prosecutor for a trumped-up charge based upon Job's verbal outburst of pain, doubt, anger, and futility. In Eliphaz's eyes, Job is condemned as a sinner by the circumstantial evidence of his intemperate speech:

> *Why does your heart carry you away,*
> *And what do your eyes wink at,*
> *That you turn your spirit against God,*
> *And let such words go out of your mouth?* (vv. 12–13).

Judgment of sin based upon symptoms is delicate and dangerous. On the one hand, we are known by our fruits. On the other hand, there are unredeemed people who seem to be examples of love, joy, peace, and longsuffering. Biographies of saints frequently reveal cantankerous, impatient, and despairing periods in their lives. If judged in those moments by those symptoms, they would be sinners rather than saints. To be fair, we must hold judgment on anyone's spirituality until we see a larger and longer picture of his life. As in Job's case, his emotional outbursts came from excruciating pain, and his irrational ranting represented his struggle with a contradiction in his concept of God that could lead him to a higher level of faith. Admittedly, it is easy to castigate Eliphaz and condemn Job in retrospect. We should, however, be slow to pass judgment upon symptoms for which the cause may be stress rather than sin. Only if we have the mind of the discerning Spirit can we know the difference.

Refuting Job's Innocence

In his first response to Eliphaz, Job posed the penetrating question, "What is man?" (7:17). At first, pessimism pervaded his answer. But as he continued to probe, he saw fleeting rays of hope in the relationship that he has known with God: "Nor is there any mediator between us" (9:33); "You will seek me diligently, But I will no longer be" (7:21); "Though He slay me, yet will I trust Him" (13:15); and "If a man dies, shall he live again?" (14:14).

We see most deeply into the theology of Eliphaz when he answers the same question, "What is man?" So anxious to defend his own theology and refute Job's claim of innocence, he sees man as a creature who is born *"abominable and filthy"* and *"who drinks iniquity like water"* (15:16). Not to our surprise, Eliphaz's pessimistic view of man is directly linked to his pessimistic view of God. If, he says, God does not trust His saints or make the heavens pure, *"How much less* [is] *man?"* (v. 16). What a depressing outlook! While Job is searching for a crack in the door of human futility, Eliphaz slams it shut in his face.

Highs and lows of human history are written by extremes in the theology of man. If viewed as utterly depraved and without hope, civilization turns into a jungle of brute survival. If viewed as inherently good and capable of self-redemption, a false aura of human progress prevails until the reality of our sinful nature catches up. How well I remember the esteemed university president who was honored for his "unfailing confidence in the goodness of human nature and our educational system." The day came when student rebels trashed his office, bombed his administration building, and demanded his resignation. As he went to the campus to try and reason with the rebels, only vulgarity and vegetables greeted him. Watching the scene on television, the thought passed through my mind, "Does he still have unfailing confidence in the goodness of man and our educational system?"

Eliphaz went to the other extreme under the pressure to discredit Job. He shows us that he knows nothing about a personal relationship with God and that he has no growing edge for changing circumstances. How ironic! Eliphaz's own words condemn him.

Refuting Job's Reasoning

A chuckle remains in our throats as we witness Eliphaz falling into another one of his own traps. With the same fatherly condescension, he invokes the authority of his age and experience. Interestingly, he reinforces his authority with the words of wise men who have not hidden anything that they have received from the fathers (v. 18). In other words, Eliphaz reminds Job that he has access to *all the truth* he needs and it is futile, even sinful, to search beyond.

Eliphaz is not as confident as he claims. Ignoring his own standard of wisdom once again, he indulges in excessive words and endless repetition in his attempt to illustrate his doctrine that pain, dread, darkness, trouble, anguish, desolation, ruin, loneliness, and futility are the automatic and inevitable wages for wickedness (vv. 20–31). The only new element in Eliphaz's argument is a concession on timing. God's judgment may not be immediate, but Eliphaz knows without a shadow of doubt that "it will be accomplished before his time" (v. 32).

In keeping with his wise and fatherly self-image, Eliphaz does not directly describe Job as a wicked man. He leaves that to his younger compatriots, whose rashness is forgivable. Eliphaz's tactic is to lean back, draw deeply on his pipe, and fashion lazy, rising smoke rings whose perfect circles are intended to bring Job to his own conclusion.

Job—The Resolution of Will

Exhaustion has taken its toll on Job. With a weak sigh, he suggests that he could speak as glibly as his friends if their circumstances were reversed. The sigh becomes a plea when Job asks them to understand that he is exhausted by God, reproached by friends, and delivered into the hands of the ungodly. If only he had a mediator! Instead, Job has only his uncondemned integrity and his unconquerable faith in God to hold him. What else? If he gives up, death holds no hope.

16:1 Then Job answered and said:
2 "I have heard many such things;
Miserable comforters are you all!
3 Shall words of wind have an end?
Or what provokes you that you answer?
4 I also could speak as you do,
If your soul were in my soul's place.
I could heap up words against you,
And shake my head at you;
5 But I would strengthen you with my mouth,
And the comfort of my lips would relieve your grief.
6 "Though I speak, my grief is not relieved;
And if I remain silent, how am I eased?
7 But now He has worn me out;
You have made desolate all my company.
8 You have shriveled me up,
And it is a witness against me;
My leanness rises up against me
And bears witness to my face.

9 He tears me in His wrath, and hates me;
He gnashes at me with His teeth;
My adversary sharpens His gaze on me.
10 They gape at me with their mouth,
They strike me reproachfully on the cheek,
They gather together against me.
11 God has delivered me to the ungodly,
And turned me over to the hands of the wicked.
12 I was at ease, but He has shattered me;
He also has taken me by my neck, and shaken me to pieces;
He has set me up for His target,
13 His archers surround me.
He pierces my heart and does not pity;
He pours out my gall on the ground.
14 He breaks me with wound upon wound;
He runs at me like a warrior.
15 "I have sewn sackcloth over my skin,
And laid my head in the dust.
16 My face is flushed from weeping,
And on my eyelids is the shadow of death;
17 Although no violence is in my hands,
And my prayer is pure.
18 "O earth, do not cover my blood,
And let my cry have no resting place!
19 Surely even now my witness is in heaven,
And my evidence is on high.
20 My friends scorn me;
My eyes pour out tears to God.
21 Oh, that one might plead for a man with God,
As a man pleads for his neighbor!
22 For when a few years are finished,
I shall go the way of no return.
17:1 "My spirit is broken,
My days are extinguished,
the grave is ready for me.
2 Are not mockers with me?
And does not my eye dwell on their provocation?
3 "Now put down a pledge for me with Yourself.
Who is he who will shake hands with me?
4 For You have hidden their heart from understanding;
Therefore You will not exalt them.

5 He who speaks flattery to his friends,
Even the eyes of his children will fail.
6 "But He has made me a byword of the people,
And I have become one in whose face men spit.
7 My eye has also grown dim because of sorrow,
And all my members are like shadows.
8 Upright men are astonished at this,
And the innocent stirs himself up against the hypocrite.
9 Yet the righteous will hold to his way,
And he who has clean hands will be stronger and stronger.
10 "But please, come back again, all of you,
For I shall not find one wise man among you.
11 My days are past,
My purposes are broken off,
Even the thoughts of my heart.
12 They change the night into day;
'The light is near,' they say, in the face of darkness.
13 If I wait for the grave as my house,
If I make my bed in the darkness,
14 If I say to corruption, 'You are my father,'
And to the worm, 'You are my mother and my sister,'
15 Where then is my hope?
As for my hope, who can see it?
16 Will they go down to the gates of Sheol?
Shall we have rest together in the dust?"

Job 16:1—17:16

The Suffering of Loneliness

Loneliness is the deepest kind of suffering. As Job's world falls apart bit by bit, he runs the gamut of emotions—agony and anger, depression and doubt, hostility and futility. Behind each of these reactions, however, is the hidden assumption that his relationship with God and his three friends, even though reduced to a fraying thread, remains intact. Not until the very end of his previous response to Zophar (chapters 12–14) does Job give us the hint that the spectre of loneliness is creeping into his soul. Looking backward through nostalgic eyes, he speaks the pain of realizing that he will never see his sons come to maturity (14:21).

What father does not know the same pain of being cut off from a future with his children? I myself am not afraid to die, but the thought of never seeing my children and grandchildren come to their maturity drives a stake of lonely dread deep into my heart.

Something in Eliphaz's second speech (chapter 15) magnifies this early hint of loneliness into the haunting, dominating theme of Job's answer to him. In a classic study of the dynamics of loneliness, we see Job suffering from alienation, seeing through isolation, and searching for intimacy.

Suffering from Alienation

What does Eliphaz say or do that sinks Job into the pit of lonely despair? One possibility is that Eliphaz snips the line of mutual trust between him and Job when he calls his friend a "hypocrite." Eliphaz and his two compatriots have been searching for a sin to explain Job's suffering. Without success, they have accused him of everything from open rebellion to secret pride. Hypocrisy is different. When Job's friends accuse him of sin, the burden of proof rests upon them, but when Eliphaz calls him a "hypocrite," how can Job attest his sincerity? If the witness of a lifetime before his friends is not sufficient, he has no recourse. Eliphaz has cut Job adrift.

Another possible explanation is Job's life-long respect for Eliphaz's age and authority. One of the major causes of loneliness is to be alienated from significant people in your life. When my father died, I sensed an inexplicable loneliness. At the time, I explained my feeling with the thought that the mantle of fatherhood had passed down to me, the eldest and only son of the family. A mystical awe always accompanies the passing of the generations. Still, the gaping hole in my soul remained. Not until I began to recall the events of our life together as father and son did the reason for my loneliness come clear. Memory after memory broke through to my consciousness to remind me that my father had served as the most significant person in my developing years. Although I had declared my independence and established my own family years earlier, an invisible bond of love and respect held us together across a continent. Death broke that bond, leaving me temporarily lost and lonely.

Job, too, may have been surprised to discover that he was not as independent and secure as he thought. Even while contesting with Eliphaz, he counted upon him for support. When Eliphaz condemned Job's character and denied his sincerity, he severed the final bond of love and respect that bound him to Job as a father figure. In turn, Job reacts like a son who has been disinherited without warning: *"What provokes you that you answer . . . as you do?"* (16:3–4). Human intimacy is defined as a relationship in which one's deepest feelings can be given and received with acceptance and understanding. Job's plaintive question tells us that he did not expect Eliphaz to condemn him for expressing his honest feelings. He needs acceptance; he gets alienation. He needs intimacy; he gets loneliness.

Alienation from human contact is the primary cause of loneliness. Literally translated, alienation means *no bond.* Job speaks first of alienation from his friends. Instead of accepting his show of feelings and understanding his anguish, they ignore his emotions and reject his cry for help. After repeated pleas, Job gives up on them as *"miserable comforters"* (v. 2).

Job's suffering from alienation has a deeper cause. God becomes his enemy. In a description that would be rated "R" for violence if made into a movie, Job portrays God as a vicious animal tearing at his flesh and clawing at the remains:

He tears me in His wrath, and hates me;
He gnashes at me with His teeth;
. . . .
He has also taken me by my neck, and
shaken me to pieces (vv. 9–12).

As if God acting like a wild animal were not enough, Job also sees His attack as a cold, premeditated act:

He has set me up for His target,
His archers surround me.
He pierces my heart and does not pity;
He pours out my gall on the ground.
He breaks me with wound upon wound;
He runs at me like a warrior (vv. 12–14).

All of this leads Job to speak of the symptoms from which the lonely suffer. Pathos fills the scene as Job says that he is worn out, desolate, shriveled up, emaciated, shattered, weeping, and broken (16:7–17:1).

Still, Job's alienation is not complete. His friends have abandoned him and God has attacked him. One last support remains—Job's community. For the Hebrew in particular, a sense of racial and religious identity has served as a holding power through exile and holocaust. To be born a Jew is to count upon the inherent right of membership in the Hebrew community. No sin can cancel this relationship except the denial of the birthright. In such cases, the person is pronounced "dead."

Job finds himself subjected to a fate worse than death. Although he never denies his birthright, his community cuts him off:

> *But He has made me a byword of the people,*
> *And I have become one in whose face men spit* (17:6).

Job's alienation is thus complete. He is abandoned by his friends, attacked by God, and estranged from his community. We understand now the totality of the suffering from the pain of loneliness. Intellectually, he is adrift,

> *Though I speak,*
> *my grief is not relieved;*
> *And if I remain silent,*
> *how am I eased?* (16:6).

Physically, Job is exhausted, *"But now He has worn me out"* (16:7).

Socially, he is an island, *"You have made desolate all my company"* (v. 7).

Spiritually, he is as good as dead,

> *My spirit is broken,*
> *My days are extinguished,*
> *The grave is ready for me"* (17:1).

Who would not join Job in putting on sackcloth (the *symbol* of suffering), in laying his head in the dust (the *posture* of suffering), and in apologizing for a face swollen from uncontrolled weeping and eyes sunken from the shadow of death (the *symptoms* of suffering)? (16:15–16).

Seeing through Suffering

Utter loneliness is not without compensation. Like attendance at your own hanging, the mind is wonderfully cleared. Hidden behind Job's pathetic pleas are insights that break through to a mind that is sharpened by suffering and focused by loneliness.

For the first time in his search to understand God's strange silence and contradictory behavior, Job seems to see another force at work in his suffering. Although the insight is momentary, Job objectifies his anguish by introducing the idea that

> *My adversary sharpens His gaze on me.*
> *They gape at me with their mouth,*
> *They strike me reproachfully on the cheek,*
> *They gather together against me* (16:9, 10).

Adversary is the key word. It implies the personification of evil and points to Satan himself. Although Job quickly lapses back into a gory description of God acting like a wild animal and a vengeful archer, the concept of *adversary* will not be lost. In the suffering of His loneliness, Christ will come face to face with Job's "adversary" and our common enemy—Satan.

Another insight that comes through Job's pain-sharpened mind is the confidence that his *"witness is in heaven"* (16:19). In his earlier pleadings, he cries for a "mediator" who will intervene for him while he is still alive and on earth. Now, Job seems reconciled to the fact that he may die without vindication. If so, he is convinced that his faith in God and his claim of innocence will carry over into eternity where he will be vindicated. Therefore, like an attorney appealing to a higher court, Job says, *"My evidence is on high"* (v. 19). Through suffering, he sees with the eyes of faith.

Once again, Job humbles us when he foresees the death of Christ as "ransom" for our sins. Does Job really know the meaning of his prayer when he asks God,

> *Now put down a pledge for me with Yourself.*
> *Who is he who will shake hands with me?* (17:3).

Job is appealing to a God of justice in the setting of a courtroom. He dares to ask God to post the bail bond for him and shake hands as a sign of mutual trust. He knows that only God can ransom and reconcile him. Although he will not live to see the coming of Christ, he foresees the plan of redemption through the eyes of suffering.

One more insight breaks through to the consciousness of Job as he stands alone with the severed bonds of his relationship with his friends, God, and community lying limp at his feet. In an astounding declaration of faith, Job gives the witness,

> *Yet the righteous will hold to his way,*
> *And he who has clean hands will be stronger and*
> *stronger* (v. 9).

With these words, Job sees that righteousness is more than an external discipline, it is an intrinsic quality! All else has failed Job. Alienated from human intimacy, attacked by God, exhausted in body, and broken in spirit, Job is driven back to the center of his soul where he finds the "purity" of heart (16:17) that gives him strength upon strength to *"hold to his way"* (17:9). How far he has come from the original description of a righteousness based upon a moral discipline of fearing God and shunning evil (1:1). Although none of us would choose the suffering of loneliness in order to sharpen our spiritual vision, there is some compensation in knowing that those who suffer acutely can also see more clearly.

Searching for Intimacy

Spiritual vision is not enough for a person suffering from loneliness. Job is like Adam in the Garden, of whom God said, "It is not good that man should be alone" (Gen. 2:18). Not even God can meet the need for human intimacy. Back in my college days, I remember the testimony of a girl whose heart had just been broken when her boyfriend called off their engagement. Sobbing, she said, "God is all I need." At the time, I played the budding psychologist who instantly diagnosed her case as a form of spiritual projection—substituting God for her fiancé. My analysis was confirmed when she married the next man that came along. Evidently, she needed more than God.

Job's desperate need for human intimacy is related to his expectations that death is imminent for him. In his earlier references to Sheol, Job buys into the prevailing notion that life after death is a land of dark shadows, impersonal beings, and spiritual "nothingness." His need for human intimacy even changes his view of eternity. We can feel his desperation in reaching out for human contact when he says,

> *If I say to corruption,*
> *"You are my father,"*
> *And to the worm,*
> *"You are my mother and my sister,"*
> *Where then is my hope?* (17:14–15).

In these words, Job reveals the loneliness of suffering that borders on hell itself. He has reached the point that even the nether-nether world of Sheol is better than life. At least it holds the promise that Job will be at *"rest together* [with others] *in the dust"* (v. 16).

During an international psychiatric conference in 1971, the psychiatrist Eric Fromm said that widespread loneliness will be the result if society does not meet the basic human needs for relatedness, transcendence, rootedness, identity, and a frame of reference.

Job comes close to that breaking point of loneliness. He loses the relatedness of his friends, the bond with his transcendent God, the rootedness of his community, and the identity of his family. Only his own frame of reference remains intact. When he says, "I will hold my way" (17:9), he is hanging on to the last thread of meaning in his life. Loneliness comes in two forms—existential and essential. Existential loneliness is to be cut off from all human relationships. It is devastating, but it is not fatal. Essential loneliness, however, is to be cut off from God without hope. When this happens, life loses its meaning. Job comes close to essential loneliness. Only a shred of faith remains, but it is enough to keep him miserable, which in itself means that life still has meaning.

Bildad—The Rebuke of Tradition

No sympathy for Job's suffering can be found in Bildad. He is still stung by Job's insult when he said that beasts knew as much about the ways of God as Bildad did. In a cowardly counterattack, Bildad describes the punishment of the wicked by citing the symptoms of Job's suffering. His loss of health, family, and reputation are proof that sin is behind his suffering. The conclusion is bitter revenge for Job's insult. If all of us are stupid, Bildad says, then you, Job, do not even know God.

1 Then Bildad the Shuhite answered and said:
2 "How long till you put an end to words?
Gain understanding, and afterward we will speak.
3 Why are we counted as beasts,
And regarded as stupid in your sight?
4 You who tear yourself in anger,
Shall the earth be forsaken for you?
Or shall the rock be removed from its place?
5 "The light of the wicked indeed goes out,
And the flame of his fire does not shine.
6 The light is dark in his tent,
And his lamp beside him is put out.
7 The steps of his strength are shortened,
And his own counsel casts him down.
8 For he is cast into a net by his own feet,
And he walks into a snare.
9 The net takes him by the heel,
And a snare lays hold of him.
10 A noose is hidden for him on the ground,
And a trap for him in the road.
11 Terrors frighten him on every side,
And drive him to his feet.
12 His strength is starved,
And destruction is ready at his side.
13 It devours patches of his skin;
The firstborn of death devours his limbs.
14 He is uprooted from the shelter of his tent,
And they parade him before the king of terrors.
15 They dwell in his tent who are none of his;
Brimstone is scattered on his dwelling.
16 His roots are dried out below,
And his branch withers above.
17 The memory of him perishes from the earth,
And he has no name among the renowned.

18 He is driven from light into darkness,
And chased out of the world.
19 He has neither son nor posterity among his people,
Nor any remaining in his dwellings.
20 Those in the west are astonished at his day,
As those in the east are frightened.
21 Surely such are the dwellings of the wicked,
And this is the place of him who does not know God."

Job 18:1–21

The Barbs of Bildad

We remember Bildad as the traditionalist with the barbed tongue. His blunt and violent language has a way of escalating conflict beyond resolution. Whereas Eliphaz the Elder retains a modicum of diplomacy, Bildad minces no words in his condemnation of Job. He is the "hatchet man" among the three friends. Under the guise of defending the faith, he would not hesitate to send Job to the stake and wield the torch himself.

Bildad's first and second speeches have the same purpose. His goal is to reduce Job to silence. Accordingly, he opens his second address with the snarling question, *"How long till you put an end to words?"* (18:2). Impatiently, then, he implies that he will waste no more time talking with Job who lacks understanding, likens his friends to dumb animals, and expects God to change the nature of the universe to accommodate Job's claim that he is an exception to the moral order (vv. 2–4).

Rigid traditionalism is a prison for Bildad's mind. He adds nothing new to the debate. In fact, his second speech is more stilted than the first one. In each case, he tries to prove the doctrine that sin causes suffering by reciting evidence of calamity in the lives of the wicked. At least in the first speech, he balances his gloomy picture with the promise of prosperity if Job would repent. Now, with the short fuse of his patience burned out, he offers no hope to his friend. Instead, he resorts to a tactic that is intended to shut the mouth of his protagonist once and for all. Quoting Job's own words of anguish, Bildad turns them into proof that his "former" friend is wicked.

Words can be weapons. For my doctoral examination in the German language, I chose a book on higher education that was written during the Nazi era. After studying it for several weeks, I took it to my tutor for the test. One look and he said, "You can never pass the examination with this book. The Nazis twisted the meaning of all the terms in education in order to fit them to their own propaganda." Bildad has a Nazi knack for quoting Job out of context in order to twist the meaning of the words to his own advantage. For instance, Job has just said of his three friends,

> They change the night into day;
> "The light is near," they say,
> in the face of darkness (17:12).

Bildad accepts the analogy but turns it into a statement of proof that Job is one in whom the light is gone out and through whom the flame no longer shines (18:5). Therefore, Bildad infers that it is no surprise to hear Job accuse his friends of being in the dark. Who can see in his own darkness?

Job has also confessed that God "has worn me out" (16:7). Bildad jumps on the confession as a characteristic of the wicked,

> *The steps of his strength are shortened,*
> *And his own counsel casts him down* (18:7).

Relishing his accusations now, Bildad takes on Job's lament that he has become the prey of God the hunter (10:6) and set up as the target for His piercing arrows (16:12). "Of course," Bildad seems to say, "how else can you defend the fact that you stumble in the darkness and fall victim to your own snares?" In an exercise of overkill, Bildad identifies six different kinds of hunting traps that Job might set and then catch himself in in the darkness. Perhaps Bildad has in mind the proverb,

> The wicked is ensnared by the transgression of his lips,
> But the righteous will come through trouble (Prov. 12:13).

The list of twisted quotations continues as Bildad recalls Job's terror-stricken description of God tearing at him like an animal and then collapsing with a weak whisper, "And on my eyelids is the shadow of death" (16:16). Glee must have curled Bildad's lip as he informed Job that his own words constitute a confession of sin. Terrors of mind, exhaustion of strength, readiness for destruction, blotches of the skin, and eating of the limbs—these are the symptoms of sin (18:11–13). According to Bildad, Job is snared in the teeth of his own trap.

Something in Bildad will not let him rest his case against Job. After emasculating Job's most recent speech by turning his own words against him, Bildad recalls some other evidence that will quiet Job once and for all. He opens old wounds by reminding Job of past events: his exile to an ash heap, the strangers in his tents, the fire that took his cattle and servants, the loss of his reputation, the scorn of his people, the death of his sons, and the loss of his property (vv. 14–19).

Word of these calamities has gone east and west to astonish and frighten those who hear the story. Bildad tells Job that he has become the tragic example that suffering is caused by sin (v. 20). In Bildad's logic-tight compartment, only one conclusion can be drawn—Job is wicked and he does not know God (v. 21).

Lock-step traditionalism carries in its nature the seeds of paranoia. We think of a paranoid as a person who feels persecuted. The process by which the paranoid comes to that conclusion is a conundrum. All of the facts can be marshalled to show the paranoid that no one is out to get him. Step by step, he will follow the reasoning and agree. But then, when it comes time to draw the conclusion, the paranoid will invariably say, "They're still out to get me."

Bildad follows the same process. He lines up all the facts in logical order but comes to his own preconceived conclusion. In Bildad's hands, Job never has a chance. He does not feel the anguish of a friend, he has no room for questions about his doctrine, and he will resort to any means to justify his position. Without so much as a tear of remorse or a twinge of regret, Bildad consigns Job to the dwelling of the wicked and a place among fools (v. 21). In Bildad's mind, the debate is over.

Job—The Resolution of Trust

Violence begets violence. Job expected his friends to help him. Instead, they turn into his tormentors. The issue is between him and God, not between him and them. It is God who has taken away his health, his family, and his reputation. Why do they add to his torture?

With all of the supports of the past and the present taken from him, Job can appeal only to the future. If only he could engrave his case in stone, he knows that ultimately he will be vindicated. Suddenly, in a flash of prophetic insight, Job knows that God is alive and will be his redeemer as well as his mediator and vindicator. While he is yearning for that moment, the reality of his torment takes over again. Turning back to his friends, he warns them that they too are open to God's wrath because of their cruelty toward him. The initiative now belongs to Job.

1 Then Job answered and said:
2 "How long will you torment my soul,
And break me in pieces with words?
3 These ten times you have reproached me;
You are not ashamed that you have
wronged me.
4 And if indeed I have erred,
My error remains with me.
5 If indeed you exalt yourselves against me,
And plead my disgrace against me,
6 Know then that God has wronged me,
And has surrounded me with His net.
7 "If I cry out concerning wrong, I am not heard.
If I cry aloud, there is no justice.
8 He has fenced up my way, so that I cannot pass;
And He has set darkness in my paths.
9 He has stripped me of my glory,
And taken the crown from my head.
10 He breaks me down on every side,
And I am gone;
My hope He has uprooted like a tree.
11 He has also kindled His wrath against me,
And He counts me as one of His enemies.
12 His troops come together
And build up their road against me;
They encamp all around my tent.
13 "He has removed my brothers far from me,

And my acquaintances are completely estranged
from me.
14 My relatives have failed,
And my close friends have forgotten me.
15 Those who dwell in my house, and my
maidservants,
Count me as a stranger;
I am an alien in their sight.
16 I call my servant, but he gives no answer;
I beg him with my mouth.
17 My breath is offensive to my wife,
And I am repulsive to the children of my own
body.
18 Even young children despise me;
I arise, and they speak against me.
19 All my close friends abhor me,
And those whom I love have turned against me.
20 My bone clings to my skin and to my flesh,
And I have escaped by the skin of my teeth.
21 "Have pity on me, have pity on me, O you my
friends,
For the hand of God has struck me!
22 Why do you persecute me as God does,
And are not satisfied with my flesh?
23 "Oh, that my words were written!
Oh, that they were inscribed in a book!
24 That they were engraved on a rock
With an iron pen and lead, forever!
25 For I know that my Redeemer lives,
And He shall stand at last on the earth;
26 And after my skin is destroyed, this I know,
That in my flesh I shall see God,
27 Whom I shall see for myself,
And my eyes shall behold, and not another.
How my heart yearns within me!
28 If you should say, 'How shall we persecute
him?'—
Since the root of the matter is found in me,
29 Be afraid of the sword for yourselves;
For wrath brings the punishment of the sword,
That you may know there is a judgment."

Job 19:1–29

The Pit and the Pinnacle

The barbs of Bildad take their toll upon Job. He admits that the verbal accusations of his friends multiply his torment, brokenness, and loneliness (19:2–3). Tacitly, Job also admits that Bildad may have a point when he identifies the symptoms of his suffering as evidence of sin. Adopting a debater's tactic, Job queries, "Let's suppose that you are right and my suffering is the result of sin, what then?" By posing the hypothetical question, Job is able to step outside his pain and objectify his argument. In itself, this is evidence that Job has given up on his friends. They have proven their inability to feel his anguish or understand his suffering. Therefore, Job chooses to meet them on the common ground of the hypothetical question and the theoretical answer.

A young woman spoke her dilemma to me. As she anticipated her future, disaster seemed inevitable. I answered by saying, "You need to have faith." Disappointment clouded her face as she spoke in return, "That's easy for you to say." Academic answers are of little help to suffering persons. When Jesus ministered to the sick and the sinful, He never stayed outside their suffering by reciting theology or theory. Yet, in His debate with the Pharisees, Jesus did not hesitate to confront and confound them on their own ground. Football coaches employ the same tactic. They take the game to their opponents by attacking them with a run or pass at the point of their strength.

The Pronouncement of Prejudice

Having agreed to debate on Bildad's terms, Job argues,

> *And if indeed I have erred,*
> *My error remains with me* (v. 4).

Suddenly, Bildad is the one who is snared by his own words. In his first speech, he shows his frustration at being unable to pin down Job's sin. Consequently, he strikes upon the idea that Job is guilty of secret sins (8:11–18). Yet, he, along with Eliphaz and Zophar, has tried to make Job's sin a public issue because he threatens the doctrine that holds their world together. In fact, Bildad goes a step farther.

He contends that Job's sin has become a cosmic issue because Job demands that the God of justice set aside the moral order and make him an exception. Job's rejoinder is twofold: First, he says, "If the issue is sin, it's my problem." No evidence has been presented to show that Job has harmed anyone—personally or socially. Sin is never so isolated. Its harmful effects resound through the universe. As someone said, "If you stub your toe on Earth, it is felt on Mars."

Job's case is just the opposite. If he has sinned, as his friends contend, it is a sin without social or cosmic impact. Therefore, the issue remains in him. Dhorme's translation of verse 4 is blunt:

> Even if it were a fact that I have gone astray,
> that would remain my own business.[1]

The second part of Job's rejoinder is equally blunt. He scorns his friends for "magnifying" their personal case against him (19:5) and persecuting him as if they were God. The fatal flaw in their logic is exposed. Job reasons that if the sin in him is his own business, then the issue is a matter between him and God. True, it is God who assails and surrounds him (19:6), but the telling point is that *God has not pronounced him guilty.* Job's friends are not only playing God by their persecution, but they are presuming to know the conclusion of God's mind by pronouncing Job guilty. It is bad enough to persecute people in the name of religion, but it is unforgivable to pronounce them guilty before God does.

The Process of Judgment

Little comfort comes to Job as he scores debating points against his human opposition. No logic will suffice to say why God remains silent while assailing him from every side. We feel Job's utter futility as he portrays his plight as being entangled in a net, walled in by a fence, set on a dark path, stripped of his crown, broken into rubble, uprooted like a tree, counted as an enemy, and under siege by armies (vv. 6–12).

Job is a man with "no exit" except for one point. With his objectivity comes a sense of humor. The final picture in his slide show of the wrongs that God is working against him shows a mighty army surrounding an enemy fortress and building a road for giant catapults and battering rams to break down the walls. But in cartoonlike fashion, Job shows us that the object of the siege is not a walled fortress, it is only his one little tent! Later on, God will use that sense of humor to reveal Himself to Job. For now, it is Job's turn to show God as the ludicrous one.

The Pit of Humiliation

Job has plummeted to the depths of physical pain, emotional despair, spiritual futility, and relational loneliness. Now, as a result of God's pursuit and his friends' persecution, he voices the pain of suffering from humiliation. From his community, he needs solace; from his household, he needs respect; and from his family, he needs intimacy. Instead, he is avoided by brothers, estranged by acquaintances, failed by relatives, forgotten by friends, alienated by maidservants, ignored by manservants, rejected by his wife, repulsed by his children, despised by urchins, abhorred by friends, and betrayed by loved ones (vv. 13–19).

To whom can Job turn? His humiliation is complete. On the list of those who have turned against him are even the urchins of the street. In Eastern tradition, children must give common courtesy to their elders, no matter how decrepit or despicable they are. The forty-two little children, for instance, who mocked Elisha for his bald head were cursed by the prophet and torn apart by two she-bears. In Job's case, there is no retaliation. It is he who "bears" the humiliation.

There is a moral lesson in Job's humiliation. Once the friends of Job, who were respected as the wise leaders of the East, ridiculed and rejected him, they set the tone for a response to Job from every person in the community, even to the street urchins! Leaders of the church, whether clergy or laity, must anticipate the multiplying effect of what they say and how they react to those whom they are called upon to lead. Like the "Pass-It-On" game we used to play as children, facts are distorted and feelings are aggravated as they circulate in ever-widening circles.

Just when we are convinced that Job has suffered every pain known to man, he falls into a new and deeper pit. Humiliation is the deepest and darkest of all because of the heights of love, honor, and respect from which he fell. As low as Job has been before, in the pit of humiliation he touches bottom. Our minds immediately reach back to the thought that he is the "Intermediate Adam" and prefigures the prophesy of Isaiah concerning Christ the suffering servant,

> He is despised and rejected by men,
> A man of sorrows and acquainted with grief.
> And we hid, as it were, our faces from Him;
> He was despised, and we did not esteem Him (Isa. 53:3).

The Pinnacle of Faith

What is it that brings the pits and pinnacles of life together? Is it simply an emotional lurch from high to low? Is it an intellectual flash that lets us see clearly when we are stripped of pretense? Or is it the spiritual principle expounded by the apostle when he wrote, "If we endure [with Him], we shall also reign with Him" (2 Tim. 2:12)? In his book, *Holy Company,* Elliott Wright creates a hall of fame for the faithful whom we extol as saints. Through the biographies of the book, there is the overriding and underlying theme that saints are those who "hobble toward holiness."[2] They are not perfect, they are not without personal doubt and public persecution, yet they continue to walk sharing their insights and giving themselves as they go. Each of them goes down into the pit of humiliation; each of them rises to the pinnacle of faith. Job is not alone.

When Job hits the bottom of the pit of humiliation, he has no place to go but to stand and look up. His stance is represented by his unshaken confidence in his innocence before God. Yet, for the first time, he deals with the shock of recognition that he may not be vindicated while still alive. The odds are too great and the time is too short. His only recourse is to turn the clock ahead to eternity. Sheol, the land of shadows, has slowly changed its meaning for him. At first, it meant nothing more than impersonal suspension between worlds (6:7–10). Then, he dared to suggest that he would retain his personhood so that God would miss him (9:21). Another flash of insight lets him see the potential of personhood even in death (17:13–16). Not until Job touches the bottom of the pit of humiliation, however, do the eyes of his faith open wide. With no place to go in human existence, he can only wish that his words were written in a book, *"engraved on a rock / With an iron pen and lead, forever!"* (19:24).

Deferred gratification of our most urgent desires is a sign of emotional and spiritual maturity. Instant gratification is its opposite and the sign of a secular attitude that cannot see beyond the "radical now." In the give-and-take of exaggerated words and the intricacies of logical debate between Job and his friends, we dare not lose sight of the fact that Job has been "hobbling toward the holy," usually with two steps forward and one step back.

From the pit of humiliation, however, Job becomes the Neil Armstrong of faith exploration by taking "one small step for man; one giant step for mankind." Bursting into the reality of revelation known only to the prophet, Job declares:

> *For I know that my Redeemer lives,*
> *And He shall stand at last on the earth;*
> *And after my skin is destroyed,*
> *this I know,*
> *That in my flesh I shall see God* (vv. 25–26).

Scholars warn us against overspiritualizing Job's revelation. At the same time, there is the danger of missing the meaning of this prophetic insight by becoming bogged down in the sticky details of specific words. In between the extremes are the farsighted affirmations of faith to which Job says, *"I know."* In this moment, Job joins Isaiah the Prophet when he "saw the Lord sitting on a throne, high and lifted up" (Isa. 6:1), and John in his Revelation when he was "in the Spirit on the Lord's Day" (1:10). As the veil of Truth goes up, Job foresees the hope of the Atonement, the Incarnation, and the Resurrection.

Out of the pit of humiliation, Job prophesies the Atonement with his affirmation *"I know that my Redeemer lives."* His choice of the word *redeemer* is proof of God's inspiration. The Hebrew word is *gâ'al,* a term that generally means "vindicator," but always in the specific context of a "kinsman" in close blood relationship who stands in defense of a brother. Earlier, Job had appealed for an independent umpire to plead his case. Now he knows that he cannot stand before God in his own righteousness. His blameless behavior is not enough to redeem him. A brother who is willing to shed his blood on Job's behalf is his only hope. He dares to believe that such a brother exists and will vindicate him in the future. Job foresees the Atonement.

The eyes of faith stay wide open as Job advances to a vision of the Incarnation when he affirms, *"I know that . . . He shall stand at last on the earth"* (19:25). God has spoken through Job! How else can a man who has not even received the law and the covenant envision the time when "the Word became flesh and dwelt among us" (John 1:14)? God and man, heaven and earth, life and death are all conjoined in the Incarnation of Christ. Although Job is centuries from the birth of the Savior, he lives in that hope by faith!

Job's eyes open widest, however, when he announces from the pinnacle of faith, *"This I know, / That in my flesh I shall see God"* (19:26). Questions abound. Does Job mean that he shall see God while alive? Or does he anticipate the bodily resurrection which is so far advanced beyond the shadowy Sheol in which the Hebrews believed? The answer comes to us when Job reinforces his original insight with the details,

Whom I shall see for myself,
And my eyes shall behold,
and not another (v. 27).

For Job, the hope of resurrection is personal. His choice of the eyes as the sensory organ that will give him a first-hand witness of his Redeemer is significant. To behold the face of God in the Hebrew tradition meant instant death. But, with the coming of Christ, John tells us that "we beheld His glory, the glory as of the only begotten of the Father, full of grace and truth" (John 1:14). Throughout the New Testament, "seeing" Christ with the eyes is evidence of credibility—whether with the disciples who lived with Him or the apostles to whom He appeared. Job has only the vision to foresee that day, but it is sufficient to anchor his hope and help him through his suffering.

Job's journey of faith has come to the turning point. Like Martin Luther King, Jr., he has "climbed to the top of the mountain and seen the other side." The vision will never let him turn back. From here on out, the revelation of the Redeemer will be the reference point to which Job returns when pain and pressure become intolerable.

George Frederick Handel composed the oratorio *Messiah* in twenty-four days. A servant who came in while he was writing the "Hallelujah Chorus" found the composer weeping copious tears. When Handel could speak, he told the servant, "I think I did see all heaven before me and the great God Himself." Is it any wonder that the resurrection passage that immediately follows the "Hallelujah Chorus" is opened with the unforgettable soprano aria, "I know that my Redeemer liveth"? Perhaps not as clearly as Handel, but just as surely, Job saw all heaven before him and the great God Himself. He, too, must have spoken through a flood of tears when he wept, *"How my heart yearns within me!"* (19:27).

The Projection of Judgment

Just as quickly as Job rises in the Spirit to the pinnacle of faith, he falls back again. Perhaps a piercing pain reminds him of the debate with his friends over the justice of God. His perspective, however, has changed. If he is to be vindicated by the God of justice, even in the future life, it means that his friends will also have to stand under the scrutiny of judgment for the way they have treated him. Sternly, Job warns them against playing God. If they persist in persecuting him and continue to judge him guilty of sin, they themselves will know the meaning of judgment when they feel the wrath of God and fall under his sword (v. 29). The debate has come down to the hard but simple truth: If his friends are right, Job is wrong; but if Job is right, his friends are wrong. Job is willing to let God be the judge.

Zophar—The Rebuke of Common Sense

Although Zophar is enraged by Job's words and insulted by his warning, he reenters the debate with the confidence of his simple answers. In a condescending tone, he repeats the cause-and-effect relationship between man's wickedness and God's wrath. Admitting that the wicked may enjoy temporary prosperity, he speaks of the terror that pursues him and turns all his gain into misery. Zophar strikes a keynote for further accusations when he cruelly states that God's justice is vindicated by the calamity that came from heaven to destroy Job's possessions and kill his children. Essentially, Zophar has nothing new to say.

1 Then Zophar the Naamathite answered and said:
2 "Therefore my anxious thoughts make me
answer,
Because of the turmoil within me.
3 I have heard the rebuke that reproaches me,
And the spirit of my understanding causes me
to answer.
4 "Do you not know this of old,
Since man was placed on earth,
5 That the triumphing of the wicked is short,
And the joy of the hypocrite is but for a moment?
6 Though his haughtiness mounts up to the
heavens,
And his head reaches to the clouds,
7 Yet he will perish forever like his own refuse;
Those who have seen him will say, 'Where
is he?'
8 He will fly away like a dream, and not be found;
Yes, he will be chased away like a vision of the
night.
9 The eye that saw him will see him no more,
Nor will his place behold him anymore.
10 His children will seek the favor of the poor,
And his hands will restore his wealth.
11 His bones are full of his youthful vigor,
But it will lie down with him in the dust.
12 "Though evil is sweet in his mouth,
And he hides it under his tongue,
13 Though he spares it and does not forsake it,
But still keeps it in his mouth,
14 Yet his food in his stomach turns sour;
It becomes cobra venom within him.
15 He swallows down riches
And vomits them up again;
God casts them out of his belly.
16 He will suck the poison of cobras;
The viper's tongue will slay him.
17 He will not see the streams,
The rivers flowing with honey and cream.
18 He will restore that for which he labored,
And will not swallow it down;

From the proceeds of business
He will get no enjoyment.
19 For he has oppressed and forsaken the poor,
He has violently seized a house which he did
not build.
20 "Because he knows no quietness in his heart,
He will not save anything he desires.
21 Nothing is left for him to eat;
Therefore his well-being will not last.
22 In his self-sufficiency he will be in distress;
Every hand of misery will come against him.
23 When he is about to fill his stomach,
God will cast on him the fury of His wrath,
And will rain it on him while he is eating.
24 He will flee from the iron weapon;
A bronze bow will pierce him through.
25 It is drawn, and comes out of the body;
Yes, the glittering point comes out of his gall.
Terrors come upon him;
26 Total darkness is reserved for his treasures.
An unfanned fire will consume him;
It shall go ill with him who is left in his tent.
27 The heavens will reveal his iniquity,
And the earth will rise up against him.
28 The increase of his house will depart,
and his goods will flow away in the day of His
wrath.
29 This is the portion from God for a wicked man,
The heritage appointed to him by God."

Job 20:1–29

The Almost-Perfect Sermon

Frenzy drives Zophar back into the fray. Job's warning that he and his friends will come under the judgment of God's wrath is more than Zophar can take. Pleading a personal sensitivity that has been insulted by the censure, he promises to speak magnanimously from a spirit of understanding. Zophar does neither. He reverts to a hell-fire-and-brimstone sermon on sin that adds the heat of hostility but not the light of understanding to the debate. Stylistically, however, he presents a model for good preaching that is worthy of study by students in homiletics classes. If outlined on a blackboard, Zophar's sermon would look like this:

TITLE: The Way of the Wicked

TEXT: *Do you not know this of old,*
Since man was placed on earth,
That the triumphing of the wicked is short,
And the joy of the hypocrite is but for a moment? (20:4–5).

OUTLINE:
- I. The joy of the wicked is brief (vv. 6–11)
  - A. His fall is great (vv. 6–7)
  - B. His name will disappear (v. 8)
  - C. His children will suffer (v. 10)
  - D. His death will be premature (v. 11)
- II. The sin of the wicked is self-destructive (vv. 12–19)
  - A. His evil desires turn to poison (vv. 12–16)
  - B. His dreams will not come true (v. 17)
  - C. His ill-gained profits will bring no joy (vv. 18–19)
- III. The judgment of God is sure (vv. 20–28)
  - A. His conscience condemns him (vv. 20–21)
  - B. His success repudiates him (v. 22)
  - C. His destruction is imminent (vv. 23–28)
    1. God will impale him (vv. 24–25)
    2. Darkness will cover him (v. 26)
    3. Fire will consume him (v. 26)
    4. Heaven will expose him (v. 27)
    5. Earth will resist him (v. 27)

CONCLUSION: *This is the portion from God for a wicked man,*
The heritage appointed to him by God (v. 29).

In contrast to the rambling thoughts and poetic flights that characterize most of the speeches given by Job and his friends so far, Zophar's sermon is precise and pointed. His portrayal of "the way of the wicked" is classic, not unlike Jonathan Edwards's best-known sermon, "Sinners in the Hands of an Angry God." When Edwards preached to his Puritan congregation in New England, it is said that his description of the wrath of God was so realistic that sinners hung on to the pews with white knuckles for fear of slipping into hell.

If Job had a guilty conscience, Zophar's sermon might have been equally effective. It is almost a perfect sermon except:

The motive is wrong. Zophar admits that he has been personally insulted by Job's warning of judgment. Retaliation is the misguided motive for his preaching. Worse yet, he misreads the revelation of Job's pinnacle experience as a temporary triumph of a wicked man and the momentary joy of a hypocrite. His text may be true, but his motive is wrong. Handling the word of truth is an awesome responsibility. Motive must match the message.

The hope is missing. In his first sermon, Zophar spoke of wickedness as well, but he finished his preaching with a song of restoration if Job would repent. Not even the slightest sound of hope is found in his second sermon. The true Zophar stands up. In defense of his own ego, he easily forgets the other side of his own doctrine of justice; namely, that a return to righteousness will restore prosperity. In his heart of hearts, Zophar is more capable than Bildad of burning Job at the stake because his passion for righteousness is nothing more than a coverup for protecting his own ego.

The materialism is evident. A long time ago, a camp meeting evangelist spent ten days and twenty sermons preaching against immodesty in women's dress. Afterward, my grandmother reflected on the experience, "Watch out for preachers who ride hobbies. They are revealing their own problem." Sure enough, the news came back a year or two later that the hobby-riding evangelist ran away with one of his new converts. Zophar also rides a hobby. He is obsessed with wealth, success, and possessions. Code words tell us where his heart is: wealth (v. 11), proceeds from business (v. 18), well-being (v. 21), self-sufficiency (v. 22), treasures (v. 26), increase of his house (v. 28), and his goods (v. 28).

Is it possible that Zophar is jealous of Job's prosperity? The sad fact is that he misses Job's need by miles. The loss of prosperity is not Job's fear, it is his loss of fellowship with God. In his obsession with possessions, Zophar has no spiritual word for Job. He is a materialist of the first order.

The accusation is aggravated. In general, Zophar's sermon sounds like a broken record. He is simply repeating the hard-line doctrine of God's justice in a narrow context. In specifics, however, he slips in a new accusation that changes the ground rules for the debate. Job has claimed that his sin, if there is any, is a private matter between him and God. Rather than confronting that question head-on with a factual rebuttal, Zophar comes at it obliquely by suggesting that Job is a "robber baron" who has come to wealth by oppressing the poor and engaging in unethical business practices:

> *From the proceeds of his business*
> *He will get no enjoyment.*
> *For he has oppressed*
> *and forsaken the poor,*
> *He has violently seized a house*
> *which he did not build* (vv. 18–19).

In casting about for a sin of which to accuse Job and justify his position, Zophar has overextended his reach. If Job is guilty of oppressing, forsaking, and robbing the poor, he has committed the unpardonable sin against his people. Zophar presents no proof of his charge. Perhaps he knows that his accusation will be overruled by the lack of evidence, but, like a wily prosecutor in a courtroom, he wants to put a shadow of doubt in the minds of the jury.

The charge is cowardly. In all his passion for details, Zophar never mentions the name of Job or points the finger at him. Cowering behind his role as a preacher, he pontificates in generalities so that he can claim immunity from personal attack. In my senior year of high school, I heard a preacher attack from the pulpit my choice of a Christian college. Although he never mentioned my name or pointed his finger, it so happened that I was the only young person in the church who planned to attend college. With a boldness that baffles me now, I called him on the telephone, "You were preaching against me." As gentle and harmless as a dove, he demurred. When I pressed the point that I was the only young person in the congregation with college plans, he then defended his attack by saying, "I only preach the truth. If the shoe fits, wear it!" We can expect the cowardly Zophar to give the same answer if Job presses him to name a name, point a finger, and prove the charge that he has sinned against the poor.

The bad news is that Zophar and Job are talking past each other. Job's problem is suffering; Zophar's solution is sin. Job's question is with God; Zophar's answer is with man. Job's need is spiritual; Zophar's fixation is material. The only good news is the fact that they are still talking. As long as the lines of communication are up, even when they are hot with hostility, there is still a glimmer of hope for reconciliation.

Job—The Resolution of History

Zophar's one-sided view of the wicked pushes Job to show the other extreme. Point by point, he shows that the wicked are happy, not despairing; prosperous, not poor; mighty, not weak; healthy, not afflicted; and peaceful, not terrorized. Furthermore, their families are safe and joyous. Job also destroys the argument that the judgment of the wicked is passed on to future generations. Why, he asks, should the children suffer when they are not guilty? With final irony, Job points out that the wicked have a quick and easy death attended by an elaborate funeral. For the first time, Job pronounces the whole theory of suffering false.

1 Then Job answered and said:
2 "Listen carefully to my speech,
And let this be your consolation.
3 Bear with me that I may speak,
And after I have spoken, keep mocking.
4 "As for me, is my complaint against man?
And if it were, why should I not be impatient?
5 Look at me and be astonished;
Put your hand over your mouth.
6 Even when I remember I am terrified,
And trembling takes hold of my flesh.
7 Why do the wicked live and become old,
Yes, become mighty in power?
8 Their descendants are established with them in their sight,
And their offspring before their eyes.
9 Their houses are safe from fear,
Neither is the rod of God upon them.
10 Their bull breeds without failure;
Their cow calves without miscarriage.
11 They send forth their little ones like a flock,
And their children dance.

12 They sing to the tambourine and harp,
And rejoice to the sound of the flute.
13 They spend their days in wealth,
And in a moment go down to the grave.
14 Yet they say to God, 'Depart from us,
For we do not desire the knowledge of Your ways.
15 Who is the Almighty, that we should serve Him?
And what profit do we have if we pray to Him?'
16 Indeed their prosperity is not in their hand;
The counsel of the wicked is far from me.
17 "How often is the lamp of the wicked put out?
How often does their destruction come upon them,
The sorrows God distributes in His anger?
18 They are like straw before the wind,
And like chaff that a storm carries away.
19 They say, 'God lays up one's iniquity for his children';
Let Him recompense him, that he may know it.
20 Let his eyes see his destruction,
And let him drink of the wrath of the Almighty.
21 For what does he care about his household after him,
When the number of his months is cut in half?
22 "Can anyone teach God knowledge,
Since He judges those on high?
23 One dies in his full strength,
Being wholly at ease and secure;
24 His pails are full of milk,
And the marrow of his bones is moist.
25 Another man dies in the bitterness of his soul,
Never having eaten with pleasure.
26 They lie down alike in the dust,
And worms cover them.
27 "Look, I know your thoughts,
And the schemes with which you would wrong me.
28 For you say,
'Where is the house of the prince?
And where is the tent,
The dwelling place of the wicked?'

29 Have you not asked those who travel the road?
And do you not know their signs?
30 For the wicked are reserved for the day of doom;
They shall be brought out on the day of wrath.
31 Who condemns his way to his face?
And who repays him for what he has done?
32 Yet he shall be brought to the grave,
And a vigil kept over the tomb.
33 The clods of the valley shall be sweet to him;
Everyone shall follow him,
As countless have gone before him.
34 How then can you comfort me with empty words,
Since falsehood remains in your answers?"

Job 21:1–34

Stop, Look, and Listen!

Nothing that Zophar says can dim Job's vision of God. With an objectivity that reflects his new perspective, Job says, "Stop, look, and listen!"

Stop the attack!
Look at me!
Listen to the facts!

A vision of God is practical as well as inspirational. Moses came down from Mt. Sinai with a code for divine–human relationships. Saul, after seeing Jesus on the Damascus road, asked, "Lord, what do You want me to do?" John not only saw Christ as Alpha and Omega, but heard the instruction to write down his visions in a book to the seven churches of Asia. The test of authenticity for a personal revelation is its practical application.

Job's momentary glimpse of the glory of God helps him see what he must do. The debate has degenerated into a contest of adversaries talking past each other in a climate of hostility. Under the inspiration of God, Job sees it as his task to *reduce* the hostility, *reestablish* the primary issues of the debate, and, if at all possible, *restore* the broken relationships.

"Stop," Job says. The word *listen* often has a double meaning. When someone says, "Listen!" they want undivided attention from the person to whom they are speaking, as well as a fair hearing for their case. When Job opens his response to Zophar with the word *listen,* he calls a halt to the hostility that has turned the debate into childish mocking.

Children are cruel when they taunt each other. Mocking a boy as a "sissy" or taunting a girl as a "cow" can cause permanent scars. Adults are expected to be more mature. They may get angry, they may resort to sarcasm, but mockery is an insult to their humanity as well as to their maturity. The mob who mocked Jesus on the cross betrayed their animal instincts.

Job knows that mockery is the last step before a permanent break in the relationship with his friends. If allowed to continue, they will destroy each other. Like the nuclear arms race, each side justifies the escalation of weapons as a defense against the build-up of the other side. Bilateral arms reduction is an ideal goal, but the truth of the matter is that one side or the other must call a halt to the race by taking the initiative of "unilateral" action to change the climate for Strategic Arms Limitation Talks. Such a move goes against human nature but not against the nature of God. Without God's initiative, there would be no redemption for us sinners and enemies (Rom. 5:10).

Job's motive is not as pure as God's when he calls for a halt to the hostility. In fact, he engages in a bit of sarcasm himself when he chides his friends with the word *consolation* (21:2). They came to console him and failed. Reversing roles, Job offers his friends the consolation of continuing their mockery if they reject his position on the issues. Job only asks for a détente—a climate in which he gets a hearing without hostility.

"Look at me," Job says (21:5). Zophar has created a mythical image of the wicked man. One can imagine him looking past the diseased face and beyond the pain-filled eyes of Job as he relates suffering with wickedness in generic terms. The language of the lips is always more violent when the eyes of the adversaries do not meet. So, for the second time, Job commands, *"Look at me."* The first time he appealed to the integrity of a life-long relationship with his friends,

> Now therefore, . . . look at me;
> For I would never lie to your face (6:28).

This time, Job wants his friends to see the evidence of suffering on his countenance and let the language of the eyes be the means of communication. Job knows that they will be astonished by a face that has turned into a hideous mask and awed into silence by eyes that flash innocence. Prefiguring Jesus as the "Intermediate Adam," he too has no form nor comeliness (Isa. 53:2). Jesus knows what it means for men to turn their faces from Him (Isa. 53:3).

Not enough can be said about the importance of the language of the face and eyes in communicating with those who suffer. Experts in communication tell us that the language of the lips transmits only 7 percent of what we say. The tone of voice accounts for 33 percent, and the language of the body, especially the face, speaks 60 percent of what is heard.

As a hospital chaplain, I was often called to counsel with the family of a patient whose illness had just been diagnosed as terminal. If the patient had not been informed of the diagnosis, the family usually agreed that they would go into the hospital room and act as if nothing had happened. After they left, the patient would call for me and say through tight lips, "Tell me the truth." While the family had tried to talk as if nothing had happened, the tone of their voices and the language of their eyes betrayed the message of doom.

With the command, *"Look at me,"* Job challenges his friends to move from superficial talk to in-depth communication. They had been conversing verbally at the 7 percent level of communication. By calling a halt to the hostility of the debate, Job wants to change the tone of voice which accounts for 33 percent of their communication. Now, he is willing to open up the depths of the final 60 percent of the message we transmit by asking that they speak the language of the eyes.

When President John F. Kennedy confronted Russia in the Cuban missile crisis, Secretary of State Dean Rusk said, "We stood eyeball to eyeball with the enemy." The daring confrontation convinced the Russians that the United States meant business. They withdrew the missiles and expressed a willingness to talk again. Job is willing to take the same risk. In an open test of truth and courage, he wants to talk "eyeball to eyeball."

"Listen," Job says again by inference as he begins to summarize the issues of the debate. This time he invokes the other side of the meaning of the word *listen.* He asks that his friends "hear" the evidence

and "understand" him (21:2–3). Up to now, Job and his friends have been talking past each other. They have either ignored what is being said or selectively have chosen words and phrases for rebuttal.

A group of authors and experts met to discuss the issues of the future. No agenda was set. Like banty-roosters posturing for position, the participants went through the necessary process of repeating what they had written or reciting what they knew. The first speech lasted twelve minutes, the second one lasted twenty minutes! The tone was set and dialogue died. For two days, authorities in written and spoken communication talked past each other. Well-known educator Jean Piaget sees this kind of communication in children and calls it "collective monologue."

Job says *"Listen"* because he wants to get the debate back on track. He wants to replace personal attack with substantive issues and a "collective monologue" with genuine dialogue. "Stop, look, and listen" calls for a complete change of the climate for communication. Assuming this climate, Job sums up the debate by returning to the question *why*.

Why do the wicked continue to prosper? Zophar's portrayal of the wicked man assumes swift retribution from God. This is a half-truth that cannot be generalized. Job presents the facts. The wicked live, grow old, and become mighty. More than that, they are blessed with maturity for their children, safety for their homes, increase in their herds, joy in their family, wealth for their days, and ease for their death (21:7–13).

Job describes the factual opposite of Zophar's mythical man. If his friends are looking into his eyes, they will see the tears of suffering that no one can deny. If they have an ounce of compassion in them, they will weep with their brother.

Yet, Job says, this is the same wicked man who rejects God, resists His ways, refuses to serve Him, and ridicules the value of prayer (vv. 14–15).

Steely truth glistens through the tears in Job's eyes. His friends must face the fact that Job has never turned away from God. Therefore, the ways of the wicked cannot account for his suffering. The doctrine of God's justice, which brings swift retribution to the wicked, cannot stand when Job and his friends eyeball the facts and each other.

Why should the children of the wicked suffer? When pushed into a corner on the evidence that the wicked are not immediately punished, Job's friends concede the point by extending the time of retribution to the suffering of the children. Here is another half-truth with which Job must deal. While it is true that the sins of the parents are frequently visited upon the second and third generations of children, it is not incontrovertible proof of God's "carry-over" justice. Too many factors are involved. Some godly parents who do their best to bring up their children in the fear and admonition of the Lord are crushed by godless sons and daughters whose rebellion is impossible to explain. God Himself is a parent whose heart takes the stabs from the wayward children of His own creation. At the same time, we know people who are miracles of grace, despite their parental influence and home environment. By all counts, they are spiritually impoverished. Yet, they attain a spiritual maturity that puts to shame those of us who are the progeny of Christian parents and the products of Christian homes. None of us who is a parent dares to claim a cause-and-effect relationship between our righteousness and our children's faith or between our sins and our children's suffering. Both the human will and God's grace are filled with surprises.

Tears appear again in Job's eyes as he remembers the violent deaths of his own children. Time and time again, we see that this memory is the deepest wound and the most tender part of his soul. Job cannot accept the fact that his children died for his sin. If God is just, he says, then let the wicked man himself know God's recompense, see God's destruction, and drink of His wrath (vv. 19–21).

Now for the telling fact. Eyeball to eyeball, Job asks his friends the penetrating question:

> *For what does he* [the wicked man] *care*
> *about his household after him,*
> *When the number of his months is*
> *cut in half?* (v. 21).

Again, through the tears in Job's eyes, they see just the opposite—a caring love that made Job's children the priority of his life (1:5). The contradiction is obvious. The justice of God cannot be defended by carrying over the time of retribution from the wicked man to his children.

Why do the wicked not die differently? The time line of retribution is extended once again. If the argument cannot stand that the wicked are punished immediately or by transfer to their children, Job's friends argue that retribution will come at the time of death. Pointedly, now, Job accuses his friends of arrogance. By twisting the facts to fit their doctrine of justice, they are guilty of trying to teach God the truth (21:22). The evidence speaks for itself. There is no set distinction between the wicked and the righteous in death. Either one may die young or old, easy or hard, prosperous or poverty-stricken:

> *They lie down alike in the dust,*
> *And worms cover them* (v. 26).

William Cullen Bryant put the same scene in poetry when he wrote "Thanatopsis":

> As the long train,
> Of ages glide away, the sons of men—
> The youth in life's green spring and he who goes
> In the full strength of years . . .
> Shall one by one be gathered to thy side,
> By those who in their turn shall follow them.

If Job's friends are looking him in the eye when he makes this point, in their minds and hearts they know that he is right.

Why do you include me among the wicked? Job calls for a personal point of order in the debate. Perhaps his friends have dropped their eyes or turned them away from his face. "Look," Job calls them back to the language of the eyes. Do they assume that he is naive? Do they not have the courage to say what they mean? Job confronts them with the fact that he knows that all of their thoughts and schemes, inferences and innuendoes are directed personally at him. He knows about whom they speak when they ask the questions,

> *Where is the house of the prince?*
> *And where is the tent,*
> *The dwelling place of the wicked?* (v. 28).

Furthermore, he can make the connection between what has happened to him and their earlier conclusion, "And the dwelling place of the wicked will come to nothing" (8:22).

Sarcasm returns to Job's voice when he counters their conclusion. Their wisdom, he says, is limited to the small circle of their personal perception and their local tradition. If only they would consult the common sense of the itinerant travelers who write their impressions of life on signposts at the intersections of the roads, they would see the wisdom of the wider world. Graffiti on a signpost can be mind-stretching truth. In a New York subway, someone wrote, "Jesus is the answer." Underneath it someone else scrawled, "What is the question?"

Our perspective of life changes when we see the bigger picture. Television is maligned as a medium that corrupts taste and values, but we cannot forget the good side of the tube. Instant news from around the world gives us a global view of life that changes the way we think, feel, and act toward our world neighbors. Children starving in Africa pull at our hearts and open our pursestrings. Russians who have faces just like ours are difficult to hate. Industrial pollution that rides on the jet stream and falls upon other nations becomes our responsibility.

Job knows from experience that a glimpse of the bigger picture challenges easy answers and opens new horizons. Even the tramp along the road has something to teach us from the experience of moving in the wider world. If only Eliphaz, Bildad, and Zophar could see beyond their prejudice and provincialism, they would know that Job could not be counted among the wicked.

Why do the wicked not fear life after death? Returning to the time line of retribution, Job refutes the assumption of his friends that the wicked who are not punished immediately, through their children or at the time of death, will suffer in eternity:

> *For the wicked are reserved*
> *for the day of doom;*
> *They shall be brought out*
> *on the day of wrath* (21:30).

Not so, Job says. The evidence shows that the wicked are as prosperous in death as they are in life. A grand procession brings them to their graves, an honor guard stands vigil over their tombs, and the dirt that covers their bodies *"shall be sweet"* (v. 33). Although death is the common experience of all humankind, the wicked flaunt the high cost of dying. But then, eternity makes no distinction. In the faceless land of shadows there is no retribution. By reminding them of their doctrine of Sheol, Job shows that the history of the wicked in eternity, as well as in life and death, cannot be used to defend their narrow view of the justice of God or their cruel explanation of his suffering. For Job, the friends who came to counsel him have only brought empty words and false answers (v. 34).

In the closing speech of the second round of debate, Job has tried to reduce the hostility, raise the understanding, and restate the question: *Why?*

NOTES

1. Edouard Dhorme, *A Commentary on the Book of Job* (Nashville: Thomas Nelson, 1984), p. 182.
2. Elliott Wright, *Holy Company* (New York: Macmillan, 1980), p. 1.

CHAPTER FIVE

His Friends' Reproach/Job's Rebuttal

Job 22:1—27:23

A stalemate has developed between Job and his friends. Their arguments have been pushed to opposite extremes and neither will concede a point. Confusion is represented by the fact that the arguments are now partial and disjointed. One point is clear. Eliphaz and Bildad do not hesitate to indict Job, not just as a sinner who has rebelled against God but as the epitome of evil who wreaks havoc upon the most helpless of creatures—the poor, the widows, and the orphans.

Eliphaz—The Reproach of Experience

Frustration has cracked the thin shell of courtesy with which Eliphaz first spoke. As the oldest and wisest of Job's friends, he had expected that his prophecy from God, telling him that sin causes suffering, would be sufficient to bring Job to repentance. Instead, the hammering of reality has shattered his source of authority. Still, he pronounces Job a sinner and proceeds to justify his conclusion. The weakness of his position is exposed by his search through the catalog of social sins that might apply to Job. In an implausible stretch of logic, he reasons that Job has concocted the idea of God's absence in order to cover his secret sins.

Cocksure once again, Eliphaz admonishes Job to repent and be restored to God's favor. Prophetically, Eliphaz forsees Job restored, not just to prosperity, but also to the honored role as an intercessor for others—a role that Eliphaz thinks God has given to *him* in order to help Job.

1 Then Eliphaz the Temanite answered and said:
2 "Can a man be profitable to God,

Though he who is wise may be profitable to himself?
3 Is it any pleasure to the Almighty that you are righteous?
Or is it gain to Him that you make your ways blameless?
4 "Is it because of your fear of Him that He corrects you,
And enters into judgment with you?
5 Is not your wickedness great,
And your iniquity without end?
6 For you have taken pledges from your brother for no reason,
And stripped the naked of their clothing.
7 You have not given the weary water to drink,
And you have withheld bread from the hungry.
8 But the mighty man possessed the land,
And the honorable man dwelt in it.
9 You have sent widows away empty,
And the strength of the fatherless was crushed.
10 Therefore snares are all around you,
And sudden fear troubles you,
11 Or darkness so that you cannot see;
And an abundance of water covers you.
12 "Is not God in the height of heaven?
And see the highest stars, how lofty they are!
13 And you say, 'What does God know?
Can He judge through the deep darkness?
14 Thick clouds cover Him, so that He cannot see,
And He walks above the circle of heaven.'
15 Will you keep to the old way
Which wicked men have trod,
16 Who were cut down before their time,
Whose foundations were swept away by a flood?
17 They said to God, 'Depart from us!
What can the Almighty do to them?'
18 Yet He filled their houses with good things;
But the counsel of the wicked is far from me.
19 "The righteous see it and are glad,
And the innocent laugh at them:
20 'Surely our adversaries are cut down,
And the fire consumes their remnant.'

21 "Now acquaint yourself with Him, and be at peace;
Thereby good will come to you.
22 Receive, please, instruction from His mouth,
And lay up His words in your heart.
23 If you return to the Almighty, you will be built up;
You will remove iniquity far from your tents.
24 Then you will lay your gold in the dust,
And the gold of Ophir among the stones of the brooks.
25 Yes, the Almighty will be your gold
And your precious silver;
26 For then you will have your delight in the Almighty,
And lift up your face to God.
27 You will make your prayer to Him,
He will hear you,
And you will pay your vows.
28 You will also declare a thing,
And it will be established for you;
So light will shine on your ways.
29 When they cast you down, and you say, 'Exaltation will come!'
Then He will save the humble person.
30 He will even deliver one who is not innocent;
Yes, he will be delivered by the purity of your hands."

Job 22:1–30

The Tyranny of a Private Vision

Protocol again dictates that Eliphaz the Elder open the third round of debate. His earlier responses have shown us that he is the statesman of the three friends—gentle, calm, reasonable, and diplomatic. His task at the beginning of each round of the debate is to state the issues and set the tone for the discussion. He has also assumed that it is his responsibility as the elder statesman to seal the case.

For the first time, Eliphaz is unnerved. Job's "Stop, Look, and Listen" speech shook the foundations of his theology and threatened to topple his authority. If what Job says is true, Eliphaz's world is on the verge of collapse. The nature of his response reveals his panic. In self-defense, he points the finger of judgment at Job and says, "Your wickedness is great and you are hopelessly depraved!" (22:5).

With these words, Eliphaz states the issue and sets the tone for the third round. Prejudice will rule and panic will prevail in a series of personalized attacks. Eliphaz has defaulted on his leadership role by creating a chasm that will widen until the last bridge of communication is broken down.

Leaders are the value-makers and tone-setters for the people who follow them. The axiom applies to leadership at every level—from the smallest group to the largest nation. When Thomas J. Peters and Robert H. Waterman began their search for the best-run companies in the United States, they assumed that leadership made no difference. Immediately, they were proven wrong. Their best-selling book, *In Search of Excellence,* is based upon the premise that behind every company of quality there is a legendary leader who sees his or her role as the shaping of human values and communicating these values by personal style and presence.[1] Leaders still make the difference.

Eliphaz fails as a leader because his vision of God's justice is threatened by Job's vision of God's love. When Job got his glimpse of God, he exclaimed,

> For I know that my Redeemer lives,
> And He shall stand at last on the earth;
> And after my skin is destroyed, this I know,
> That in my flesh I shall see God (19:25–26).

Eliphaz had his vision in the nighttime when God said,

> Can a mortal be more righteous than God?
> . . . .
> If He charges His angels with error,
> How much more those who dwell in houses of clay
> . . . .
> Does not their own excellence go away?
> They die, even without wisdom (4:17–21).

The clashing issue and the contrasting tone of these two visions can be felt. Job's vision opens the horizon of God's future to see a healing note of hope for all people. Eliphaz's vision narrows the horizon by focusing upon a formula of faith that is divisive, pessimistic, and elitist. Like the woman who broke the alabaster box, poured the perfume over Jesus' head, and wiped his feet with her tears, her act and Job's vision are memorials to their faith wherever the gospel is preached throughout the whole world (Mark 14:9). Among nighttime visions, however, the fabled Ghost of Christmas Past who appeared to Scrooge in Charles Dickens's *Christmas Carol* is far better known than Eliphaz's self-trumpeted revelation.

In essence, Eliphaz is tyrannized by his vision of God's justice. His response to Job is symptomatic of anyone who fixates on the experience of a private vision of God.

Orthodoxy Is Sterilized

Eliphaz sees the message of suffering on Job's face and the evidence of innocence in his eyes. But if he shows compassion or agrees that his friend has integrity, his own case is lost. The only escape from the dilemma is to suppress his emotions and sterilize his thoughts. Eliphaz makes his choice and gives a classic example of defending sterile orthodoxy. Once having put the sight of Job's face and eyes out of his mind, he can fall back upon his skills as a master of logical disputation. He begins by turning Job's argument against him. In the process of eliminating the evidence that God punishes the wicked immediately through their children, at death or in eternity, Job opens the door for the conclusion that God is morally indifferent to the wicked. This is not his intention. Job only wants to show that the hard and fast rule of "cash-register justice" cannot be invoked in his case. Eliphaz's mind works only with generalizations, not exceptions. Thus, by jumping on the generalization that God is morally consistent with the wicked, he can return to the solid ground of his private vision, which views God as impartial in His justice. Suppressing his feelings and collecting his thoughts, Eliphaz begins his response to Job by paraphrasing and applying what God told him in his nighttime vision:

> Can a mortal be more righteous than God?
> Can a man be more pure than his Maker? (4:17).
> *Can a man be profitable to God, . . .*
> *Is it any pleasure to the Almighty that you are righteous?*
> *Or is it gain to Him that you make your ways blameless?* (22:2–3).

Once the vision of his experience is reestablished, Eliphaz moves with logical ease to the conclusion with which Job must agree: *God is impartial in His justice.* If so, Job must also agree that God is not punishing him for his righteousness or his "fear of the Lord" (v. 4). *Ergo!* If God's justice is impartial and He is not punishing Job for his righteousness, He must be balancing on the scales of blind justice the weight of Job's great sin with the equal weight of his great suffering:

> *Is not your wickedness great,*
> *And your iniquity without end?* (v. 5).

Notice that Eliphaz advances to this conclusion under the cover of five rhetorical questions. There is no room in his logic for Job's open question *why.* In fact, there is not even room for a yes or no answer. By stating the first four questions so that no is the only answer, Eliphaz sets up the final questions about Job's wickedness with an unequivocal yes.

Sophistry, the art of twisting truth to your own advantage, is a survival technique for a sterile orthodoxy. By ignoring changes in social circumstances, advances in human thought, and especially the conditions of human suffering, rigid orthodoxy can always give ready answers. All of those who are trying to find their way through the quicksands of suffering to a higher ground of faith are its victims.

Sin Is Stereotyped

Once Eliphaz has reestablished the validity of his doctrine of justice and the credibility of his authority, he is bound to identify Job's sin and indict him as a sinner. Eliphaz has already concluded that Job is guilty of the sin of the rich and the powerful. He has oppressed the poor. To illustrate, Eliphaz accuses Job of committing the unpardonable sin of the rich. He has unjustly taken the cloak of a poor brother as a pledge against a nonexistent debt. Worse yet, he has violated the fundamental principle of mercy by refusing to return the cloak in the nighttime to protect the brother against the cold—not unlike stripping the naked of their clothing (v. 6). Eliphaz then compounds Job's wickedness by adding to the list of his sins: refusing water to the weary, withholding bread from the hungry, sending widows away empty, and crushing the strength of the fatherless (vv. 7, 9).

No bill of particulars can be more damning. To justify his conclusion that Job's great suffering is matched by great sin, Eliphaz accuses Job of the most heinous crimes against humanity. No proof is needed to support his indictment. All Eliphaz needs to do is play upon the stereotype in the public mind that the rich are the oppressors of the poor.

Stereotyping is a product of prejudice and a device for self-protection. Sociological studies show that people who are asked to speak the first word that comes to mind when ethnic or national origins are mentioned tend to give responses that are automatic and predictable. Certain groups may evoke the description "lazy," "pushy," "dumb," "sexy," etc. Religious stereotypes also persist in public opinion. During the years of the "Born Again" movement, a reporter asked Emily Harris, co-author of *I'm O.K., You're O.K.,* "Are you born again?" In refusing to answer, she explained, "If I say yes, you'll assume that you know everything about me." She wanted to avoid the stereotype that all "born-again" people are alike.

Eliphaz has proven once again that behind his smiling face and gentle voice he is the most devious and dangerous of the three friends. Without a shred of evidence to prove his charge, he counts upon public prejudice against the rich to indict Job for sins against society. He knows that the stereotype is so firmly fixed in the public mind that he can point the finger at Job saying, "You are the man!" without fear that the evidence will ever be required. Brazenly, before the whole world, he announces that the snares, fears, darkness, and flood of sorrows that have come over Job's soul are God's retribution for his great sin.

God as Scapegoat

Nothing is beyond Eliphaz now. The tyranny of his private vision drives him on. He puts in Job's mouth, for instance, the quotation that Job had attributed to the wicked saying,

> Depart from us,
> For we do not desire the knowledge of Your ways.
> Who is the Almighty, that we should serve Him,
> And what profit do we have if we pray to Him? (21:14–15).

Eliphaz turns these words against him. Making Job sound arrogant and incorrigible, Eliphaz quotes him out of context,

> *And you say, "What does God know?*
> *Can He judge through the deep darkness?"*
> . . . .
> *They said to God, "Depart from us!*
> *What can the Almighty do to* [us]?" (22:13, 17).

Job means just the opposite, but Eliphaz needs a motive to explain the great sins of which he has accused his friend. Dominoes of twisted logic continue to fall. Job is not only a great sinner, Eliphaz says, but he is actually the *personification of evil!* For this reason, when Job and the rest of the wicked are punished by God for their sins,

> *The righteous see it and are glad,*
> *And the innocent laugh at them* (v. 19).

What a turnabout! Job asked his friends for compassion, they give him glee for his plight. How often a quote out of context becomes the justification for a crucifixion. When the chief priests and scribes quizzed Jesus, "If You are the Christ, tell us," He said to them, "If I tell you, you will by no means believe. And if I also ask you, you will by no means answer Me or let Me go" (Luke 22:67–68).

How right He was! With just a series of twisted words, the chief priests and scribes set before Pilate the accusation that Jesus claimed to be a king in opposition to Caesar. Job must have been equally shocked to hear his words come back to him as proof that he personifies evil, rather than exemplifies good.

Salvation Is Self-Conscious

By now, we are suspicious of Eliphaz's motive in everything he says. In one breath, he snarls that Job's wickedness is great, his sin against the poor is unpardonable, and his nature is totally depraved. In the next breath, he coos like a loving father giving spiritual advice and glibly promises the restoration of Job's prosperity. Taken alone, the concluding section of Eliphaz's speech reads like a lilting psalm of redemptive hope. But placed in the context of Eliphaz's whole speech, it appears as a puzzling contradiction.

Perhaps Eliphaz is compensating for the viciousness of his personal attack on Job. Perhaps the panic is passed and having regained his confidence, he can be gracious once again. Or perhaps he feels as if he has accomplished his purpose of shaming Job into repentance. Whatever the motive, Eliphaz reveals the basic flaw in a faith based upon a personal experience and a private vision. The plan of salvation becomes a subjective, self-centered, and self-conscious scheme.

Eliphaz advises Job:

> *Now acquaint yourself with* [God], . . .
> *Receive, please, instruction from His mouth,*
> *And lay up His words in your heart* (22:21–22).

But what is the source of God's revelation? According to Eliphaz, the truth has been given to him in the nighttime vision. Therefore, he is advising Job to heed him because he is the oracle of God's word. The problem is a private vision that only defends a doctrine of man. Subjective experience is confused with objective revelation.

In a series of promises to Job, Eliphaz tells him that wealth is the evidence of man's righteousness and God's favor. Having concluded that Job has committed the sin of the rich, he fills his speech from beginning to end with economic terms. In his original questions to Job, he chose the words, *"profitable," "pleasure,"* and *"gain"* (vv. 2–3). When describing Job's sins, he talks about *"pledges,"* the resources of *"clothing," "water," "bread,"* alms, and possessions (vv. 6–9). Even in pronouncing him totally depraved, Eliphaz acknowledges that God has filled the houses of the wicked with *"good things"* (v. 18). Not surprisingly, we also read his remedy in the promises of economic gain:

> *If you return to the Almighty,*
> *you will be built up; . . .*
> *Then you will lay your gold*
> *in the dust,*
> *And the gold of Ophir among the stones of the*
> *brooks.*
> *Yes, the Almighty will be your gold*
> *And your precious silver;*
> . . . .
> *And you will pay your vows* (vv. 23–27).

The fallacy of this approach is that Job has long ago settled the issue of riches. When he loses his wealth in the calamities of enemy raids and fire from heaven, he says,

> The LORD gave, and the LORD has taken away;
> Blessed be the name of the LORD (1:21).

Is it possible that Eliphaz's obsession with wealth is a projection of his own desires? If so, his promise of prosperity is self-centered rather than God-centered.

The closing sentences of Eliphaz's speech are equally revealing. He promises Job authority, wisdom, confidence, humility, power, and purity (22:28–30).

These are the qualities of a wise and righteous man who is honored by God with the role of being an intercessor for others. Is not this the precise image with which Eliphaz conceives himself? In other words, if Job repents and is restored, he will become the spiritual clone of Eliphaz. After all, when religion is based upon a private vision, the only model is the person who has had the experience.

How will Job respond to this speech in which Eliphaz coils like a snake, claws like a hawk, and coos like a dove? Will he answer in kind or hold his course? Eliphaz has challenged Job's vision of God.

JOB—THE REBUTTAL OF INNOCENCE

In response to Eliphaz's charge, Job contends that he does not hide his secret sins by arguing that God is far away. Rather, he seeks a hearing with God in order to prove his innocence. Given such a hearing, he has no doubt that God will vindicate him. Then, turning Eliphaz's argument against him, Job reveals his understanding of the violence of the world—the weak who suffer, the rich who rob, the poor who are miserable, and the criminals who go free. God does not bring judgment on them. In fact, He appears to be indifferent to their sins. How, then, can you say that suffering is God's retribution for sin? With one final fling, Job throws out the challenge, *"Prove me a liar."*

> 23:1 Then Job answered and said:
> 2 "Even today my complaint is bitter;
> My hand is listless because of my groaning.

3 Oh, that I knew where I might find Him,
That I might come to His seat!
4 I would present my case before Him,
And fill my mouth with arguments.
5 I would know the words which He would answer me,
And understand what He would say to me.
6 Would He contend with me in His great power?
No! But He would take note of me.
7 There the upright could reason with Him,
And I would be delivered forever from my Judge.
8 "Look, I go forward, but He is not there,
And backward, but I cannot perceive Him;
9 When He works on the left hand, I cannot behold Him;
When He turns to the right hand, I cannot see Him.
10 But He knows the way that I take;
when He has tested me, I shall come forth as gold.
11 My foot has held fast to His steps;
I have kept His way and not turned aside.
12 I have not departed from the commandment of His lips;
I have treasured the words of His mouth
More than my necessary food.
13 "But He is unique, and who can make Him change?
And whatever His soul desires, that He does.
14 For He performs what is appointed for me,
And many such things are with Him.
15 Therefore I am terrified at His presence;
When I consider this, I am afraid of Him.
16 For God made my heart weak,
And the Almighty terrifies me;
17 Because I was not cut off from the presence of darkness,
And He did not hide deep darkness from my face.
24:1 "Since times are not hidden from the Almighty,
Why do those who know Him see not His days?
2 "Some remove landmarks;

They seize flocks violently and feed on them;
3 They drive away the donkey of the fatherless;
They take the widow's ox as a pledge.
4 They push the needy off the road;
All the poor of the land are forced to hide.
5 Indeed, like wild donkeys in the desert,
They go out to their work, searching for food.
The wilderness yields food for them and for their children.
6 They gather their fodder in the field
And glean in the vineyard of the wicked.
7 They spend the night naked, without clothing,
And have no covering in the cold.
8 They are wet with the showers of the mountains,
And huddle around the rock for want of shelter.
9 "Some snatch the fatherless from the breast,
And take a pledge from the poor.
10 They cause the poor to go naked, without clothing;
And they take away the sheaves from the hungry.
11 They press out oil within their walls,
And tread winepresses, yet suffer thirst.
12 The dying groan in the city,
And the souls of the wounded cry out;
Yet God does not charge them with wrong.
13 "There are those who rebel against the light;
They do not know its ways
Nor abide in its paths.
14 The murderer rises with the light;
He kills the poor and needy;
And in the night he is like a thief.
15 The eye of the adulterer waits for the twilight,
Saying, 'No eye will see me';
And he disguises his face.
16 In the dark they break into houses
Which they marked for themselves in the daytime;
They do not know the light.
17 For the morning is the same to them as the shadow of death;
If someone recognizes them,

They are in the terrors of the shadow of death.
18 "They should be swift on the face of the waters,
Their portion should be cursed in the earth,
So that no one would turn into the way of their
vineyards.
19 As drought and heat consume the snow waters,
So the grave consumes those who have sinned.
20 The womb should forget him,
The worm should feed sweetly on him;
He should be remembered no more,
And wickedness should be broken like a tree.
21 For he preys on the barren who do not bear,
And does no good for the widow.
22 "But God draws the mighty away with His
power;
He rises up, but no man is sure of life.
23 He gives them security, and they rely on it;
Yet His eyes are on their ways.
24 They are exalted for a little while,
Then they are gone.
They are brought low;
They are taken out of the way like all others;
They dry out like the heads of grain.
25 "Now if it is not so, who will prove me a liar,
And make my speech worth nothing?"

Job 23:1—24:25

Glimpses of the Hidden God

The false accusations of Eliphaz are so ridiculous that they collapse under their own weight. Job is wise in not dignifying them with a direct response. Besides, he has other things on his mind. From the summit of his new-found faith, he catches glimpses of the character and purpose of God. More often than not, his view is still clouded by his suffering and hazed by his humanity. Yet, in the fleeting moments when there is a break in the clouds and Job's eyes open, it is like a clear day on which he can see forever.

Many commentators interpret Job's "response" to Eliphaz as the words of a man who is alienated from God and arrogant in his own righteousness. To come to that conclusion is to disregard the context and misread the text. Job is a pioneer on a journey of faith. It is a struggle of contradictions but not without flashes of spiritual insight, each of which is a step of preparation for an audience with God. Therefore, when Job confesses that he is still a rebel who is bitter and powerless before God, his honesty clears the way for him to ask the question that nags at all of us when we suffer. *"Oh, that I knew where I might find Him"* (23:3).

C. S. Lewis, in grieving for his wife, spoke the same desire:

> Meanwhile, where is God? This is one of the most disquieting symptoms. When you are happy, so happy that you have no sense of needing Him, so happy that you are tempted to feel His claims upon you as an interruption, if you remember yourself and turn to Him with gratitude and praise, you will be—or so it feels—welcomed with open arms. But go to Him when your need is desperate, when all other help is vain, and what do you find? A door slammed in your face and a sound of bolting and double bolting on the inside. After that, silence. You may as well turn away. The longer you wait, the more emphatic the silence will become. . . . What does this mean? *Why is He so present a commander in our time of prosperity and so very absent a help in time of trouble?* (emphasis mine).[2]

Phillip Yancey asked the same question in the title of his best-selling book, *Where Is God When It Hurts?* Some of us have never felt the pain and emptiness behind that question. Sooner or later we will. It is the universal question of those who suffer.

Job helps us learn that the absence of God does not necessarily mean alienation from God. In answer to his own question, *"Oh, that I knew where I might find Him,"* Job gives us insights of faith that show him moving closer to God rather than broadening the breach of an uncrossable chasm.

After repeated appeals to appear before God, Job has given up on being vindicated while still alive. Once he sees the future hope of a Redeemer, his desire for vindication comes alive again. Therefore, he reopens his plea to appear before the seat of God and present his case (vv. 3, 4). Faith tells him that God and he will understand each other now (v. 5) and that God will not use His great power to make the hearing a mismatch (vv. 6, 7).

Going on, Job again speaks for all humankind in its search for God. Wherever he looks, he cannot see Him—forward, backward, right hand, left hand, North, or South (vv. 8–9). The eyes of faith open again. Job exclaims, *"But He knows the way that I take"* (v. 10).

Even when we cannot see God, He sees us! Suddenly, Job's eyes open wide. For the first time, he sees the reason for his suffering. God is not punishing him or acting by whimsy—*He is testing Job.* This realization changes Job's whole perspective. Even though the reason for his suffering is still hidden, in the mind of God it has a purpose. Job's confidence in God tells him that the purpose is good and, therefore, the suffering is bearable. Anticipating the end, Job witnesses by faith,

> *When He has tested me,*
> *I shall come forth as gold* (v. 10).

Suffering with a purpose is endured and forgotten. When our daughter had her first baby, she chose natural childbirth. Immediately after the baby was born, she said that she had never known such pain. An hour later, when she held her baby in her arms, she beamed, "It was worth it. I want six more babies."

Still, suffering is not easy. When Job realizes that the test is not yet over, he shudders at the thought of God—unique, unchangeable, unfettered, inscrutable, and sovereign—administering the test (vv. 13–14). Fear, weakness, and sheer terror strike at his heart again (vv. 15–16). He has already felt the "black dog of despair" within his being and experienced an impenetrable darkness all around him. Job has reason to be terrified at the thought, *What's next?*

Why Doesn't God Do Something?

"Seeing" continues to be the subject of Job's thoughts as he talks aloud to himself. Eliphaz has wrongly accused him of saying that God does not see the ways of the wicked because He is too distant to see through the darkness and the clouds between heaven and earth (22:12–14). Inspired insight has shown Job that this is wrong. Although he cannot see God, he knows that God sees him and the way he takes (23:10). But, as so often happens, new faith creates new frustration. If God sees human affairs without myopia or blurred vision, then why doesn't He do something about them?

The question applies to both suffering and sin. Job has already answered the question with regard to his own suffering. He believes that God has not intervened to give him relief because his suffering is a test that is not yet finished, and with a purpose that is not yet known.

Sin is another story. To paraphrase Job's dilemma, If God sees wickedness, then why do we not see Him act? Job is questioning the governance of God. While he has disputed the doctrine of justice that is based upon automatic rewards and punishment, he still expects God to act like a judge who periodically holds sessions and sets the docket to deal with the righteous and the wicked. Rather arrogantly, Job expects to see as God sees because of his righteousness. He is preoccupied with the *means* rather than the *ends* of justice. Jesus will straighten out that expectation when He reveals the certainty of the final judgment, but He leaves the timing to the Father (Matt. 24:36).

Job is impatient with God because he sees wickedness rampant on the earth. Eliphaz portrayed only the sins of the rich. Job enlarges the picture to include the rich as well as the poor, the city as well as the country, agriculture as well as industry, crimes against people as well as crimes against property, and sins of the spirit as well as sins of the flesh. He sees three categories of wickedness.

Renegades against the Helpless

For people who live off the land and exist at the mercy of the seasons, there is a common code of survival. Mutual respect is given to the boundaries of the scrubbiest farms, the sustenance value of the smallest flocks of sheep, the carrying power of a single donkey, and the working power of a cumbersome ox. To violate this code is a crime punishable by death. The Law of Moses, for instance, invokes the commandment from God, "Thou shalt not remove thy neighbor's landmark" (Deut. 19:14, KJV), curses the violator (Deut. 27:17), and condemns the guilty to death (Deut. 19:21).

A similar code prevailed on the frontier of the Old West in America. Only the land, horses, and cattle stood between the pioneers and death. Consequently, land-grabbers, horse thieves, and cattle-rustlers found no mercy for their crimes. Vigilantes took justice into their own hands and "hanging trees" were plentiful.

Renegades roamed the land of Job also. Their victims were not the rich and the powerful who could protect themselves against marauding raids, but the fatherless, the widow, and the needy (24:2–4). Without any resources upon which to fall back, helpless people whose land, flocks, and cattle were stolen had no recourse but to scavenge for food like animals, without clothing or shelter in the burning heat, freezing cold, and drenching wet of the wilderness (vv. 5–8).

Profiteers against the Poor

Another category of the wicked is the respectable man who exploits the poor. Often, he is an executive who makes policy decisions that affect the lives of those who work for him. By fudging on fair wages, extracting usurious interest on debts, treating laborers like pieces of property, and failing to consider their human needs, he joins the group known in contemporary terminology as the "robber baron." He works within the loopholes and the margins of the law so that he cannot be formally charged with a crime. In the eyes of God, however, his greed is evident and his victims are orphans, widows, and the poor who are naked, hungry, thirsty, wounded, and dying (vv. 9–12). Job cannot understand why *"God does not charge them with wrong"* (v. 12).

Rebels against the Light

Separate from renegades and profiteers who perpetrate crimes against the helpless and the poor are the wicked who count on the darkness to cover their sins. Job names murderers, adulterers, and thieves as rebels against the light. Not only do they seek the cover of physical darkness to carry out their nefarious deeds, but, symbolically, they also avoid the moral light of conscience and the spiritual light of God. Murder, for instance, is a sin against the sanctity of life; adultery is a sin against the sanctity of marriage; and thievery is a sin against the sanctity of property. Each is a sacred right fundamental to the survival of the society. Each is a sacred revelation inherent in the "light" of natural law and individual conscience. Each is a specific commandment of God who is the Light. Therefore, murderers, adulterers, and thieves have one consuming dread—the intrusion of light upon them and their deeds. Like the dawn of the morning, a ray of conscience or a beam of truth casts the *"shadow of death"* over their souls and strikes terror into their hearts for fear of being exposed (24:17).

Jesus brings this image of the wicked rebelling against the light to fulfillment when He teaches, "And this is the condemnation, that light has come into the world, and men loved darkness rather than light, because their deeds were evil" (John 3:19).

Renegades, profiteers, and rebels are a roster of the wicked and perpetrate a catalog of sins against property, people, and sacred rights. Job is outraged to think that God sees their wickedness and does nothing about it. Speaking for all people, he insists that God act upon the wicked: their lives should be brief, their portion should be cursed, their grave should be unmarked, their family should forget them, their body should be eaten by worms, their name should be erased, and their wickedness should be stopped (24:18–20).

The common reason for bringing them to judgment is that, in one way or another, each of their sins is a threat to society, *"For he preys upon the barren who do not bear,"* and a crime against innocent people, *"And does no good for the widow"* (v. 21).

Job's conundrum is complete when he reasons that God seems to make no distinction between the wicked and the righteous in His judgments. When he acts, *"no man is sure of life"* (v. 22). Worse yet, God even appears to be in collusion with the wicked. By refusing to bring them to swift and automatic judgment, God seems to give them a sense of security upon which they rely to continue their sins and their crimes (v. 23).

"Yet," Job says whenever he is on the verge of an insight, *"His eyes are on their ways"* (v. 23). The God who sees the ways of man will act in His own time and in His own way (v. 24). Some scholars believe that Job has acquiesced to his friends' doctrine of justice that equates sin with suffering. To the contrary, he has never denied his faith in the justice of God. The issue is whether God's justice fits the formula of automatic, swift, and obvious punishment upon the wicked with equal evidence of prosperity for the righteous. Job is so sure of his case that he closes his speech by throwing down the dare:

> *Now if it is not so,*
> *who will prove me a liar,*
> *And make my speech worth nothing?* (v. 25).

BILDAD—THE REPROACH OF TRADITION

Tradition has no answer for radical changes in the circumstances of life. Unable to refute Job's argument that violence is rampant on the earth, Bildad resorts to a doxology, extolling the greatness of God in contrast with the sinfulness of man. Pointedly, but indirectly, he calls Job a maggot and a worm.

> 1 Then Bildad the Shuhite answered and said:
> 2 "Dominion and fear belong to Him;
> He makes peace in His high places.
> 3 Is there any number to His armies?
> Upon whom does His light not rise?
> 4 How then can man be righteous before God?
> Or how can he be pure who is born of a woman?
> 5 If even the moon does not shine,
> And the stars are not pure in His sight,
> 6 How much less man, who is a maggot,
> And a son of man, who is a worm?"
>
> *Job 25:1–6*

Man the Maggot

By now, we expect the debaters to talk past each other. Bildad's response to Job is no exception. Rather than taking the challenge to prove him a "liar" for arguing that God seems to be indifferent to rampant wickedness, Bildad's simplistic mind leads him to speak the logical extremes of his traditional doctrine. His view of God, man, and creation not only summarizes the position of the three friends but dead-ends the debate.

God Is Unapproachable

A brief and beautiful doxology with the rhythm of poetry and the majesty of music sums up Bildad's view of the nature of God. God rules over all authority, maintains all peace, commands all forces, radiates all light, perfects all holiness, and possesses all purity (25: 2–4).

Every attribute is true. The God of Bildad is power, peace, perfection, and purity; but He is also the God of Job—immanent presence and interacting personality. Bildad, however, must keep God at a safe distance in order to create Him in his own image. Teetering on the brink of deism and agnosticism is preferable to admitting that God sees and cares about His human creation in terms other than blind justice.

Man Is Irredeemable

Our theology determines our anthropology. Therefore, an unapproachable God results in an unredeemable man. No matter what he does, righteousness and purity will escape him. All of the frustration in man's quest for God prior to the advent of Christ comes into intense focus at this point. Of course, Bildad is half-right. Man cannot redeem himself. Isaiah spoke of the same futility:

> But we are all like an unclean thing,
> And all our righteousnesses are like filthy rags;
> We all fade as a leaf
> And our iniquities, like the wind,
> Have taken us away (Isa. 64:6).

But Isaiah also forsaw the Savior who bridges the gap between God and man:

> All we like sheep have gone astray;
> We have turned, every one, to his own way;
> And the Lord has laid on Him the
> Iniquity of us all (Isa. 53:6).

Paradoxically, Bildad is closer to the truth than Job when he contends that man is powerless to redeem himself. Job still believes that he can stand before God in his own righteousness and blamelessness. The difference is between a static faith and a dynamic faith. Bildad has fixed an unapproachable God in the heavens and an irredeemable man on earth—never the twain shall meet. Job, however, is a man who is spiritually on the move. Although he has a problem of his own righteous conceit, he has demonstrated that he is open to change. If Bildad and Job were alive at the advent of Christ, we could expect that Bildad would side with the Pharisees while Job would cry, "Lord, be merciful to me a sinner."

Creation Is Imperfect

Bildad's opinion of man continues to deteriorate as he draws a comparison between the creation of the universe and the creation of man. Even though God pronounces both of these creative works as "good," Bildad sees the flaws through pessimistic eyes. Again, he speaks half a truth when he declares,

> *If even the moon does not shine,*
> *And the stars are not pure in His sight* (25:5).

Adam's sin in the Garden of Eden not only affected man's nature but corrupted all the universe. Paul wrote to the Romans, "For we know that the whole creation groans and labors with birth pangs together until now" (Rom. 8:22).

Bildad is neither so insightful nor hopeful. He uses the imperfection of the moon and the stars to set up a comparison with man. In his mind, he has created a step-down universe in which God walks above "the circle of heaven"(22:14), the physical universe reflects His power and majesty (25:2, 3), and man, by comparison, is the "runt" of His creation.

Man Is Insignificant

David the Psalmist and Bildad the Shuhite asked the same question,

> When I consider Your heavens,
> the work of Your fingers,
> The moon and the stars,
> which You have ordained,
> What is man that You are mindful of him,
> And the son of man that You visit him? (Ps. 8:3–4).

They came to opposite conclusions. David realized the uniqueness of man as distinguished from the physical universe. He also recognized the exalted position of man as created "a little lower than the angels, and . . . crowned . . . with glory and honor" (Ps. 8:5).

Bildad, however, fails to see the uniqueness of man or the glory of his potential. As he compares the nature of man with the nature of God, he has already pronounced him "irredeemable." Now, he compares the nature of man with the nature of the universe and pronounces him "insignificant":

> *How much less man, who is a maggot,*
> *And a son of man, who is a worm?* (25:6).

A worm's-eye-view of man is the most extreme kind of pessimism. Periodically, this idea surfaces in both secular and spiritual viewpoints. James Jones, the novelist, said that a man is a cruel trick of God who gets his dealings from the bottom of the deck. After World War II, pessimism about the nature of man produced a flurry of books and plays that dwelt upon the "existential despair" of man whose life is meaningless and whose future is empty. During my college days, there was a popular book by Hession, *The Calvary Road,* that was used to promote the idea that holy people become "worms" upon whom others step.[3]

Today, the pendulum has swung to the other extreme. As part of the "me" generation that exalts the self, sin and guilt are played down. Spiritual self-esteem is having a heyday. Although we prefer to soar in the realm of angels rather than grub on earth with apes, sooner or later we can expect to stub our toes and skin our noses on the reality that man is neither a worm nor a god.

On the dismal note that man is a maggot, Bildad closes the case against Job, "not with a bang but a whimper." Some commentators argue that Bildad's speech is not over. Portions of Job's final response are brought forward to become part of Bildad's continuing speech. Other portions of Job's next response are attributed to Zophar who does not appear to speak again. Without doubt, textual difficulties abound throughout this closing section of the third round of debate. Despite the difficulties, a good argument can be made for the fact that Bildad's abbreviated speech and Zophar's strange silence represent their withdrawal from the conflict. Try as they might, they fail to comfort Job's suffering, condemn him for sin, or convince him that he is wrong. Bildad's closing words support the alternative that the debate has come to a dead end. After all, when Bildad pronounces man a maggot and the son of man a worm, what else can he say? For Eliphaz, Bildad, and Zophar, they have nothing more to offer Job.

JOB—THE REBUTTAL OF DILEMMA

Bildad's tradition is bankrupt. No help has been given to ease Job's suffering—or anyone else who needs strength and wisdom. Therefore, Job reverses roles with Bildad and becomes the teacher. In masterful style, he recreates the dilemma in which they have placed him. On the one hand, there is an all-powerful God whom they cannot know or understand (26:5–14). On the other hand, there is the orthodox answer that puts sin and suffering in a direct cause-and-effect relationship. The gulf is fixed—one extreme leads to agnosticism, the other to nihilism or utter futility. In between is Job's integrity that will not let him accept either extreme. Come what may, Job vows that he will not sin (27:2–10). Rather, from his suspended position between the extremes, he is ready to teach.

26:1 But Job answered and said:
2 "How have you helped him who is without power?
How have you saved the arm that has no strength?
3 How have you counseled one who has no wisdom?
And how have you declared sound advice to many?
4 To whom have you uttered words?
And whose spirit came from you?
5 "The dead tremble,
Those under the waters and those inhabiting them.
6 Sheol is naked before Him,
And Destruction has no covering.
7 He stretches out the north over empty space;
He hangs the earth on nothing.
8 He binds up the water in His thick clouds,
Yet the clouds are not broken under it.
9 He covers the face of His throne,
And spreads His cloud over it.
10 He drew a circular horizon on the face of the waters,

At the boundary of light and darkness.
11 The pillars of heaven tremble,
And are astonished at His rebuke.
12 He stirs up the sea with His power,
And by His understanding He breaks up the storm.
13 By His Spirit He adorned the heavens;
His hand pierced the fleeing serpent.
14 Indeed these are the mere edges of His ways,
And how small a whisper we hear of Him!
But the thunder of His power who can understand?"
27:1 Moreover Job continued his discourse, and said:
2 "As God lives, who has taken away my justice,
And the Almighty, who has made my soul bitter,
3 As long as my breath is in me,
And the breath of God in my nostrils,
4 My lips will not speak wickedness,
Nor my tongue utter deceit.
5 Far be it from me
That I should say you are right;
Till I die I will not put away my integrity from me.
6 My righteousness I hold fast, and will not let it go;
My heart shall not reproach me as long as I live.
7 "May my enemy be like the wicked,
And he who rises up against me like the unrighteous.
8 For what is the hope of the hypocrite,
Though he may gain much,
If God takes away his life?
9 Will God hear his cry
When trouble comes upon him?
10 Will he delight himself in the Almighty?
Will he always call on God?
11 "I will teach you about the hand of God;
What is with the Almighty I will not conceal.
12 Surely all of you have seen it;
Why then do you behave with complete nonsense?

13 "This is the portion of a wicked man with God,
And the heritage of oppressors, received from
the Almighty:
14 If his children are multiplied, it is for the sword;
And his offspring shall not be satisfied with
bread.
15 Those who survive him shall be buried in death,
And their widows shall not weep,
16 Though he heaps up silver like dust,
And piles up clothing like clay—
17 He may pile it up, but the just will wear it,
And the innocent will divide the silver.
18 He builds his house like a moth,
Like a booth which a watchman makes.
19 The rich man will lie down,
But not be gathered up;
He opens his eyes,
And he is no more.
20 Terrors overtake him like a flood;
A tempest steals him away in the night.
21 The east wind carries him away, and he is gone;
It sweeps him out of his place.
22 It hurls against him and does not spare;
He flees desperately from its power.
23 Men shall clap their hands at him,
And shall hiss him out of his place.

Job 26:1—27:23

Let Me Teach You!

Disgust spreads across Job's face when he hears Bildad speak his disdain for man as a "maggot" and a "worm." Although Job is the one being trampled like a worm, his mind and spirit are rising to the realization that he is unique in creation, special in relationship to God, and capable of dignity even in distress. Furthermore, having seen the vision of God, he has put self-pity behind him. The stubborn ounces of his own weight as a man prod him to taunt Bildad for his position. Contempt fills Job's voice as he speaks for the first time using the singular pronoun *"you."* Bildad is the object of his contempt.

Job identifies his own position as powerless, weak, and without wisdom to deal with the mysterious circumstances of his suffering.

Bildad, however, is commended as the one who could help him, hold him up, and counsel him (26:2, 3). But, rather than meeting his needs, Bildad charges him with sin, labels him as wicked, and reduces him to a worm. Thus, three biting questions escape through Job's clenched teeth:

> *How* in the world did you ever develop a reputation for giving sound advice?
> *Who* in the world do you think you are talking to?
> *What* in the world prompts you to speak with the tone that you do? (vv. 2–3).

Job resents the fact that Bildad has a reputation for wisdom that has failed under test. Deeper yet, he resents being treated as a worm by Bildad whom he identifies as a friend. And deepest of all, he resents the hostile tone of voice that reflects not the spirit of God but the spirit of a self-defensive man tainted with a touch of the demonic (vv. 3–4).

People who are suffering count upon our strength and wisdom for help. Often I write this note on a "get well" card for a sick person who is known for ministering to others: "As you have given yourself to so many for their healing, we now give ourselves to you."

Job does not expect too much from his friends. If only they had supported him with their strength and showed him compassion for his suffering, they would have served him well. To treat him as a great sinner and a despicable worm, however, is indefensible.

Job pauses to await an answer from Bildad. G. Campbell Morgan suggests that the long discourses given by Job in chapters 26–31 are punctuated by pauses. As we have noted, the first pause follows Job's taunting of Bildad (26:4). A second pause comes after Job taunts all three of his friends and awaits Zophar's response (27:23). Then, just after Job concludes his "Hymn on Wisdom" (chapter 28) and before he proceeds with a lengthy summary of his defense (chapters 29–31), he pauses again to permit rebuttal. In each case, the pause is greeted by silence. All of the initiative has been passed to Job.

Returning to our immediate text (26:1–4), Job is stung by Bildad's inference that he is a maggot and a worm. His first reaction is to sting back with a sharp-edged and sarcastic tongue (vv. 1–4). Then he pauses, as if to breathe a soul-cleansing sigh and await Bildad's retort. When nothing happens, Job takes up his taunt once again. His attention shifts from Bildad to all three friends, and his tone modifies from sarcasm to satire. By literal definition, *sarcasm* means a tearing of the flesh. *Satire* means a plate of mixed ingredients—some emotional, some intellectual, some witty, some wise, some cutting, and some healing. In literature, satire is a delicate tool for exposing vice and folly in behavior as well as absurdities and inconsistencies in thought. Job chooses satire to taunt his friends. They have failed to comfort or convince him by their teaching, so he needles them by suggesting, "Let me teach you!"

Let Me Teach You about God's Power

Eliphaz, Bildad, and Zophar pride themselves on their knowledge of the power of God. Eliphaz sings about it (5:8–16), Zophar invokes it (11:7–12), and Bildad trumpets it (25:2–3). Without denying what they have said, Job teaches them how little they really know about the power of God.

Beginning with the underworld of the dead, going down into the shades of Sheol, and bottoming out in the lowest and blackest of hells (*"Destruction"* or "Abaddon"), Job teaches that these mysterious realms are *"naked"* and without *"covering"* before the power of God (26:5–6). This knowledge goes far beyond the teaching of his friends, who speak of God's power in heaven and on earth but seem baffled by the dark underworld beyond Sheol and the sea.

Again, Job informs his friends that the power of God is centered in the spiritual rather than the physical realm:

He stretches out the north
over empty space;
He hangs the earth on nothing (v. 7).

Eliphaz, Bildad, and Zophar built their case for the power of God primarily on physical evidence—sun, moon, stars, earthquakes, storms, and seasons. All religions must decide on the primary element in the universe. Hindus, for instance, believe that the universe is carried on the back of an elephant who rides on the back of a tortoise. They lack the revelation of Genesis that tells us, "In the beginning God created the heavens and the earth" (1:1). Job's friends either forgot that truth or denied it. In any case, Job brings it back to them with the declaration that God in His power created the universe out of nothing and holds it together by His Spirit.

Other word pictures come forward in Job's teaching about the power of God. Sometimes, he draws from the Genesis account as he speaks of the separation of sea and sky (vv. 8–9), the division of light and darkness (v. 10), and the decorating of the heavens by His Spirit (v. 13). Other times, he brings in images from various creation accounts, such as drawing the horizon of the waters as a circle with a caliper (v. 10), or shaking the pillars of heaven with His reproof (v. 11). Job envisions God as a divine architect at work. While his friends portray the power of God in broad sketches, Job tutors them in the specifications of the Divine blueprint. Even then, he quickly draws the limits of his own knowledge of God by bowing in humility,

> *Indeed these are the mere edges*
> *of His ways,*
> *And how small a whisper we hear of Him!* (v. 14).

Faith always has a future. Paul sees far when he says, "For now we see in a mirror, dimly, but then face to face. Now I know in part, but then I shall know just as I also am known" (1 Cor. 13:12).

Such a future cannot be seen if the power of God is restricted to its physical dimensions. Scientists, for instance, have a theory that a wandering star called Nemesis upsets our universe every thirty-three billion years or so and, in rain of fire, destroys the earth. What then? The power of God cannot be limited to its expression in nature. Only faith in the God who *"hangs the earth on nothing"* is adequate to even approach the knowledge of his infinite power.

Let Me Teach You about the Fear of God

Strange as it seems, in all of the wordy discourses of Eliphaz, Bildad, and Zophar, not one of them has addressed God or prayed to Him! Evidently, He is so distant and they are so fearful, there is no communication. Job is quite the opposite. He prays to God, speaks to God, complains to God, and fights with God. Professor Mathias A. H. Zahniser, in a chapel address at Asbury Theological Seminary, noted that Jesus had a stormy prayer life but a calm public life. Dr. Zahniser confessed that his prayer life and public life were just the reverse. He prayed in calm and stormed in public. We share his confession. We also learn why Job withstood the onslaught of brutal personal attack from his friends. He had a stormy prayer life!

As evidence of Job's daring with God, he takes an oath that is filled with contradiction before the Almighty. To teach his friends that a relationship with God goes beyond fear, he swears by his innocence on the justice of God—the same God who he says has *"taken away my justice"* and *"has made my soul bitter"* (27:2).

Despite his complaints about the justice of God, he still has the confidence to swear by Him. Backing up his oath, Job risks everything he has, is, or will be on the character of God—my justice, my soul, my breath, my lips, my tongue, my integrity, my righteousness, and my heart (vv. 2–6).

In contrast to his friends who tremble in fear at the thought of God, Job goes to the other extreme with a confidence that almost makes God an equal with him, a man. As a teacher, however, he gets his point across.

Let Me Teach You about God's Justice

Job's final lesson for his friends is a satirical passage couched in the mixed ingredients of personal vengeance and hard truth. Uncharacteristically, Job puts a curse upon his friends by wishing that they could receive a taste of the medicine that they have given to him when they charge him with great sin and total depravity.

May my enemy be like the wicked,
And he who rises up against me
like the unrighteous (v. 7).

Job has talked earlier about reversing roles with his friends,

I also could speak as you do,
If your soul were in my soul's place (16:4).

He has also posted a warning for them. If he is right and they are wrong, Job reminds them that they should:

> Be afraid of the sword for yourselves;
> For wrath brings the punishment
> of the sword,
> That you may know there is a judgment (19:29).

Now, Job sets out to teach his three friends the implications of his warning if their roles are reversed (27:11). His purpose is to show them that they have behaved toward him with *"complete nonsense"* (v. 12).

Role playing is an effective technique for understanding the position of another person. In Harper Lee's novel *To Kill a Mockingbird,* Scout's teacher, Miss Caroline, tells her that Scout's father, Atticus, taught her to read incorrectly. Atticus sits her down and says, "You never really understand a person . . . until you climb into his skin and walk around in it."[4]

The advice is particularly good for married couples. In marriage enrichment workshops, husbands and wives are asked to reverse roles and respond to each other as they perceive the way each other talks. Quick insight comes when you hear your shouts and see your stubbornness acted out before your eyes. Healing starts when laughter breaks out.

Job is not laughing though as he lets his friends hear their own words about *"the portion of the wicked man with God"* (v. 13)—devastation for his family (vv. 14–15), dust for his riches (vv. 16–17), destruction for his house (v. 18), death for his body (v. 19), dread for his soul (v. 20), dissolution for his name (v. 21), and desperation for his days (v. 22).

Envisioning the world as a stage upon which the wicked man has performed, Job foresees the curtain call as the moment of truth:

> *Men shall clap their hands at him,*
> *And shall hiss him out of his place* (v. 23).

Stark contrast is one of the most powerful of all dramatic effects. Producers of great films have the genius for taking their audience from triumphant heights to tragic depths. Job felt the stab of those emotions when Eliphaz lifted him to see God in the glory of His highest heavens (22:12) and then cast him down among the company of the wicked who defy God and dare Him to wield His sword of judgment against them (22:17). Eliphaz went on to warn Job that God does wreak His vengeance upon the wicked and when He does,

> The righteous see it and are glad,
> And the innocent laugh them to scorn (22:19).

Eliphaz's words now come back to haunt him. If Job is right and Eliphaz is wrong, he and his two friends will be clapped, hissed, and laughed off the stage when God weighs them on the balances of justice and finds them wanting (27:23).

It is Zophar's turn to speak. There is a pause, but he has nothing to say. Perhaps the dread sound of clapping and hissing has already driven him off the stage.

NOTES

1. Thomas J. Peters and Robert H. Waterman, Jr., *In Search of Excellence* (New York: Harper and Row, 1982).
2. Lewis, *A Grief Observed,* pp. 4–5.
3. Roy Hession and Revel Hession, *The Calvary Road* (Fort Washington, Pa.: Christian Literature Crusade, 1950).
4. Harper Lee, *To Kill a Mockingbird* (Philadelphia: J. B. Lippincott Co., 1960), p. 36.

CHAPTER SIX

Job's Reflection/Review

Job 28:1—31:40

Zophar has fallen silent. Either he has nothing further to contribute to the conversation or Job's eloquence overwhelms him. In either case, Job is fully in control as he steps back from the conflict to sing a beautiful three-verse hymn to wisdom. Verse one extols the ingenuity of man in mining the hidden riches of the earth (28:1–11). Verse two confesses that wisdom is beyond the ingenuity of man—neither to be found nor purchased (vv. 12–19). Verse three confirms the fundamental fact that wisdom belongs to God alone (vv. 20–27). In the final refrain, Job sings the theme that man can find wisdom only as he fears God and turns from evil.

On the Source of Wisdom

As the sounds of Job's taunts echo and reecho against the stony silence of Eliphaz, Bildad, and Zophar, there is a need to bring order out of chaos. In drama, it is time for the curtain to fall, a musical interlude to be played, and the scene to change.

Most scholars dispute the value and purpose of Job's "Hymn of Wisdom" in this chapter. They do not dispute the quality of the poetry or the importance of the truth that is presented with unsurpassed eloquence. The contention is that the poem is not consistent with Job's style of speech, the sequence of his reasoning, or the mood of his temperament. In other speeches, he tends to be more Socratic than poetic in his style, more linear than discrete in his argument, and more volatile than serene in his mood. The content of the poem is of greater concern to the scholars. Looking ahead to the speeches of Elihu and God, they find advanced conclusions in the poem, therefore rendering the rest of the Book of Job redundant. The same scholars, however, keep reminding us that we cannot impose our Western way of thinking upon the Eastern mind of Job. He has shown us, for instance, his tendency to rise and fall in emotions, change subjects at will, and move back and forth with bits and pieces of the argument. Furthermore, we know that he is a man in the midst of a struggle, who has had a vision of God. He is a soul on a journey. Therefore, the strongest case can be made that Job himself sings as a poet, speaks as a philosopher, and sees as a prophet in this "Hymn of Wisdom."

Job the Poet

1 "Surely there is a mine for silver,
And a place where gold is refined.
2 Iron is taken from the earth,
And copper is smelted from ore.
3 Man puts an end to darkness,
And searches every recess
For ore in the darkness and the shadow of death.
4 He breaks open a shaft away from people;
In places forgotten by feet
They hang far away from men;
They swing to and fro.
5 As for the earth, from it comes bread,
But underneath it is turned up as by fire;
6 Its stones are the source of sapphires,
And it contains gold dust.
7 That path no bird knows,
Nor has the falcon's eye seen it.
8 The proud lions have not trodden it,
Nor has the fierce lion passed over it.
9 He puts his hand on the flint;
He overturns the mountains at the roots.
10 He cuts out channels in the rocks,
And his eye sees every precious thing.
11 He dams up the streams from trickling;
What is hidden he brings forth to light.
12 "But where can wisdom be found?
And where is the place of understanding?
13 Man does not know its value,
Nor is it found in the land of the living.

14 The deep says, 'It is not in me';
And the sea says, 'It is not with me.'
15 It cannot be purchased for gold,
Nor can silver be weighed for its price.
16 It cannot be valued in the gold of Ophir,
In precious onyx or sapphire.
17 Neither gold nor crystal can equal it,
Nor can it be exchanged for jewelry of fine gold.
18 No mention shall be made of coral or quartz,
For the price of wisdom is above rubies.
19 The topaz of Ethiopia cannot equal it,
Nor can it be valued in pure gold.
20 "From where then does wisdom come?
And where is the place of understanding?
21 It is hidden from the eyes of all living,
And concealed from the birds of the air.
22 Destruction and Death say,
'We have heard a report about it with our ears.'
23 God understands its way,
And He knows its place.
24 For He looks to the ends of the earth,
And sees under the whole heavens,
25 To establish a weight for the wind,
And apportion the waters by measure.
26 When He made a law for the rain,
And a path for the thunderbolt,
27 Then He saw wisdom and declared it;
He prepared it, indeed, He searched it out.
28 And to man He said,
'Behold, the fear of the Lord, that is wisdom,
And to depart from evil is understanding.' "

Job 28:1–28

A musical interlude is so appropriate after the curtain falls on the heavy and hostile silence that speaks of a stalemate between Job and his friends. Music is not only a universal language, it is a way of speaking the truth in gentle tones. Protagonists cannot shout at each other and sing together at the same time. William Congreve sees the power of reconciliation in a song when he says, "Music hath charms to soothe the savage breast."[1]

After a harrowing and harried day at the office, I often listen to a symphony, read a poem, or simply sit in my easy chair to bask in the serene setting of the watercolor painting entitled "Homecoming" that hangs above the fireplace. I call it my "soul-cleansing" time—which usually ends with a snore!

Job the Philosopher

A philosopher is a person who asks fundamental questions from an objective viewpoint. Stepping back from the fray, Job draws upon the resources of his learning to ask the quintessential question,

> *But where can wisdom be found?*
> *And where is the place of understanding?* (28:12).

This question is consistent with his journey of faith. As he has had a glimpse of God's purpose from the pinnacle of faith, he has applied that vision in practical terms to his personal situation and found new hope. It is also expected that he will ask how the vision of God relates to the philosophical question that has been primary to the debate. One can argue that Job turns philosopher as well as poet in this chapter.

Job the Prophet

God always comes in the "fullness of time." Why then assume that Job's song is an end in itself, canceling out the value of the speeches of Elihu and God that are to follow? Why not see the song as a prophecy, a preparation, and a prelude for the truth that is yet to come? Even the truth of revelation needs to be repeated time and time again in order to be learned. Jesus, for instance, repeated Himself five hundred times in His teaching.

Heresy lurks in the wings whenever revelation is isolated from adequate preparation for the truth and from ongoing progress toward greater truth. Eliphaz fell into that trap by making his nighttime vision of God a private experience without past preparation or future progress. So it is whenever we use God to confirm our own opinion. One man, whom I know, destroyed the fledgling faith of a terminally ill hospital patient by announcing, "God told me that you will be healed." When the man took a turn for the worse, he renounced his faith and died with a curse. His well-meaning brother failed to see how God was preparing the patient through small steps of faith to make a declaration of trust in Him, whether in life or in death. So Job is a prophet who prepares the way for the coming of God when he repeats the refrain,

> *From where then does wisdom come?*
> *And where is the place of understanding?* (v. 20).

Through the heart of the poet, the mind of the philosopher, and the eyes of the prophet, Job sings his "Hymn of Wisdom" in three stanzas—two refrains and one finale.

Stanza One: Man's Genius Cannot Discover Wisdom

Scholars who argue that Job's hymn lacks continuity with the preceding debate fail to remember that Bildad has denounced man as a maggot and the son of man as a worm. Job not only refutes that pessimism from the standpoint of his own integrity (27:2–6), but now with a recitation on the genius of man (28:1–11). He extols such virtues as: *intellect* that *"puts an end to darkness"* (v. 3); *persistence* that *"searches every recess"* (v. 3); *curiosity* that explores the unknown (v. 4); *vision* that sees better than the falcon (v. 7); *courage* that acts more fiercely than the lion (v. 8); *inventiveness* that makes tools out of flint (v. 9); *industry* that levels mountains and cuts through rocks (vv. 9–10); *discernment* that perceives the precious (v. 10); *creativity* that provides productive alternatives (v. 10); and *insight* that brings the hidden into light (v. 11).

How can anyone say that Job's hymn is a non sequitur with the earlier debate? Bildad makes man a grub in the rotting carcass of the earth; Job exalts him as a mind and spirit created in the image of God!

The product of man's genius is high technology. As Job describes the marvels of the mining (vv. 1–8), toolmaking (v. 9), earthmoving (v. 10), and conservation (v. 11) industries, we learn again how wide and how far he sees from his pinnacle of faith. Today, "high-tech" is a term that is used in connection with the mind-boggling computer industry. We are short-sighted and arrogant to think that the genius of man culminates in our age. Job humbles us with a high-tech view of advanced industry more than two thousand years before Christ! Only the speed and sophistication of high technology has changed. The genius of man remains the same.

To understand the prophetic insight of Job's exaltation of the genius of man, apply the characteristics of his mind, heart, and hand to our advanced technology.

Today's High Technology	*Job's Man of Genius*
World-wide communication	*Intellect* that puts an end to darkness
Cancer research	*Persistence* that searches every recess
Oceanography	*Curiosity* that explores the unknown
Laser technology	*Vision* that sees better than the falcon
Space exploration	*Courage* that is greater than the lion's
Microchip circuitry	*Inventiveness* that creates new tools
Urban development	*Industry* that reshapes the environment
Organ transplants	*Discernment* that perceives the precious
Solar power	*Creativity* that produces new alternatives

Underscoring the point, only the speed and sophistication of high technology changes. The genius of man remains the same. So does the question of truth that Job sings in his first refrain,

> *But where can wisdom be found?*
> *And where* is *the place of understanding?* (v. 12).

Thousands of years of technological advancement have not changed the question. The genius of man still cannot discover wisdom. A wag commenting on new advancements in human knowledge quipped, "We know more and more about less and less; soon we will know everything about nothing."

The discovery of nuclear energy illustrates this dilemma. In the

1930s, a scientist predicted that the atom would never be smashed. In 1945, the first nuclear bomb devastated Hiroshima. Later, Albert Einstein, one of the fathers of the nuclear breakthrough, said that if he had known the consequences, he would have preferred to be a plumber. Wisdom does not necessarily advance with technology. In fact, the higher the technology, the greater the need for wisdom.

Stanza Two: Man's Resources Cannot Buy Wisdom

Increasing affluence is the other side of advancing technology. At least in the Western world, we live in an "Age of Affluence." As our confidence in technology prompts us to say, "Anything can be done," our affluence tempts us to say, "Anything can be bought."

Here is another area where human nature does not change. Job dispels any thought in the minds of his hearers that wisdom can be bought. It has no market value when weighed against the most precious of metals and stones—gold, silver, the gold of Ophir, onyx, sapphire, crystal, coral, quartz, rubies, or topaz (vv. 15–19).

Furthermore, wisdom cannot be put on the market to be purchased, weighed, valued, equaled, exchanged, or priced (vv. 15–19). Affluence has been struck a fatal blow.

Earlier in this commentary, we noted the dread disease "affluenza" and its frequent presence among children of rich parents. With everything these children want at their fingertips—homes, cars, servants, clubs, travel, food, clothes, and entertainment—they still suffer from the same symptoms as the children of the poor—loneliness, depression, disillusionment, stress, and sickness. Only high-cost drugs divide the rich from the poor.

When the disease of "affluenza" is diagnosed among rich children, the cause is found to be parents who try to substitute "things" they can buy for their presence and their relationship with their children. As one lost and lonely rich boy exploded at his father, "Love is one thing that you cannot buy for me, Dad!"

Job has the same thought about buying wisdom when he breaks into the refrain of his song once again,

> *From where then does wisdom come?*
> *And where is the place of understanding?* (v. 20).

God Alone Is the Source and Site of Wisdom

Picking up a theme that he introduced in the previous section, Job declares that wisdom is "hidden from the eyes of all the living" (compare v. 13 with v. 21). He has already had the "deep" and the "sea"—figures of speech for the world of mystery—say, *"It is not in me"* (v. 14). Now, Job adds the birds of the air from whom wisdom is concealed in order to encompass the whole of man and animal in the living universe. Taking the next step, he calls upon destruction (Abaddon, the deepest hell) and death (Sheol, the land of shadows) for their testimony. Even in the "other world," wisdom is only a rumor.

Having exhausted the witness of the natural and the preternatural worlds, Job turns to God who alone understands the "way" of wisdom and knows the "place" of understanding (v. 23). But "how" does God know wisdom? Job develops a significant parallel between the science of man, which advances technology, and the science of God, which discovers wisdom. The "scientific method" is a discipline of discovery in human knowledge that follows these steps: (1) *observing* the facts, (2) *defining* the problem, (3) *testing* the alternatives, (4) *analyzing* the evidence, (5) *reporting* the results, and (6) *applying* the principles.

Job says that God follows a similar discipline in the discovery of wisdom. He (1) *looks* to the ends of the earth and *sees* under all the heavens (v. 24); (2) *establishes* a weight for the wind (v. 25); (3) *measures* out a mete for the waters (v. 25); (4) *sets* a law for the rain and a path for the thunderbolt (v. 26); (5) *declares* the discovery of wisdom that He has seen, prepared, and explored (v. 27); and then (6) *applies* his finding to man by saying,

> *Behold, the fear of the Lord,*
> *that is wisdom,*
> *And to depart from evil is*
> *understanding* (v. 28).

Critical scholars discount the value of this grand finale in Job's "Hymn of Wisdom." To the contrary, according to the scientific method that God uses to discover wisdom, we see that the hymn would not be complete without it.

Through all his anguish and through all the chaos of debate, Job has come back to the fundamentals of his relationship with God.

At the beginning of the story, he was commended as "one who feared God and shunned evil" (1:1). God honored and defended him against Satan in the council of heaven for these same qualities. Job still does not have the answer to his suffering, but he is on the solid ground where he can remember the past, rue the present, attest his innocence, and take the advice, "Don't just do something, stand there."

On the Glory of the Past

Like an actor in a one-man drama, Job becomes the defendant, prosecutor, witness, judge, and jury for the case of his integrity. Returning to the setting with which the book began, Job elaborates on his righteousness, his prosperity, his piety, his justice, and his fame (29:1–25). Then, with dramatic flair, he outlines the contradiction of his current condition—ridiculed by outcasts, devastated by affliction, rejected by God, attacked by friends, ostracized by neighbors, and destined for death. No wonder he mourns!

1 Job further continued his discourse, and said:
2 "Oh, that I were as in months past,
As in the days when God watched over me;
3 When His lamp shone upon my head,
and when by His light I walked through
darkness;
4 Just as I was in the days of my prime,
When the friendly counsel of God was over
my tent;
5 When the Almighty was yet with me,
When my children were around me;
6 When my steps were bathed with cream,
And the rock poured out rivers of oil for me!
7 "When I went out to the gate by the city,
When I took my seat in the open square,
8 The young men saw me and hid,
And the aged arose and stood;
9 The princes refrained from talking,
And put their hand on their mouth;
10 The voice of nobles was hushed,
And their tongue stuck to the roof of their mouth.

11 When the ear heard, then it blessed me,
And when the eye saw, then it approved me;
12 Because I delivered the poor who cried out,
The fatherless and the one who had no helper.
13 The blessing of a perishing man came upon me,
And I caused the widow's heart to sing for joy.
14 I put on righteousness, and it clothed me;
My justice was like a robe and a turban.
15 I was eyes to the blind,
And I was feet to the lame.
16 I was a father to the poor,
And I searched out the case that I did not know.
17 I broke the fangs of the wicked,
And plucked the victim from his teeth.
18 "Then I said, 'I shall die in my nest,
And multiply my days as the sand.
19 My root is spread out to the waters,
And the dew lies all night on my branch.
20 My glory is fresh within me,
And my bow is renewed in my hand.'
21 "Men listened to me and waited,
And kept silence for my counsel.
22 After my words they did not speak again,
And my speech settled on them as dew.
23 They waited for me as for the rain,
And they opened their mouth wide as for the spring rain.
24 If I mocked at them, they did not believe it,
And the light of my countenance they did not cast down.
25 I chose the way for them, and sat as chief;
So I dwelt as a king in the army,
As one who comforts mourners.

Job 29:1–25

Another pause signals a shift in Job's role. Having performed with the grandeur of the poet, philosopher, and prophet, he either changes masks on stage like a Greek actor or steps into the wings while the backdrop revolves to a new setting. Job now appears before us as an attorney summing up his case in a courtroom scene. Momentarily, at least, he appears to have fallen back from the insights of his vision of God that had been taking him forward step by step on a journey of faith. He seems to revert to a legalistic view of the justice of God and a defensive position on his own righteousness. When we first met Job, we admired him; when he suffered from calamity, our hearts went out to him; when he stood his ground against cruel friends, we sided with him; but now, when he builds around himself a picket fence of "I's," he is hard to like. We must remember his purpose. Although his "Hymn of Wisdom" seems to be so far removed in tone from his legalistic summary in these chapters, they are common in purpose. Both are statements of fundamentals. In the "Hymn of Wisdom," Job leads us to the fundamental truth that "the fear of the Lord is the beginning of wisdom." Now, in his final statement closing the debate with his friends, he leads us to the fundamental truth that the "cash-register" doctrine of God's justice argued by his friends does not apply to his case.

Job begins his defense by recalling the glory of his past. If anyone exemplified prosperity as a proof of righteousness, it was he. Wistfully, Job remembers every detail of his glorious past.

God favored him. Job enjoyed more than a ritualistic relationship with God in the days of his prosperity. He remembers that God watched over him, lighted his path, befriended his family, surrounded him with children, increased his herds, and multiplied the fruit of his fields (29:2–6).

One can imagine a wistful gleam in Job's eyes as he recalls *"the days of my prime, . . . When the Almighty was yet with me"* (vv. 4, 5).

Fame followed him. As God's favor centered on Job's *"tent"* (or household) (v. 4), his fame followed him *"to the gate by the city"* (v. 7) where all civic and commercial transactions took place. When Job took his reserved seat in the gate to give his counsel and make his trades,

> *The young men saw me and hid,*
> *And the aged arose and stood;*
> *The princes refrained from talking,*
> *And . . .*
> *The voice of nobles was hushed* (vv. 8–10).

All ears were tuned to hear him and all eyes were turned to see him. Nods of blessing affirmed his words and gleams of admiration approved his appearance (v. 11).

Righteousness covered him. Job's fame did not come from his political power and economic wealth. In direct refutation of Eliphaz's charge that he committed the sin of the rich by oppressing the poor, Job remembers the reason for his fame. He was known for his deeds of compassion: delivering the poor, helping the fatherless, saving the perishing, and bringing joy to the widow's heart (vv. 12–13).

His compassion went deeper than charity. Wearing righteousness as his clothes and justice as his robe and turban (v. 14), he gave himself so completely to the needs of the oppressed that he became *"eyes to the blind," "feet to the lame,"* and *"father to the poor"* (vv. 15–16).

Even more, Job recalled his fame as the "Champion of the Oppressed." He not only responded to the obvious needs of the poor with deeds of compassion and an attitude of empathy, but he served as an activist for justice. He actually took it upon himself to search out the cases of injustice, identify the causes of oppression, break the evil power of those who were responsible, and free the victims (vv. 16–17).

Job gives us a pattern for our responsibility to the oppressed. Motivation for Christian social action arises out of compassion, righteousness, and a sense of justice. Compassion is an act by which we relieve the needs of the poor. Righteousness is an attitude by which we identify with the poor. A sense of justice calls for activism against the causes of oppression. Conservative Christians are well-known for their acts of mercy to relieve hunger, disease, poverty, and suffering, especially in Third World missions. Dollars sent at a distance, however, may become a substitute for identifying with the needy and pursuing the cause of justice in those nations. Liberal Christians tend to show their concern for the oppressed by trying to change the institutional structures, public and private, which are perceived to be the causes of injustice. Again, by working with faceless institutions, personal identification with the needy may be avoided. By his example, Job teaches us that we must accept our responsibility for the poor and the oppressed by combining acts of compassion, an attitude of empathy, and an activism to eliminate the causes of injustice.

Youthfulness encouraged him. Job must have been a man who was young for his years. In the days of his prime, he enjoyed the energy and outlook of the young. Like most of us, he took his health, safety, and longevity for granted,

> *I shall die in my nest,*
> *And multiply my days as the sand* (v. 18).

Job's choice of the word *nest* reminds us once again of his love for home and family. He imagines dying a peaceful death in his own bed surrounded by his children. This is a natural wish for every man. When President Lyndon Johnson left the White House for the last time and headed back to his Texas ranch, he gave a homespun farewell that tugs at the strings of every human heart, "I want to go home where folks care when you're sick and know when you die."

Physical well-being gave Job the hope that he would live long and die in peace at home. He uses the analogy of the *"root"* spreading out to reach the waters as evidence of internal vigor, the *"dew"* on the branch as the picture of the well-preserved body, and the *"bow"* in his hand to symbolize the daily renewal of his strength (vv. 19–20).

Leadership pursued him (vv. 21–25). *Charisma* is the term that described Job's prestige as a leader before calamity struck him. Three qualities characterized his leadership. Men esteemed him as a *visionary leader,* whose counsel they awaited in silence and accepted with enthusiasm (v. 21–23). Men looked to him as an *affirmative leader* whose sense of humor and smiling face made people feel good about themselves (v. 24). Men saw Job as a *decisive leader* whose governance they accepted and whose leadership they legitimized with the position and title of *"chief"* (v. 25). Remembering those days of greatness, Job likens his role to a king leading an army or a comforter bringing hope to those who mourn the dead (v. 25).

A leader, according to David Rockefeller, must "see the vision, state the mission, and set the tone" if others are to follow. Job's counsel provided the vision, his decisions defined the mission, and his countenance set the tone for men to follow him. But the honor of leadership does not stand alone. His relationship with God, his witness of the home, his compassion for the poor, his zeal for justice, his reputation for righteousness, and his youthful vigor are qualities that undergird the effective leader.

Thus ends the glory that was Job.

On the Agony of the Present

For just a moment or two, Job has escaped the ash heap in a flight of memory back to the days of his glory. His eyes are closed, his head is back, and even his diseased face shows the trace of his old smile when he remembers,

> So I dwelt as a king in the army,
> As one who comforts mourners (29:25).

His own words about comfort and mourning shock him back to reality. Job opens his eyes to see the ash heap, drops his head as he hears the taunts of the passing crowd, and loses his smile as he feels his pain again.

> 1 "But now they mock at me, men younger than I,
> Whose fathers I disdained to put with the dogs of my flock.
> 2 Indeed, what profit is the strength of their hands to me?
> Their vigor has perished.
> 3 They are gaunt from want and famine,
> Fleeing late to the wilderness, desolate and waste,
> 4 Who pluck mallow by the bushes,
> And broom tree roots for their food.
> 5 They were driven out from among men,
> They shouted at them as at a thief.
> 6 They had to live in the clefts of the valleys,
> In caves of the earth and the rocks.
> 7 Among the bushes they brayed,
> Under the nettles they nestled.
> 8 They were sons of fools,
> Yes, sons of vile men;
> They were scourged from the land.
> 9 "And now I am their taunting song;
> Yes, I am their byword.
> 10 They abhor me, they keep far from me;
> They do not hesitate to spit in my face.
> 11 Because He has loosed my bowstring and afflicted me,
> They have cast off restraint before me.
> 12 At my right hand the rabble arises;
> They push away my feet,
> And they raise against me their ways of destruction.

13 They break up my path,
They promote my calamity;
They have no helper.
14 They come as broad breakers;
Under the ruinous storm they roll along.
15 Terrors are turned upon me;
They pursue my honor as the wind,
And my prosperity has passed like a cloud.
16 "And now my soul is poured out because of my plight;
The days of affliction take hold of me.
17 My bones are pierced in me at night,
And my gnawing pains take no rest.
18 By great force my garment is disfigured;
It binds me about as the collar of my coat.
19 He has cast me into the mire,
And I have become like dust and ashes.
20 "I cry out to You, but You do not answer me;
I stand up, and You regard me.
21 But You have become cruel to me;
With the strength of Your hand You oppose me.
22 You lift me up to the wind and cause me to ride on it;
You spoil my success.
23 For I know that You will bring me to death,
And to the house appointed for all living.
24 "Surely He would not stretch out His hand against a heap of ruins,
If they cry out when He destroys it.
25 Have I not wept for him who was in trouble?
Has not my soul grieved for the poor?
26 But when I looked for good, evil came to me;
And when I waited for light, then came darkness.
27 My heart is in turmoil and cannot rest;
Days of affliction confront me.
28 I go about mourning, but not in the sun;
I stand up in the assembly and cry out for help.
29 I am a brother of jackals,
And a companion of ostriches.
30 My skin grows black and falls from me;
My bones burn with fever.

31 My harp is turned to mourning,
And my flute to the voice of those who weep.
Job 30:1–31

A change of worlds is spoken in Job's opening words, *"But now"* (v. 1). How far is it from being the famed leader of men to the butt of the fool's joke? How far is it from enjoying the blush of youth to standing at death's door? How far is it from prospering as God's favorite son to suffering as a victim of God's apparent brutality? Job has learned that the distance is as far as from the highest heaven to the lowest hell, and it is as near as the unexpected calamity that turns life upside down in a split second.

"But Now"—From Man's Fame to the Fool's Joke

Job's ego is crushed by the fall from his exalted position of greatest fame to being debased as the butt of the grossest of jokes. Successful people at the top of their profession are often victimized by dreams in which they have a fear of falling. People of fame and fortune may outwardly show the gloss of confidence, but, inwardly, there is the nagging knowledge that fame and fortune are fickle friends. Subconsciously, they also know that the higher the heights, the greater the fall.

No one other than Christ Himself has experienced a greater fall from fame than Job. Symbolically, he fell from the best seat in the city gate (29:7) and the governor's chair (29:25) to the exile of an ash heap outside the city walls (30:19). Young men who had fallen silent before him in reverence (29:8–9) are now replaced by the mocking crowd of the dregs of humanity (30:1). Instead of the aged standing in honor of him, princes falling in silence, and nobles whispering in his presence (29:8–10), Job is the object of ridicule from the rabble. They sing taunting songs about him, swear vulgar words by him, treat him as untouchable, and spit in his face (30:9–10). Worst of all, his tormentors are the young men upon whom all the rest of the society looks down with contempt. At one time, Job would not even hire their fathers to watch his dogs (v. 1). They represent all the waste and wickedness that he avoided in his disciplined and righteous life. They are wastrels, indolent, exiles, scavengers, outcasts, and aborigines (vv. 3–7).

Job may have the contrast with his own children in mind when he ascribes to his mockers the consequences of being the *"sons of fools"* and *"vile men,"* who are driven by whips from the presence of civilized people (v. 8).

A sad note follows as Job thinks about the reason why he is the butt of the fool's joke. Straight out, he charges God with the responsibility. The analogy of the "bow string" comes back to his mind. In the past, he gloried in his manly strength as symbolized by the "bow," which was daily renewed with the resiliency that produced its power (29:20). Now, however, Job's manly strength has been cut off. He is as weak as a man whose bow string has been snapped and whose body has gone limp (30:13). Consequently, he is helpless to defend himself against the siege of the rabble who attack on Job's right hand by setting snares for his feet, laying siege to his walls, and destroying the roads for his escape (vv. 12–13).

Then, by frontal assault, the army of the rabble rushes his fortress and advances through the breach in the walls to destroy him because he is powerless and no one comes to his defense (v. 14). Thus, his fame has vanished like a breath of wind and his prosperity has passed like the wisp of a cloud (v. 15). Sheer terror is the only legacy that remains from his glorious past (v. 15).

But Now—From the Blush of Youth to the Door of Death

Having prided himself in his robust health and youthful vigor, Job has a hard time coping with his current physical condition. Earlier, he had been blessed with high energy, youthful appearance, a glow of well-being, and the continuous renewal of his strength (29:19–20). Now, he cries out from the depths of suffering that has ravished every part of his being.

Sooner or later, physical suffering takes its toll upon our spiritual and mental well-being. Job knows pain in every form. Spiritually, he draws the contrast between the time when he said, "My glory is fresh within me" (29:20), and his present outlook, when his soul is poured out and he can only cry from his emptiness (30:16). His resources are exhausted; yet his pain does not let up. In fact, he knows every form of human pain—days of prolonged pain, nights of piercing pain, and days and nights of gnawing pain (vv. 16–17).

Only those who have lived with the totality of pain in its many forms can identify with Job. As medical science has created the techniques to prolong life, it has also created the potential for prolonged and total pain. One of the most critical moral issues of the future will be related to pain. How much pain can a person take? How much can a family accept? Are addictive drugs an answer? Is negotiated death the only way out?

Job experiences the limits of psychological as well as physical pain. By analogy, he describes the psychological impact of pain when he says,

> *By great force my garment is disfigured;*
> *It binds me about as the collar of my coat* (v. 18).

Scholars disagree on the meaning of this analogy. Some say Job is referring to his emaciated condition that makes his garment hang on him like an ill-fitting and out-sized tent. Others believe that Job is picturing the violent effects of pain—writhing until the clothes are knotted around the body to choke the victim. Anyone who has battled through a night with high fever will lean toward this latter interpretation.

Whichever the case, the result is the same. Job blames God for destroying his health and casting him into the *"mire"* as if he were no more than *"dust and ashes"* (v. 19). We live Job's shock with him. Not many months ago, he had the health and the hope to live long and die in his "nest." Now, having lost his health and his hope, he will die in the mire.

But Now—From God's Favor to God's Brutality

As Job praised God during the time of his exaltation, he now blames God for his debasement. Many scholars read his words as blasphemy. Certainly, he is on the borderline again. But before being too hard on Job, we must remember that he had known a relationship with God who watched over him, lighted his path, befriended his family, surrounded him with children, increased his herds, and multiplied the fruit of his fields (29:2–6).

Remember also that Job has no explanation for God's change of attitude. No wonder he is baffled. He did not change; evidently, God did. Therefore, we can understand the anguish of his complaint,

I cry out to You,
but You do not answer me;
I stand up, and You regard me (30:20).

Job no longer doubts that God hears and sees him, but the knowledge only adds to his dilemma. If God hears his earnest prayer and sees his blameless life, Job asks again and again,

Why have You become cruel to me?
Why do You oppose me?
Why did You lift me up to ride on the wind? and then,
Why did You spoil my success?

Only one conclusion remains for Job. The same God who gave "friendly counsel" over his "tent" (29:4) will bring him to death in the *"house appointed for all the living"* (30:23). Then, with the desperation of a dying man, Job tries to strike a responsive chord in God's heart. Appealing to His compassion, he believes that no one would lay a hand on a man who cries for mercy when he is already broken and ruined (v. 24). After all, Job followed God's example when he wept with the troubled and grieved for the poor (v. 25). *"But,"* Job says for the third time,

when I looked for good, evil came to me;
And when I waited for light, then came darkness (v. 26).

All of Job's world has been turned upside down. For peace, he has turmoil; for health, he has pain; for joy, he has mourning; for confidence, he has helplessness; for fame, he has the company of jackals and ostriches; for beauty, he has blackened skin and dermatitis; and for strength, he has weakness (vv. 27–31). Only the humiliation of Christ exceeds the humiliation of Job. Job would understand what Isaiah meant when he portrayed the suffering Christ as "despised and rejected by men, a man of sorrows and acquainted with grief" (Isa. 53:3). Christ would know what Job means when he sums up the reversal of his world in the poetic plight,

My harp is turned to mourning,
And my flute to the voice of those who weep (30:31).

Thus ends the humiliation of Job. As does the apostle Paul, Job also knows how "to be abased . . . how to abound. . . . to be full and to be hungry, both to abound and to suffer need" (Phil. 4:12).

Job also knows what it means to be an example of the suffering that is supposedly reserved for the most wicked of men according to the cause-and-effect doctrine of the justice of God.

On the Oath of Innocence

Again, Job positions himself between his magnificent past and his miserable present with an oath of innocence. As he elaborated earlier upon his blessings, he now outlines in detail his righteousness. Through a series of oaths encompassing the whole of his life, he attests freedom from sin. At the level of the flesh, he is free from lust, cheating, and adultery. Equally sinful, but less violent, are the sins of the rich—mistreating or neglecting servants, the poor, beggars, and orphans. Sins of attitude are also included—the sin of arrogance that often accompanies riches. Then, Job cites the sin of idolatry when the sun and moon are worshiped. Job even claims freedom from the sin of rejoicing at his enemies' misfortune. Earlier, Job set his signature on his innocence. Now, he makes his mark, risking his honor upon his innocence. This is another way of saying that if God would hear him, he would be vindicated.

Job's conclusion is an afterthought—a sin he forgot to mention. If he has raped the land or polluted the environment to the hazard of man, he invites the wrath of God upon his head.

1 "I have made a covenant with my eyes;
Why then should I look upon a young woman?
2 For what is the allotment of God from above,
And the inheritance of the Almighty from on high?
3 Is it not destruction for the wicked,
And disaster for the workers of iniquity?
4 Does He not see my ways,
And count all my steps?
5 "If I have walked with falsehood,
Or if my foot has hastened to deceit,

6 Let me be weighed on honest scales,
That God may know my integrity.
7 If my step has turned from the way,
Or my heart walked after my eyes,
Or if any spot adheres to my hands,
8 Then let me sow, and another eat;
Yes, let my harvest be rooted out.
9 "If my heart has been enticed by a woman,
Or if I have lurked at my neighbor's door,
10 Then let my wife grind for another,
And let others bow down over her.
11 For that would be wickedness;
Yes, it would be iniquity deserving of judgment.
12 For that would be a fire that consumes to destruction,
And would root out all my increase.
13 "If I have despised the cause of my male or female servant
When they complained against me,
14 What then shall I do when God rises up?
When He punishes, how shall I answer Him?
15 Did not He who made me in the womb make them?
Did not the same One fashion us in the womb?
16 "If I have kept the poor from their desire,
Or caused the eyes of the widow to fail,
17 Or eaten my morsel by myself,
So that the fatherless could not eat of it
18 (But from my youth I reared him as a father,
And from my mother's womb I guided the widow);
19 If I have seen anyone perish for lack of clothing,
Or any poor man without covering;
20 If his heart has not blessed me,
And if he was not warmed with the fleece of my sheep;
21 If I have raised my hand against the fatherless,
When I saw I had help in the gate;
22 Then let my arm fall from my shoulder,
Let my arm be torn from the socket.
23 For destruction from God is a terror to me,
And because of His magnificence I cannot endure.

24 "If I have made gold my hope,
Or said to fine gold, 'You are my confidence';
25 If I have rejoiced because my wealth was great,
And because my hand had gained much;
26 If I have observed the sun when it shines,
Or the moon moving in brightness,
27 So that my heart has been secretly enticed,
And my mouth has kissed my hand;
28 This also would be an iniquity deserving of judgment,
For I would have denied God who is above.
29 "If I have rejoiced at the destruction of him who hated me,
Or lifted myself up when evil found him
30 (Indeed I have not allowed my mouth to sin
By asking for a curse on his soul);
31 If the men of my tent have not said,
'Who is there that has not been satisfied with his meat?'
32 (But no sojourner had to lodge in the street,
For I have opened my doors to the traveler);
33 If I have covered my transgressions as Adam,
By hiding my iniquity in my bosom,
34 Because I feared the great multitude,
And dreaded the contempt of families,
So that I kept silence
And did not go out of the door—
35 Oh, that I had one to hear me!
Here is my mark.
Oh, that the Almighty would answer me,
That my Prosecutor had written a book!
36 Surely I would carry it on my shoulder,
and bind it on me like a crown;
37 I would declare to Him the number of my steps;
Like a prince I would approach Him.
38 "If my land cries out against me,
And its furrows weep together;
39 If I have eaten its fruit without money,
Or caused its owners to lose their lives;
40 Then let thistles grow instead of wheat,
And weeds instead of barley."
The words of Job are ended.

Job 31:1–40

"If I Have Sinned, Let Me Be Cursed"

By remembering his glorious past and describing his ignominious present, Job has created an "either-or" bind. Either he has sinned and his downfall is the retribution of God, or he has not sinned and his suffering remains a mystery. Job, of course, is adamant about his innocence. Thus, his final statement is an elaborate defense of his own righteousness, sworn on an oath and sealed by his signature.

When was the key word that Job used as he recalled the glory of his past (chapter 29). *But now* sets the stage for the woeful description of his calamitous reversal and current condition (chapter 30). To understand the passionate, poetic, and sometimes rambling defense of his innocence in this final chapter of his soliloquy, the key words are *if . . . , then. If* is the conjunction that sets up a condition. *Then* is its companion that spells out the consequences if the condition is enacted. By building his defense around the *if . . . . then* sequence, Job adopts the cause-and-effect doctrine with which Eliphaz, Bildad, and Zophar defended the justice of God and condemned him of sin. According to their simplistic doctrine or formula, *if* Job sins, *then* he will suffer, and, conversely, *if* he is righteous, *then* he will prosper.

A courtroom scene again appears before us. In the legal practice of Job's day, a person accused of a crime was entitled to hear the charges against him. Job invoked that right by asking God,

> How many are my iniquities and sins?
> Make me know my transgression and my sin (13:23).

Eliphaz answered for God with his charge that Job had committed the sin of the rich by oppressing the poor (22:5–11). In turn, Job exercises the right of denying the charges by affirming his innocence,

> My foot has held fast to His steps;
> I have kept His way
>   and not turned aside.
> I have not departed from the commandment
>   of His lips;
> I have treasured the words of His mouth
> More than my necessary food (23:11–12).

Still another right is exercised when Job contends that the issue is between him and God (19:4) and, therefore, claims that his condemnation or vindication belongs to God alone (27:2–6).

One final right belongs to the accused in the due process of ancient law. An oath of clearance could be taken in which the accused pleads "not guilty" by setting up the *if . . . , then* sequence of a negative confession, "*if* I have committed this crime," and a negative consequence, "*then* let me be cursed by man and God." This oath applied to each of the crimes of which the defendant was accused and became a legal document to which the defendant affixed his signature. The document was then posted in public as a call for the persons who were wronged to come forward and testify against the accused. If none came forward, the judge accepted the "not guilty" plea and announced acquittal.

Job cites a full catalog of sins in the *if . . . , then* sequence. Each is a personal and a public sin against the rights of man and the law of God. Each bears the consequences of severe punishment by human and divine justice here and in the hereafter. To trace through the sixteen sins and Job's oath of clearance, the following chart shows the condition of sin, the person who is wronged, and the consequences of judgment:

Condition	*Person Wronged*	*Consequence*	*Text*
"If I have lusted,"	Virgin	"then destruction and disaster will befall me."	31:1–4
"If I have lied,"	Neighbor	"then I will lose my harvest."	vv. 5–8
"If I have seduced,"	Neighbor's wife	"then I will lose my wife to my neighbor."	vv. 9–12
"If I have oppressed,"	Servants	"then how will I answer God?"	vv. 13–15
"If I have neglected,"	Poor, widows, and orphans	"then let my arm be torn from its socket."	vv. 16–23
"If I have committed idolatry" (gold or sun and moon),	God	"then God will judge me."	vv. 24–28
"If I have shown malice,"	Enemies	. . .	vv. 29–30
"If I have slighted,"	Strangers	. . .	vv. 31–32
"If I have been hypocritical,"	Public	. . .	vv. 33–34
"If I have exploited,"	Land	"then let thistles grow instead of wheat and weeds instead of barley."	vv. 38–40

Who can doubt that Job is a rare person? How many other persons in human history other than Christ would dare to submit their character and conduct to the scrutiny of both man and God? Job is hard to like because he puts us to shame. We charge him with self-righteousness in our own self-defense. We read his religion as a series of negatives based upon fearing God and shunning evil. A deeper look into the motive and principles behind his righteousness, however, reveals an enlightened man far ahead of his time.

Job confesses his weakness. In opening his defense, he admits the need for a covenant with his eyes in order to avoid the sin of lust. Job takes a risk with the only part of his defense that implies a confession. He fronts the issue of lust as the first item on his agenda. Otherwise, he cannot declare his life an open book and seal it with his signature.

Job believes in the equality of persons. Behind his understanding of the causes of his servants and his fair treatment of their complaints is the enlightened principle that all persons are created equal by God:

> *Did not He who made me in the womb*
> *make them?*
> *Did not the same One fashion*
> *us in the womb?* (31:15).

It is false to assume that persons can be treated equally only if they are the same in status, role, and compensation. The press for equality in today's society has produced the monsters of the welfare state in government, comparable worth in employment, grade inflation in education, and entitlement in the distribution of wealth. Job believed in and practiced the equality of persons without creating these monsters. His servants remained in their role as servants and their pay was related to their achievement, but they were assured that their wealthy superior respected them as persons, listened to their cause, and responded to their complaints with fair and consistent decisions. When given the opportunity, none of them came forward to charge Job with inequality.

Job's love goes beyond his duty. Each time that Job speaks, he reveals more about the quality of his home, and especially his love for his children. At the very beginning of the book, he was introduced as a loving father of a large, prosperous, and joyous family whose spiritual life was his first concern (1:4–5). At the news of his children's death, he tore his robe, shaved his head, and fell to the ground and worshiped because he had committed his family to God (1:20–21).

After Bildad suggests that his sons died because of their sins (8:4), Job is crushed under the weight of deep depression (chapters 9–10). We learn how deep the wound goes when Job bewails the fact that he will never know the pride of seeing his sons come to honor or be present to support them if they fail (14:21). Out of the same despondency, he desperately seeks the intimacy of family relationships, even in death, where corruption is envisioned as his father and the worm as his mother and sister (17:14). But the lowest point of all is the humiliation he feels by the rejection of young children (19:18).

Even as Job gains the strength to take the initiative in the debate, he still does not forget the loss of his children. In his description of the wicked, for instance, he bemoans the fact that they will see their children come to maturity and see their grandchildren, while he will not (21:8). Likewise, in refuting Eliphaz's claim that God passes His retribution on to the children of the wicked, Job answers, "For what does he [the wicked] care about his household after him?" (21:21). There is no doubt that Job is drawing the contrast between the selfishness of the wicked and the unselfish love that he gave to his family.

Eliphaz's accusation that Job has sinned by crushing the strength of the fatherless (22:9) is the last straw. Job refutes this charge by swearing,

> *If I have . . .*
>
> . . . .
>
> *Or eaten my morsel by myself,*
> *So that the fatherless could not eat of it*
>
> . . . .
>
> *Then let my arm fall from my shoulder,*
> *Let my arm be torn from the socket* (31:16–22).

In between this oath is a parenthesis that tells us of Job's love that goes beyond his duty to share his bread with orphans. Almost incidentally, Job reports, "(*But from my youth I reared him as a father*)" (v. 18).

Up to now, Job's words have revealed a man of stature and strength who takes pride in his righteousness. Indeed, self-esteem is not a problem for Job. But now we see the other side of him. In a parenthesis, he mentions the fact that his family includes orphans who have become his foster children!

A corporate executive whom I know has two shelves of family pictures in his office. One is his natural family of five children and eight grandchildren. The other shelf has scores of pictures of his adopted family—the teenagers of his high-school Sunday school class that he has taught for thirty-five years. Although his days are given to multimillion-dollar decisions in the corporation, any one of the members of his natural or adopted family has first priority on his time if they need him. He doesn't have to brag about what he is doing for God. His love for his two families is so natural that he needs no recognition. With genuine humility, he glows when he speaks of "his children." Like Job, his outward duty to the orphan is obvious; but his inward love is more like a parenthesis.

Job avoided idolatry. Eliphaz accused Job of making gold his god (22:22–25). In his own defense, Job not only denies the charge but calls on God as his witness that he has never made gold his hope, fine gold his confidence, or rejoiced because of his great wealth and because of self-made gains (31:24–25).

Astrological cults also prevailed in the land of the East. While Job could never be charged with substituting the sun and the moon for the Almighty, the temptation might be to curtsy to the lesser gods while bowing to the one God. A man carried a Bible, the Koran, and the Bhagavad-Gita under his arm. When asked to explain in which God he believed, he answered, "I believe in all of them. I'm taking no chances."

Pluralism is a code word that describes much theological thought today. While implying the spirit of tolerance among various denominations and religions, it can also be a subtle rendering of the word *syncretism,* which means the dilution of doctrine in order to accommodate various theological views and promote cooperation among religions and denominations. John Wesley gave us a principle for the pluralism of spirit without the dilution of doctrine when he advised, "In essentials, unity; in non-essentials, liberty; in all things, charity." Although he lived in the eighteenth century, Wesley's principle is especially applicable today when pluralism has become, according to one observer, "An oblong purplish blur that covers many gods."

In the same context, this observer noted that the contemporary question is not, "Do you believe in God?" but rather, "In which god do you believe?"

Even without the revelation of the Mosaic Law, Job avers that he has no other gods before or with Shaddai—the Almighty. Moreover, he refuses to greet other gods by such a customary and presumably innocent gesture as kissing his ring to acknowledge their presence. Robert Ingersoll, the atheist, tipped his hat as he passed a church one day. When a puzzled friend asked him how he could acknowledge God, in whose existence he did not believe, Ingersoll answered, "We nod, but we do not speak."

Job did not even nod to other gods, whether they were represented by the glint of gold or the cult of the sun and moon. Idolatry, to him, was a sin against God whether in practice or in admiration.

Job modeled hospitality. In the moral code of the land of the east, sojourning strangers were to be entertained as guests. Eliphaz accused Job of violating this code,

> You have not given the weary water to drink,
> And you have withheld bread from the hungry (22:7).

Evidently, the letter of the code could be met by giving strangers second-rate food, water, and lodging. Job challenges anyone to come forward with that accusation of him as their host. Rather, he again speaks parenthetically about both his servants and strangers, *"Who is there who has not been satisfied with his meat?"* (31:31). Although duty called for hospitality, Job qualified as a second-mile saint in his hospitality to strangers. His guests received the best food from the table.

Job stewarded the environment. In his passion to defend his innocence, Job interrupts his listing of sins and cries out, *"Oh, that I had one to hear me!"* (v. 35).

He then answers his oath of clearance with the seal of his signature and the call for God to write a book of charges, which he would be willing to wear in public as a challenge for any witnesses against him to come forward. He is so confident of his innocence that he presumes to approach God *"like a prince"* coming before his father, the king. At first, his princely self-image seems arrogant, but then we remember his relationship with God. In His confrontation with

Satan, God asked, "Have you considered My servant Job, that there is none like him on the earth, a blameless and upright man, one who fears God and shuns evil?" (1:8).

For Job to call himself a *"prince"* before God may have been a bit presumptuous, but he was not far off. When he actually enters the presence of God, however, he will bow as a servant.

Having sworn his oath of clearance, Job is struck with an afterthought. He forgot to mention the sins of the landowner, which undercut sustenance for the society,

> *If my land cries out against me,*
> *And its furrows weep together;*
> *If I have eaten its fruit without money,*
> *Or caused its owners to lose their lives* (31:38–39).

Two sins of landowners are mentioned. One is the obvious sin of stealing another man's crop or land. The other is the sin of raping the land. From God's instruction to Adam in the Garden through the Mosaic Law, and into the current environmental movement, the stewardship of the earth is a natural and revealed truth. During the 1970s when the interest in environmentalism peaked, accusations were leveled at Christians who aligned themselves with the capitalism that wasted resources, ruined the land, and polluted the air. Rene Dubos, the father of environmentalism, corrected his cohorts with the admonition that the stewardship is a biblical principle given by God in the Garden. Christians who foul the environment or wink at its pollution are guilty of the sin that Job avoided. He knew the consequences of *if . . . ,*

> *Then let thistles grow instead of wheat,*
> *And weeds instead of barley* (v. 40).

Each of the sins that Job mentions in his oath of clearance has external and internal dimensions. Externally, Job is referring to a discipline of conduct that can be witnessed by the public in his relationships with God and man. Internally, there is a spirit of life that God recognized when He commended Job for being "blameless" as well as "upright" (1:8). This inner spirit motivated Job to go beyond the righteousness required by the letter of the Law to the grace that flowed from the spirit of his life. On both counts, before man and God, Job swears his innocence and seals it with his signature. With that oath, *"The words of Job are ended"* (v. 40).

NOTE

1. William Congreve, *The Mourning Bride,* act 1, sc. 1.

CHAPTER SEVEN

Elihu's Remonstrance/Readiness

Job 32:1—37:24

A brash young man has been waiting in the wings to speak. All of Job's other friends have fallen silent. Their arguments have failed to convince Job of his sin. Yet, the dilemma of sin and suffering remains. Job's cry of *why* has gone unanswered. Into the silence steps Elihu, claiming to be wise and capable of serving as the mediator in the dispute. In a series of speeches, he deals directly with God's justice, Job's righteousness, and the purpose of suffering. Elihu's "Song of the Seasons," in which he proclaims the goodness of God, is a prelude to the coming of God Himself. Job has called upon God to answer him. Instead, he gets Elihu to prepare the way.

On the Right to Speak

Elihu is an angry young man. Job has justified himself rather than God and his older friends have condemned Job without answering him. Because of his age, Elihu apologizes for speaking, but claims as his authority the Spirit of understanding which is independent of age. Also, he cites the fact that he has listened patiently to all the arguments and has waited until the other three speakers have fallen silent. Now it is his turn. Ready to burst forth with words, Elihu assumes the role of the mediator—objective and wise.

> 1 So these three men ceased answering Job, because he was righteous in his own eyes.
> 2 Then the wrath of Elihu, the son of Barachel the Buzite, of the family of Ram, was aroused against

Job; his wrath was aroused because he justified himself rather than God.

3 Also against his three friends his wrath was aroused, because they had found no answer, and yet had condemned Job.

4 Now because they were years older than he, Elihu had waited to speak to Job.

5 When Elihu saw that there was no answer in the mouth of these three men, his wrath was aroused.

6 So Elihu, the son of Barachel the Buzite, answered and said:

"I am young in years, and you are very old;
Therefore I was afraid,
And dared not declare my opinion to you.
7 I said, 'Age should speak,
And multitude of years should teach wisdom.'
8 But there is a spirit in man,
And the breath of the Almighty gives him understanding.
9 Great men are not always wise,
Nor do the aged always understand justice.
10 "Therefore I say, 'Listen to me,
I also will declare my opinion.'
11 Indeed I waited for your words,
I listened to your reasonings, while you searched out what to say.
12 I paid close attention to you;
And surely not one of you convinced Job, or answered his words—
13 Lest you say,
'We have found wisdom';
God will vanquish him, not man.
14 Now he has not directed his words against me;
So I will not answer him with your words.
15 "They are dismayed and answer no more;
Words escape them.
16 And I have waited, because they did not speak,
Because they stood still and answered no more.
17 I also will answer my part,
I too will declare my opinion.
18 For I am full of words;
The spirit within me compels me.

19 Indeed my belly is like wine that has no vent;
It is ready to burst like new wineskins.
20 I will speak, that I may find relief;
I must open my lips and answer.
21 Let me not, I pray, show partiality to anyone;
Nor let me flatter any man.
22 For I do not know how to flatter,
Else my Maker would soon take me away.

Job 32:1–22

Through Eyes of Anger

The debate is over. Job stands upon his oath of clearance and his three friends do not take up the challenge. Silence is communication of its own kind. Sometimes, "silence is consent"; at other times, "silence is golden." What is the meaning of the silence into which Job's friends fall? According to our text, they cease answering Job *"because he was righteous in his own eyes"* (v. 1).

Disgust may have been the communication of their silence as they conclude that Job is self-righteous, arrogant, and intractable. Or, their silence may have spoken of their *resignation.* The third round of debate degenerated into a shouting match and a boring rerun of useless arguments. Perhaps by their silence, they were saying that there was nothing more to be said. *Concession* may also be a reason for their silence. As the elder statesman of the wise, Eliphaz has made a wild and unsubstantiated charge that Job suffers because he has committed the sin of the rich—oppressing the poor. In turn, Job took his case to the public with an oath of clearance, and thereby shifted the burden of proof to Eliphaz and the people whom he allegedly wronged. When no witnesses came forward, Eliphaz lost his case. Through silence, he and his friends confessed that Job *was* righteous, at least before men and in his own eyes.

Enter Elihu. The author of Job introduces him by name, father, region, and family. Elihu's name means "My God is He" and bespeaks a spiritual heritage. He is the son of Barachel, a name meaning "God Blesses" and suggesting a prosperous and aristocratic family. Elihu came from the land of Buz. According to genealogical tables, Buz was a brother of Uz, the forefather to Job. The names are significant. Job and Elihu are related through a common ancestry. We also learn that Elihu is a member of the family of Ram, which has roots in the tribe of Judah (Ruth 4:19), and probably explains the Hebraic connection in Elihu's theology. Scholars who consider Elihu's speeches as irrelevant to Job's journey of faith fail to take these factors into account. Elihu brings to the conversation a heritage that the three friends lack. He identifies with Job in his spiritual heritage, aristocratic position, family ancestry, and Judaean roots.

Elihu is an angry young man. His youth is revealed by the fact that he waits until all of his elders have exhausted their words. Then, his youthful anger spills onto the pages of Scripture through a phrase that is repeated four times in the brief introduction. His "*wrath was aroused*" against Job as a person, against Job's position before God, against his friends for their failure, and against his friends for their silence (32:2–5).

Elihu is mad at the world! Typical of the young, he sees flaws in what is reputed to be the wisdom of age and reacts violently against it. He is angry, impatient, and arrogant. Yet, youthful rage is not without its redeeming value. In every generation, the young serve as a check-and-balance for our ideas, values, attitudes, and tastes by their questions and causes, pranks and protests, rage and reaction, music and dress. Although we hate to admit it, youth see clearly through their anger, even though they do not see the whole picture or the long view. Time will take care of that. Young radicals often become old reactionaries. Is it possible that Eliphaz, Bildad, and Zophar see the image of their reactionary age in the mirror of Elihu's radical rage?

Elihu cites the flaws in the arguments of Job and his three friends. His wrath is aroused against Job because, in his zeal to attest his innocence, he has justified himself but not God. Elihu has reason for his rage. The chief end of man is to glorify God, not himself. In spirit, if not in fact, Job leaves an air of self-glory in his final speech when he swears to his righteousness. Isaiah declares such righteousness as "filthy rags" (Isa. 64:6), and the apostle Paul prays that he might "be found in Him, not having my own righteousness, which is from the law, but that which is through faith in Christ, the righteousness which is from God by faith" (Phil. 3:9).

Our condemnation of Job, however, must be tempered by the fact that he has served God to the outer edge of his knowledge and has no place else to stand. From our privileged post-Resurrection perspective, his head may be wrong, but we cannot deny that his heart is right.

Elihu's anger is especially justified against his three friends who pronounced Job guilty of sin without reason. Job's anguished cry *why* went unanswered through all of the rounds of debate. Yet, the three friends jumped to judgment in self-defense of their inadequate orthodoxy. The young always have a strong sense of the justice that they demand of others. Elihu comes to Job's defense in his rage. By taking his side against injustice, Elihu becomes the first friend to show some understanding of Job's plight. His task is monumental. He must walk the tightrope between the contending parties with an anger that threatens his balance.

Elihu performs fairly well. Although the substance of his speech contains little information that is new, he offers an approach that is essential in preparation for the voice of God.

Spirit, Not Age, Is the Source of Wisdom

In keeping with protocol, Elihu apologizes for speaking as a youth. He has listened carefully to the arguments of both sides of the debate and feels the frustration of the stalemate. Behind the scenes of the contest over the question, Why does Job suffer? Elihu perceives another question: What is the source of authority for wisdom?

Young people are particularly sensitive to questions of authority. In their search for identity and independence, they test authority figures, such as parents, and authority structures, such as schools. If the lines of authority are too rigid or too lax, they rebel. Some resistance is inevitable because youth need to find the limits and the lines against which they can sharpen their own identity. In a study at Harvard, a psychiatrist reported a radical swing in the emotional problems of students in the 1960s compared with those in the 1980s. In the 1960s, students reacted against authoritarian parents; in the 1980s, their emotional problems stemmed from the laxity of permissive parents, often represented by the absence of the father from the home. Neither extreme is satisfactory. The middle ground is a home with clear, high, and reasonable standards backed up by parental love, praise, and consistency.

Elihu is brash enough to challenge the authority of age as the source of wisdom:

> *Great men are not always wise,*
> *Nor do the aged always understand*
> *justice* (32:9).

Indirectly, he is also challenging the source of authority that Eliphaz, Bildad, and Zophar claimed. Eliphaz cited the experience of a personal revelation as his source of authority, while Bildad relied upon tradition, and Zophar counted upon common sense.

If there is any doubt about Elihu's role in preparation for the coming of God, it is erased by his introduction of the source of authority that goes beyond the experience, tradition, and reason upon which Job and his three friends relied:

> *But there is a spirit in man,*
> *And the breath of the Almighty*
> *gives him understanding* (v. 8).

Job is being prepared for the coming of God, who reveals Himself through His Spirit. Elihu grasps a truth that prevails from the beginning of creation when "the Spirit of God was hovering over the face of the waters" (Gen. 1:2) to the end of Revelation when "the Spirit and the bride say, 'Come!' " (Rev. 22:17). When he speaks of the *"breath of the Almighty,"* he also anticipates the revelation written by Paul, "All Scripture is given by inspiration of God" (2 Tim. 3:16). Not by coincidence, Elihu's *"breath of the Almighty"* and Paul's "inspiration of God" are synonymous and interchangeable phrases. Elihu takes a giant step toward new truth when he claims the *"breath of the Almighty"* as the authority for his words.

Openness, Not Prejudice, Is the Secret to Communication

Elihu has vented his rage against his three older friends for jumping to judgment against Job without cause. To his credit, he vows to correct in his own speaking the criticism that he has leveled against the others. Elihu can say "listen to me" because, as a good listener himself, he has earned the right to speak. The implication is that the three friends failed to listen to Job because their ears were blocked by a preconceived conclusion. If so, nothing that Job could say would make a difference. He pleaded with his friends to hear his case and let God make the judgment. His pleas fell on deaf ears and closed minds.

Elihu creates a climate for reopening the lines of communication when he says, "Listen to me, because I have listened to you." Four principles of good listening are given. Elihu says, *"I waited for your words"* (32:11). The first principle of good listening is to *let the other person speak first.* Combative conversation is like a nuclear war. Poor listeners and prejudiced speakers must vie for "first-strike capability" in order to put their opponent on the defensive. In his initial cry of anguish, Job opened himself to attack. Eliphaz took the advantage with a first-strike speech in which he fired the formula of orthodoxy from the silo of his personal authority, exploded Job's righteousness, and presumed that guilt would be the fallout leading to repentance. Elihu has witnessed this verbal devastation and wants no part of it. He will speak without vengeance and listen to Job.

Again, Elihu speaks, *"I listened to your reasonings"* (v. 11). The second principle of good listening is to *follow the thinking of the speaker through to the end.* A major fault of a poor listener is to hear the first part of an argument, leap to a premature conclusion, and stop listening. Of all people, I am most guilty. So often, the introduction, outline, or text of a good sermon sets my mind in motion with a flood of thoughts and illustrations for new sermons of my own. When I get home, my wife or son will mention a spiritual truth, a humorous punchline, or a gripping story in the pastor's sermon that I completely missed! Elihu did better. He followed the reasoning of Job and his three friends from the beginning to the end.

A third principle of good listening is given in Elihu's words, *"I listened . . . while you searched out what to say"* (v. 11). A good listener *does not interrupt the speaker who pauses to think before continuing to speak.* Count the interruptions in a good conversation between friends. Check the times that you interrupt a person in the middle of a sentence or during a pause. Many of us are rude and unfair listeners who kill ordinary conversation with our interruptions. But add the heat of conflict to the conversation and stir in a dose of hostility. Interruptions multiply, not just out of passion, but as counter-offensive weapons. The slightest pause in the opponent's speech is used as an invitation to interrupt the line of reasoning and turn the argument to one's own advantage. An interruption is a rude, selfish, and unfair tactic that Elihu refused to employ even when tempted.

Elihu says, *"I paid close attention to you"* (v. 12). The fourth principle of a good listener is to *identify with the speaker as a person, as well as hear the spoken words.* Throughout the debate, Job complained that his friends failed to understand the totality of his sufferings that went far beyond the volatility, and yet the inadequacy, of his words. Elihu heard Job's plea and applied its principle as he concentrated his attention upon Eliphaz, Bildad, and Zophar. Not only did Elihu "hang on every word" they spoke, but he tried to "get under their skin" to understand the motives, feelings, and needs behind their speaking.

Elihu must have made his three elder friends uncomfortable. Subconsciously, at least, they had to be aware of Elihu's intense listening that made them pause to choose their words. Each time they turned toward him, their gaze was met with two eyes that studied every move they made. Through those eyes, they must have detected a critical mind dissecting every proposition they advanced. Such listeners are rare, but they are invaluable to the understanding that must precede the resolution of conflict. On the principles of good listening, Elihu indicts the three debaters for an unsubstantiated conclusion that failed to convince Job and an ineffective rebuttal that failed to answer him. Furthermore, Elihu says that they cannot excuse their ineptness by saying,

> *"We have found wisdom";*
> *God will vanquish him, not man* (v. 13).

A fresh approach is needed. Elihu rejects the line of his friends' reasoning and intends to reopen communication by clearing the lines of premature judgment.

Passion, Not Detachment, Is a Sign of Caring

Elihu bit his tongue while listening to the endless rhetoric of fruitless debate. Inside of him, anger fermented and frothed like new wine that has no outlet except to explode the seams of old wineskins. The same analogy is used by Jesus when he teaches the difference between the fresh spirit of His approach and the stodgy law of the

Pharisees: "And no one puts new wine into old wineskins; or else the new wine bursts the wineskins, the wine is spilled, and the wineskins are ruined. But new wine must be put into new wineskins" (Mark 2:22).

In contrast to the sterile detachment of Eliphaz, Bildad, and Zophar from the debate, Elihu confesses his passion and admits that facts and feelings will be inseparable in his speech.

Job must have taken comfort at Elihu's confession. There is nothing more demeaning to human personality than to be ignored. Dr. Fred B. Craddock, on a *Preaching Today* tape, tells about a member of his choir who was known as the practical joker of the church. One day, he met her in the choir room after a worship service. While putting away her choir robe, she said, "I quit." Dr. Craddock thought she was kidding. But when she repeated her resignation, he asked her what could be done to make her change her mind. She answered, "I need someone to take me seriously." Although everyone laughed at her, she felt as if no one cared for her.

Even anger is preferable to a snub. Politicians say, "I would rather be stoned than ignored." With the same insight, John Studdert-Kennedy has written a verse in which Jesus returns to earth and no one cares. At one time or other, we have all felt the pain of Kennedy's concluding line, "And Jesus crouched against the wall and cried for Calvary."[1]

Job must have found some comfort in Elihu's promise to speak with passion. Even though he would be the target of Elihu's anger, he knew, for the first time, that someone took him seriously. Elihu cared.

Equality, Not Partiality, Is the Standard of Justice

Eliphaz, Bildad, and Zophar revealed their bias against Job, not just in their faulty conclusion, but in their failure to apply the standard of judgment to themselves and others. Equality is a foundational value for justice. In a just society, for instance, each person must have equal rights before the law, equal protection of life and safety, and equal opportunity to realize his or her potential as a person. Spiritual matters are also subject to the principle of justice and the practice of equality. Jesus scores the Pharisees for showing partiality to the rich, the pious, and the distant proselyte, while ignoring the poor, the sinner, and the neighbor at home. For their injustice, Jesus condemns them as hypocrites who will not "escape the condemnation of hell" (Matt. 23:33).

A person who claims to speak with *"the breath of the Almighty"* is sensitized to the principle of justice and the practice of equality. Speaking in the Spirit is not a private experience without public implication. Justice and equality can only be demonstrated in interpersonal relationships and in a social setting. Perhaps in refutation of Eliphaz's private vision and public contradiction, Elihu confirms his claim to speak with the Spirit of understanding by saying,

> *Let me not, I pray,*
> *show partiality to anyone;*
> *Nor let me flatter any man* (32:21).

His insight is prophetic. Centuries later, Paul will inform the Ephesians that when the body of Christ is one in the Spirit, they will speak the truth in love, without favor or flattery (Eph. 4:15).

Under the inspiration of the Spirit, Elihu is not only sensitive to the principle of justice, but he is humbled before the justice of God. Job has warned his three friends about the wrath of God if they failed to speak justly. Elihu heard that warning and therefore pledges that he will speak without favor or flattery, *"Else my Maker would soon take me away"* (32:22).

The climate for communication has been totally changed. Elihu will speak in the Spirit, openly, passionately, and justly. Even if the substance of his speech adds nothing new to the argument, he creates the climate in which God Himself loves to come and speak.

On the Discipline of Suffering

In his own defense, Job has advanced three contentions that are unanswered. First, he is innocent (33:8–9). Second, God's persecution is unjust (vv. 10–11). Third, God's silence shows His indifference (vv. 12–13). Quoting Job's words, Elihu refutes each of these arguments in reverse order. God does speak in many ways, beginning with dreams and visions and, if these are not effective, through suffering and pain. His purpose in each case is to chasten the spirit and save the person from perdition (vv. 19–28).

1 "But please, Job, hear my speech,
And listen to all my words.
2 Now, I open my mouth;
My tongue speaks in my mouth.
3 My words come from my upright heart;
My lips utter pure knowledge.
4 The Spirit of God has made me,
And the breath of the Almighty gives me life.
5 If you can answer me,
Set your words in order before me;
Take your stand.
6 Truly I am as your spokesman before God;
I also have been formed out of clay.
7 Surely no fear of me will terrify you,
Nor will my hand be heavy on you.
8 "Surely you have spoken in my hearing,
And I have heard the sound of your words, saying,
9 'I am pure, without transgression;
I am innocent, and there is no iniquity in me.
10 Yet He finds occasions against me,
He counts me as His enemy;
11 He puts my feet in the stocks,
He watches all my paths.'
12 "Look, in this you are not righteous.
I will answer you,
For God is greater than man.
13 Why do you contend with Him?
For He does not give an accounting of any of His words.
14 For God may speak in one way, or in another,
Yet man does not perceive it.
15 In a dream, in a vision of the night,
When deep sleep falls upon men,
While slumbering on their beds,
16 Then He opens the ears of men,
And seals their instruction.
17 In order to turn man from his deed,
And conceal pride from man,

18 He keeps back his soul from the Pit,
And his life from perishing by the sword.
19 "Man is also chastened with pain on his bed,
And with strong pain in many of his bones,
20 So that his life abhors bread,
And his soul succulent food.
21 His flesh wastes away from sight,
And his bones stick out which once were
not seen.
22 Yes, his soul draws near the Pit,
And his life to the executioners.
23 "If there is a messenger for him,
A mediator, one among a thousand,
To show man His uprightness,
24 Then He is gracious to him, and says,
'Deliver him from going down to the Pit;
I have found a ransom';
25 His flesh shall be young like a child's,
He shall return to the days of his youth.
26 He shall pray to God, and He will delight
in him,
He shall see His face with joy,
For He restores to man His righteousness.
27 Then he looks at men and says,
'I have sinned, and perverted what was right,
And it did not profit me.'
28 He will redeem his soul from going down to
the Pit,
And his life shall see the light.
29 "Behold, God works all these things,
Twice, in fact, three times with a man,
30 To bring back his soul from the Pit,
That he may be enlightened with the light
of life.
31 "Give ear, Job, listen to me;
Hold your peace, and I will speak.
32 If you have anything to say, answer me;
Speak, for I desire to justify you.
33 If not, listen to me;
Hold your peace, and I will teach you wisdom."

Job 33:1–33

With the "Breath of the Almighty"

Critics are not kind to Elihu. They accuse him of being a brash and spoiled aristocratic kid on an ego trip. In their opinion, he talks too much and contributes nothing to the content of the debate. Many scholars feel as if the Book of Job would have more integrity if Elihu and his speeches were wiped from its pages.

Something is wrong with the critics' position. True, Elihu is young, angry, aristocratic, talkative, inexperienced, and self-confident. According to the customs of the ancient East, he has no right to speak at all. Like Job, he is a rebel. Whereas Job rebels against the rigid doctrine of orthodoxy, Elihu challenges the rigid protocol of orthodoxy. The two go hand in hand. Protocol protects religious tradition as much as doctrinal presuppositions that are paraded as absolute truth. All hierarchies develop elaborate procedures of protocol to preserve their power. In the Roman Catholic tradition, for instance, the infallibility of papal decrees must be supported by the protocol that limits or channels debate on controversial issues. When Pope John XXIII opened the windows of the Roman Catholic Church to let the first fresh spiritual renewal waft through a sanctuary made musty by tradition, he changed both doctrine and protocol. For instance, English was substituted for Latin in the Mass, laypeople were encouraged to read the Bible, and nuns were given the privilege of common dress.

Elihu is essential to Job's journey of faith. Although he may contribute little toward the answer of Job's suffering, his youthful daring breaks through the barrier of religious protocol so that God may appear and Job may hear. Furthermore, according to his own claim, he speaks with the authority of the Spirit and with the *"breath of the Almighty."* God always chooses human instruments for His work. Elihu is an early illustration of Paul's insight, "But we have this treasure in earthen vessels, that the excellence of the power may be of God and not of us" (2 Cor. 4:7).

Those who want to cross out Elihu and cancel his contribution to the Book of Job need the humbling perspective of the backwoods preacher, who chuckled, "The Lord chooses earthen vessels even though He knows that most of them are cracked."

The critical test for Elihu is whether or not he demonstrates the excellence of the power of God through the Spirit rather than exalting himself. From this perspective, we must commend rather than condemn Elihu. Without glossing over his flaws, he shows us that he is the instrument of the Spirit and speaks with the *"breath of the Almighty."*

Elihu Speaks to Job Person to Person

As Elihu turns from his three elder friends to Job, his attitude changes. Critics emphasize the fact that he puffs himself up by saying,

> *My words come from my upright heart;*
> *My lips utter pure knowledge* (33:3).
> and
> *Truly I am as your spokesman before God* (v. 6).

Job has repeatedly called for a mediator and Elihu has the audacity to put himself in that position. Without doubt, his confidence takes him over the boundary of good sense and creates expectations that he cannot fulfill. His intentions, however, cannot be faulted. Elihu is trying to respond to Job's plea. Whereas Job's friends refuse to step down from their superior position to assume an intermediary role that requires an impartial understanding of both sides, the Spirit of God leads Elihu to take that balanced stance. On one side of the scale, he assumes the understanding given to him through the *"breath of the Almighty"* that qualifies him to be Job's spokesman before God (v. 6). An air of arrogance would prevail except for the values that the Spirit of God gives to Elihu on the other side of the scale. Courtesy is a value of the Spirit that Elihu shows. He addresses Job with a request, not a demand,

> *But please, Job, hear my speech,*
> *And listen to all my words* (v. 1).

How characteristic of the Spirit of God! Despite the intensity of His purpose and the immensity of His truth, the Spirit always shows respect for persons through the grace of common courtesy.

Far weightier than courtesy, however, is Elihu's willingness to put the weight of his common humanity on the balancing scale. Arrogance gives way to humility when Elihu says to Job,

The Spirit of God has made me,
And the breath of the Almighty
gives me life (v. 4).

Through their common creation in the image of God, Elihu makes it clear that he stands on Job's side as a man who understands his human nature and recognizes his spiritual potential. A strong hint of the Incarnation is given in Elihu's speech. The perfect balance of the Spirit is revealed to us when "the Word became flesh and dwelt among us" (John 1:14). A similar balance is poised when Elihu says,

Truly I am as your spokesman
before God;
I also have been formed
out of clay (33:6).

To speak with the balanced understanding of the Spirit of God and the spirit of man is the responsibility of every Christian, whether the preacher in the pulpit, the counselor in the sickroom, or the witness on the street. Then, as Elihu tells Job, there will be neither the fear of man playing God or the heavy hand of human superiority (v. 7). Elihu will speak God's truth in balance with Job's circumstance.

Elihu Confronts Job with the Critical Issue

Jesus introduces the Holy Spirit as "Comforter" (John 14:16, KJV). In describing His functions, however, He also emphasizes the "convicting" Spirit: "And when He has come, He will convict the world of sin, and of righteousness, and of judgment" (John 16:8).

Conviction requires confrontation. It is an error to assume that truth can be spoken without exposing error or that conviction can be felt without the sting of conscience. Only in the Spirit, however, can a person speak "the truth in love" (Eph. 4:15).

The *"breath of the Almighty"* is in Elihu when he confronts Job on the critical issue of his innocence. In the typical style of Eastern debate, he quotes Job as saying,

"I am pure, without transgression;
I am innocent, and there is no
iniquity in me" (33:9).

Elihu goes on to quote or paraphrase Job's complaint that God punishes him without cause, treats him like an enemy, holds him captive, and stalks his footsteps (vv. 10–11). Critics of Elihu note the fact that he overstates his case by choosing a word for *pure* that can be interpreted as *sinless.* Also, Elihu is cited for taking Job's questions out of the context in which he confesses that he is a sinner. Nevertheless, his critics agree that Elihu comes directly to the quintessential question, Why do the innocent suffer?

Talkative though he is, Elihu does not waste words in his confrontation with Job. *"Look,"* he says, *"in this you are not righteousness"* (v. 12). More literally, he means, "On this issue, you are not right." Under the guidance of the Spirit, Elihu is able to separate the issue from the person. The distinction is critical. On the basis of the issue, Job's three friends condemned his character as depraved and wicked. Elihu only confronts him with the issue of charging God with wrongdoing. Without the discerning Spirit, healthy confrontation over the issue of sin and hopeless condemnation of the person as a sinner gets confused.

As another characteristic of the *"breath of the Almighty"* at work in him, Elihu explains why Job has sinned in accusing God of wrongdoing. He may sound as arbitrary as his three friends when he asserts,

> *For God is greater than man.*
> *Why do you contend with Him?*
> *For He does not give an accounting of*
> *any of His words* (vv. 12–13).

There is more to the explanation than the fact that God is not accountable to man. Job's sin is not contending with God, but projecting the limitations of his finite human nature upon the infinite nature of God. Through the eyes of the Spirit, Elihu sees that Job is trying to remake God in his own image. With the mind of the Spirit, he confronts him with this specific issue rather than condemning him on general grounds.

Elihu Teaches Job New Truth

Job not only complained about the silence of God, but set the ground rules for His speaking. He insisted upon a personal audience with the privilege of cross-examination just as if he and God were equals. Elihu answers that God speaks through other means, including the nighttime visions and physical pain that Job has experienced. Eliphaz, Bildad, and Zophar said the same thing, except that they tied the experiences directly to God's punishment for Job's sin. Elihu starts down the same line of reasoning but keeps going beyond punishment to God's redemptive purpose.

Dreams, for instance, come at a time of night when the ears of man are open and his mind is uncluttered. In Huxley's science-fiction novel *Brave New World,* sleep-learning is a refined technique for teaching propaganda and controlling human behavior. A tape recorder under the pillow as a substitute for conscious learning is still a fantasy, but we know that subconscious learning has value that is yet to be known. Elihu informs Job that the dreams of which he speaks with terror are messages from God. Terror may be Job's reaction to the dreams, but according to Elihu, their purpose is to save the soul of man from sinful deeds, hidden pride, the pit of hell, and the sword of justice (vv. 17–18).

God also speaks to man through the medium of pain (v. 19). Elihu does not make it clear whether pain is a supplement or a complement to dreams. The inference is that pain is an advanced level of God's communication. The purpose of pain, however, is more important than the timing. Whereas God communicates through dreams to prevent sin, He uses pain to bring redemption.

Those who argue that Elihu adds nothing of substance to the argument of his three friends fail to see that he gives suffering a creative rather than a destructive purpose. Pain that has a creative purpose can be endured. Childbirth, for instance, with its severe pain, is endured and forgotten because of its creative purpose. Kidney stones, however, are reputed to cause the worst of pain. Without a creative purpose, endurance is limited and the memory lingers. Of course, it is little comfort for a person in the midst of suffering to be told that pain is God's way of speaking His redemptive purpose. Many times in my hospital experience I have had to answer emergency calls from patients who have been devastated by a well-meaning pastor or friend who informed them that God brought their suffering to teach them His goodness and bring them His joy. The understanding of the Spirit is needed to know when a person in pain is ready to see the meaning of what Tournier calls "creative suffering."

With the *"breath of the Almighty"* in him, Elihu perceives that Job is ready to learn from his suffering. Step by step, he walks him through the process of pain and introduces the work of the Spirit to him as new truth. He begins by recognizing that Job's suffering has destroyed his body and brought him to the edge of death,

> *Yes, his soul draws near the Pit,*
> *And his life to the executioners* (v. 22).

To picture his plight, Elihu draws the image of a thousand denizens of the "Pit" who are driving Job toward death and destruction (v. 23). Eliphaz, Bildad, and Zophar would be quick to agree. But Elihu sees the intervention of the Spirit of God, one angel against a thousand, who steps forward as the mediator for the condemned soul. Graciously, He reveals the righteousness of God and announces that He has found the *"ransom"* to redeem the condemned soul from the punishment of the Pit (v. 24). Most likely, Elihu does not even know what he is saying. Job has asked for a mediator to plead the case of his innocence before God; Elihu tells him that the mediator will personally pay the debt of his sin before God. How else could Elihu foresee the role of Jesus Christ as the mediator who ransoms us with his own life except as he is inspired to speak with the *"breath of the Almighty"*?

Resurrection follows. Eliphaz, Bildad, and Zophar also promised Job that he would sing paeans of praise if he would repent. Their songs, however, are set to the point and counterpoint of righteous behavior, almost in a minor key. Elihu's song of redemption is different. Even though it contains a verse in which man confesses his sin, the upbeat sound of the words *"delight"* and *"joy"* (v. 26) set a vibrant tone of rejoicing that only the redeemed can know. James Stewart, the Scottish preacher, captured the spirit of that song when I heard him say, "To be redeemed is to be awakened by the sound of a thousand trumpets and find it bliss to be alive in such a dawn as this."

He, as well as Elihu, had to be inspired by the Spirit of God to sing the song of redemption.

To the end of his speech, Elihu continues to give us insights into the person and work of the Holy Spirit. He reminds Job that the Spirit of God is a patient teacher,

> *Behold, God works all these things,*
> *Twice, in fact, three times with a man* (v. 29).

The text would not be violated to extend the times that God speaks to man to "seventy times seven" and on ad infinitum.

In his conclusion, Elihu also aligns his purpose in speaking with the purpose of God. Deliberately, he repeats the point that the purpose of God in speaking to man through dreams and pain is both preventive and redemptive,

To bring back his soul from the Pit,
That he may be enlightened with the
light of life (v. 30).

Then, consistent with his promise that he is open to dialogue, Elihu invites Job to speak to him. His purpose, however, is not to win a debate, but to work with God, *"Speak, for I desire to justify you"* (v. 32).

Ironically, the first time that Job is invited to speak, he has nothing to say. He has rested his case, and perhaps he senses that Elihu speaks with the *"breath of the Almighty."* It is time for him to listen, even though the speaker is a brash young man.

On the Price of Rebellion

Job has continued to claim that he is innocent even though he suffers. By inference, then, God is unjust. Elihu sharply defends the justice of God, asserting that He plays no favorites and even His delays in punishing the wicked are for the good purpose of bringing them to repentance. To the righteous God Job should submit, because in denying the justice of God he has added rebellion to his sins.

1 Elihu further answered and said:
2 "Hear my words, you wise men;
Give ear to me, you who have knowledge.
3 For the ear tests words
As the palate tastes food.
4 Let us choose justice for ourselves;
Let us know among ourselves what is good.
5 "For Job has said, 'I am righteous,
But God has taken away my justice;
6 Should I lie concerning my right?

My wound is incurable, though I am without transgression.'
7 What man is like Job,
Who drinks scorn like water,
8 Who goes in company with the workers of iniquity,
And walks with wicked men?
9 For he has said, 'It profits a man nothing
That he should delight in God.'
10 "Therefore listen to me, you men of understanding:
Far be it from God to do wickedness,
And from the Almighty to commit iniquity.
11 For He repays man according to his work,
And makes man to find a reward according to his way.
12 Surely God will never do wickedly,
Nor will the Almighty pervert justice.
13 Who gave Him charge over the earth?
Or who appointed Him over the whole world?
14 If He should set His heart on it,
If He should gather to Himself His Spirit and His breath,
15 All flesh would perish together,
And man would return to dust.
16 "If you have understanding, hear this;
Listen to the sound of my words:
17 Should one who hates justice govern?
Will you condemn Him who is most just?
18 Is it fitting to say to a king, 'You are worthless,'
And to nobles, 'You are wicked'?
19 Yet He is not partial to princes,
Nor does He regard the rich more than the poor;
For they are all the work of His hands.
20 In a moment they die, in the middle of the night;
The people are shaken and pass away;
The mighty are taken away without a hand.
21 "For His eyes are on the ways of man,
And He sees all his steps.
22 There is no darkness nor shadow of death
Where the workers of iniquity may hide themselves.

23 For He need not further consider a man,
That he should go before God in judgment.
24 He breaks in pieces mighty men without inquiry,
And sets others in their place.
25 Therefore He knows their works;
He overthrows them in the night,
And they are crushed.
26 He strikes them as wicked men
In the open sight of others,
27 Because they turned back from Him,
And would not consider any of His ways,
28 So that they caused the cry of the poor to come to Him;
For He hears the cry of the afflicted.
29 When He gives quietness, who then can make trouble?
And when He hides His face, who then can see Him,
Whether it is against a nation or a man alone?—
30 That the hypocrite should not reign,
Lest the people be ensnared.
31 "For has anyone said to God,
'I have borne chastening;
I will offend no more;
32 Teach me what I do not see;
If I have done iniquity, I will do no more'?
33 Should He repay it according to your terms,
Just because you disavow it?
You must choose, and not I;
Therefore speak what you know.
34 "Men of understanding say to me,
Wise men who listen to me:
35 'Job speaks without knowledge,
His words are without wisdom.'
36 Oh, that Job were tried to the utmost,
Because his answers are like those of wicked men!
37 For he adds rebellion to his sin;
He claps his hands among us,
And multiplies his words against God."

Job 34:1–37

Elihu is an enigma. Turning from Job to Eliphaz, Bildad, Zophar, and assorted bystanders, Elihu completely reverses his field. No longer does he claim to speak with the *"breath of the Almighty"*; no longer does he identify with Job on the common level of their created humanity; no longer does he claim to share God's desire to redeem Job; no longer does he express the patience of God in teaching Job His purpose; no longer does he invite Job to speak or wait for his answer.

Quite the opposite. Elihu speaks with cold reason from a position of assumed superiority, defending the justice of God and condemning Job just as bluntly and impersonally as Eliphaz, Bildad, and Zophar. What is Elihu's purpose? One thought is that he is trying to fulfill his promise to speak impartially as a mediator. Having spoken through the Spirit to show God's redemptive purpose in Job's suffering, he now takes the side of the three friends to vindicate the justice of God. Suddenly, the Spirit of redemption gives way to the arbitrary hand of the God of retribution. Either Elihu's concept of God is as small as that of his friends or he is a master of dramatic art. Is it possible that Elihu is playing the devil's advocate in acting out the attitudes and repeating the arguments of Eliphaz, Bildad, and Zophar? How else can we explain the fact that Elihu turns to defend the justice of God with stilted reasoning, exaggerated quotations, and unfeeling emotions? The only other explanation is that he agreed with the conclusion of the three friends that Job should be condemned for sin, but angrily disagreed with the line of reasoning that fell short of their conclusion. Perhaps he is trying to fill in the blanks of their argument in defense of God's justice and Job's condemnation.

Through the Inner Ear

The text supports the idea that Elihu is trying to present both sides of the argument without partiality. In keeping with the established procedure of the Wisdom School, he addresses the three friends and the company of bystanders, asking that they hear his argument with their "inner ear" (34:2) of human reason. Elihu also promises an artistic presentation that will be as pleasant to the ear as food is to the palate (v. 3). In the ancient East, oratory had developed into an art form of its own. Drama, sculpture, and painting were taboo because of the fear of graphic idolatry. So music and oratory took their place, being developed on the artistic standards of form, line, and color and judged for creativity, technique, and impact. The ancients forgot that style can become an end in itself. If substance, values, and meaning are lost in artistry, music and speech can be as idolatrous as drama, sculpture, and painting.

Whatever human nature touches can be turned into an idol. Jacques Ellul, for instance, believes that Western civilization has made an idol of technology. Under the guidance of the dictum "whatever can be done, must be done," he contends that technology is becoming an end in itself.[2] Nuclear weapons and medical research are examples. Technology in these fields rushes from discovery to discovery, propelled by its own momentum. Not until the new technology is developed do we ask about its meaning and morality. What are the trade-offs, for instance, for mechanical organs that keep patients alive? Or what are the implications of an arms race into outer space even under the proposal of a defensive strategy? Ellul denies the premise that "everything must be done that can be done." In fact, he is convinced that if questions of meaning and morality were asked in advance of technological research and development there are things we *should not* and *would not* do.

Elihu illustrates the spoken art at its best and at its worst in his speeches. His style ranges from the most intricate logic to the grandest poetry in the Book of Job. His pattern is to quote Job directly, or indirectly, and then to refute the position step-by-step from every angle. Analytical minds will savor the process, but philosophical minds will keep asking, "What is his purpose?" Further support for the idea that he is impartially advancing both sides of the argument is indicated by his challenge to his listeners to hear his case and then come to a consensus,

> *Let us choose justice for ourselves;*
> *Let us know among ourselves what is good* (v. 4).

Before advancing the argument pursued by Eliphaz, Bildad, and Zophar, Elihu must answer the question of his own anger. We remember that his wrath was aroused because the three older wise men condemned Job without adequate reason. His wordy speeches and overextended arguments tell us that his purpose is not to correct the process but to come to the same conclusion. To defend God's justice and condemn Job as a sinner requires a thorough reworking of his friends' arguments. Fairness requires Elihu to follow their line of reasoning to the logical conclusion of retribution, just as fairness requires him to follow the revelation of the Spirit to the inspired conclusion of redemption. Either we accept that or we must cast off Elihu as a spiritual schizophrenic who can speak out of both sides of his mouth with a pretense of equal sincerity, but only as a credit to his acting ability. It is preferable to read his speeches and to follow his arguments as attempts to be fair and thus clear the way for the coming of God. With this thought in mind, we can better understand how Elihu defends the justice of God.

"What Man Is Like Job?"

True to his promise, Elihu is impartially mad at Job and his friends. As the text informs us, his wrath is aroused against Job for justifying himself and thereby charging God with injustice. According to Elihu's quote, Job blames his suffering on God:

> *"I am righteous,*
> *But God has taken away my justice;*
> *Should I lie concerning my right?*
> *My wound is incurable,*
> *though I am without transgression"* (vv. 5–6).

Either Elihu's pride as a listener suffers a loss of credibility, or he is quoting Job as he believes the three friends heard him. Job has "almost" said that he is righteous and God has been unjust. With the slightest twist and the smallest step, Elihu sets up Job against God just as his three friends did. He also sets up the need for a countercharge against Job. Instead of the blameless, upright, and God-fearing man of wisdom whom we met at the beginning of the story, Job is reintroduced by Elihu as a bitter scoffer, a deliberate sinner, and a partner with Satan, saying,

> *"It profit a man nothing*
> *That he should delight in God"* (v. 9).

Job may have come close to claiming pristine innocence for himself and injustice on the part of God, but he studiously avoided the conclusion that righteousness is unprofitable. After all, this was the essence of Satan's challenge to the Lord, "Does Job fear God for nothing?"

(1:9) and the reason behind the misguided recommendation of Job's wife, "Curse God and die" (2:9). If Job had said what Elihu said he did, the test would have been over and Satan would have been vindicated.

"God Will Never Do Wickedly"

Elihu is also angry at Eliphaz, Bildad, and Zophar because they fail to substantiate their charge that Job had sinned, and consequently failed to vindicate the justice of God. He turns now to correct this fault, arguing from the nature of God. His major premise is simple and indisputable: *God is justice.* The corollary premise is equally consistent with His nature: *God cannot do injustice.*

> *Far be it from God to do wickedness,*
> *And from the Almighty to commit iniquity* (34:10).

Instead, His nature guarantees the promise that

> *He repays man according to his work,*
> *And makes man to find a reward according to his way* (v. 11).

Having laid the groundwork for his argument, Elihu sets out to prove that justice resides in the nature of God and that He cannot do injustice. *One proof is the continuing existence of man.* If God willed, He could call back His Spirit and His breath from man so that humankind would perish (vv. 14–15). The inference is that He is "just" with His creation even though His creation denies and rejects Him.

Humankind depends upon a dual "life-support system" for its existence. God continues to give us His Spirit and His breath. Almost incidentally in this speech, Elihu reminds us that he is still aware that God not only breathed into man the breath of life but also created him *imago dei,* "in His own image." Everyone knows what it would mean if God withdrew the breath of life from man—*"all flesh would perish"* (v. 15). No one, however, can fully comprehend what would happen if God withdrew His Spirit from the earth. All the atrocities and holocausts of history would be rolled into one apocalyptic catastrophe. As John the Revelator reminds us, except for the intervening presence of the Spirit of God, Armaggedon is *now.*

Another proof of God's justice is evident, according to Elihu, in His *impartial dealing* with princes and commoners, rich and poor, weak and mighty (vv. 19–20). Elihu pulls through the thread of our common destiny in birth and in death to illustrate his argument.

God's *perfect knowledge* is yet another proof that Elihu advances to show that He is the essence of justice. In direct response to Job's charge that God owes him a hearing and a bill of particulars on his sins, Elihu answers that God already sees perfectly the *"ways"* and *"steps"* of man (v. 21). Therefore, there is nothing that God needs to know and nothing that man can add to His knowledge. Justice based upon perfect knowledge requires only that God act, not defend His actions. For example,

> *He breaks in pieces*
> *mighty men* **without inquiry,**
> *And sets others in their place* (v. 24, emphasis mine).

Why? Because *"He knows their works"* (v. 25). Why? Because

> *They caused the cry of the poor*
> *to come to Him;*
> *For He hears the cry of the afflicted* (v. 28).

Contradiction fills Elihu's argument at this point. While positing a transcendent God who is so powerful, perfect, impartial, and arbitrary that He is untouchable, the cry of the poor still gets through to His heart. Sad to say, Job's comforters used this fact only to defend the justice of God.

How insensitive we become when self-defense dominates our motives. Pretending to probe the mind of God, we miss the pulsebeat of His heart. In Elihu's argument, the *"cry of the afflicted"* is nothing more than the consequence of the sin of the rich and the powerful—a call for God's justice, but not evidence of His mercy.

"Teach Me What I Do Not See"

Given the fact that God is justice and the proof that He cannot do unjustly, Elihu says that man may respond with one of two choices. The first choice is to submit to the justice of God. If God is silent, hidden, or bringing judgment upon nations or individuals, man must accept the fact that His purpose is to bring down the hypocrite and save the people (vv. 29–30). The second choice is to accept God's chastening, repent of sin, agree to His terms, and learn what God wants to teach (vv. 31–33).

Elihu puts that choice before Job. It sounds like the same, tired advice that Eliphaz, Bildad, and Zophar gave to Job, except for one factor. Elihu brings back the thought that God's purpose in Job's suffering is not just to chasten him for his sins but to teach him something that he does not yet see or know. To explain suffering as an occasion for teaching may seem to be a minor step in understanding God's purpose, but it is far beyond the limited insight of the three friends. By inserting into the argument such elements as the *"cry of the afflicted"* and the "teach me" purpose, Elihu is creating leverage for the Spirit to show the larger purpose of God.

Again, Elihu invites Job to speak. The tenderness of his first invitation is gone. In its place is the command of the conqueror ordering the vanquished to surrender. Elihu's lip is curled, his eyes are full of fire, and his voice shakes with vengeance, *"Therefore speak what you know"* (v. 33).

Momentarily, he takes on the role of Satan crying out "checkmate" over Job's soul.

"Job Speaks without Knowledge"

When Job does not answer, Elihu spins on his heel like a prosecutor in a courtroom. Having reduced the defendant to silence, he turns to the jury and flatters them with the call to attention,

> *Men of understanding say to me,*
> *Wise men who listen to me* (v. 34).

A scathing indictment follows. Job is accused of *stupidity.* Before the counsel of the wise, there is no greater embarrassment than to be singled out by name and cited for ignorance:

> *"Job speaks without knowledge,*
> *His words are without wisdom"* (v. 35).

Elihu is still dealing with Job's words, not his character. Continuing to play the God of justice, he promises to pursue to the bitter end the issue of Job's complaint against God. He justifies that pursuit because he says that Job's words sound like sin and his answers are like those given by wicked men (v. 36). In the next verse, however, we find that Elihu does far more than infer that Job has sinned with his words. He indicts Job for the *sin of claiming to be innocent* before God. *Stupidity,* the first charge, may be cured by teaching, but *sin,* the second charge, requires repentance and supports Elihu's advice that Job confess his sin and learn what God is trying to teach him (vv. 31–33).

Sedition is the third charge brought against Job. Sin relates to Job's character; sedition results from his words. By complaining that God has wronged him, Elihu says that Job has denied the justice of God—a blatant act of rebellion (v. 37). Only *scorn* is left on Elihu's bill of particulars. He closes his indictment by accusing Job of clapping his hands in their faces and "multiplying" his defiant words against God. All of the charges that Eliphaz, Bildad, and Zophar made against Job are now rolled into one. When God is defended as pure justice by human reason, man can be made into a monster.

The contrasting pictures of the nature of God between Elihu's first speech (chapter 33) and second speech (chapter 34) are worthy of study. With only the slightest change in wording, each speech addresses the same issue. Elihu is dealing with Job's claim of innocence and his complaint against God for causing him to suffer. But what a difference in the approach. In the first speech, Elihu is inspired "with the breath of the Almighty." In the second, he appeals to the inner ear of human reason as his authority. The difference is expressed in Elihu's attitude toward Job. Under the inspiration of the Spirit, he is a compassionate equal who serves as a mediator for the purpose of justifying Job. Posturing on behalf of human reason, however, Elihu represents a cold-hearted superior who is bent on defending God and condemning Job. Consistent with these contrasting attitudes, God's Spirit speaks to man time and time again, warning and teaching him through dreams and pain. The purpose is to save him from destruction. Human reason posits just the opposite. A God of justice has no need to speak, but only to act impartially, rewarding the righteous and punishing the wicked. Yet, in neither case can man justify himself before God. Therefore, the Spirit of God brings a ransom for man's redemption, but human reason falters because there is no adequate repayment that man can put on the scale to counterbalance the weight of his sin with the justice of God. No wonder that Elihu's first speech concludes with a song of joy while his second speech ends on a note of doom. If we speak "with the breath of the Almighty," we will invariably bring our listeners to the joy of man's redemption. But if we rely upon the inner ear of human reason, a well-worn path will lead us into the pain of God's retribution. The authority that we bring to our witness in the world or to our counsel with those who suffer will determine whether we present a God of retribution or redemption.

If Elihu's purpose is to put into balance, fairly and fully, the contrasting arguments for justifying Job and vindicating God, he has given us a masterful performance.

On the Question of Motive

Job has argued that religion is profitless. His suffering shows that it does no good to serve God. Elihu takes the opposite position. God is so far beyond man that He is not affected by human action of good or evil. The evidence is in God's creative power. Why, then, the delay in God's response to suffering? Elihu says that the cry for God often arises out of the pain of suffering, not out of genuine desire for God. In other words, Job's motive is wrong.

1 Moreover Elihu answered and said:
2 "Do you think this is right?
Do you say,
'My righteousness is more than God's'?
3 For you say,
'What advantage will it be to You?
What profit shall I have, more than if I had sinned?'
4 "I will answer you,
And your companions with you.
5 Look to the heavens and see;
And behold the clouds—
They are higher than you.
6 If you sin, what do you accomplish against Him?
Or, if your transgressions are multiplied, what do you do to Him?
7 If you are righteous, what do you give Him?
Or what does He receive from your hand?

8 Your wickedness affects a man such as you,
And your righteousness a son of man.
9 "Because of the multitude of oppressions they cry out;
They cry out for help because of the arm of the mighty.
10 But no one says, 'Where is God my Maker,
Who gives songs in the night,
11 Who teaches us more than the beasts of the earth,
And makes us wiser than the birds of heaven?'
12 There they cry out, but He does not answer,
Because of the pride of evil men.
13 Surely God will not listen to empty talk,
Nor will the Almighty regard it.
14 Although you say you do not see Him,
Yet justice is before Him, and you must wait for Him.
15 And now, because He has not punished in His anger,
Nor taken much notice of folly,
16 Therefore Job opens his mouth in vain;
He multiplies words without knowledge."

Job 35:1–16

Songs in the Night

As he promised, Elihu continues to pursue Job's complaints against God. In his last speech, he quotes Job as saying,

"It profits a man nothing
That he should delight in God" (34:9).

Elihu is particularly galled by this alleged affront to the justice of God. His anger causes him to put more aggravated words in Job's mouth.

For you say,
"What advantage will it be to You?
What profit shall I have,
more than if I had sinned?" (35:3).

Out of this quotation come two practical questions that Elihu attributes to Job and chooses to answer, *What's the use of being good?* and *Why doesn't God answer prayer?* These are universal questions that every person asks at one time or another. They are the contemporary questions that helped sell millions of copies of Rabbi Harold Kushner's book, *When Bad Things Happen to Good People.* Elihu may not have the most enlightened answers for these problems, but he does show us again that he has the mind of the Spirit in posing pertinent questions.

What's the Use of Being Good?

Abstract, oblique, and calloused answers are now expected of Elihu as he pursues the condemnation of Job through the course of human reason. Rather than dealing directly with Job's question or understanding the depth of suffering from which the question arises, he looks away to the heavens, points up to the lofty clouds, and invokes the transcendence of God as his latest authority. Certainly, he says, the nature of God cannot be affected by the actions of human beings whether righteous or wicked. Otherwise, God is not God. Elihu's first answer to the question is to say that as far as God is concerned, there is no benefit in being evil or good; sin doesn't change Him, trangressions do not affect Him, and righteousness does not benefit Him (vv. 6–7).

Elihu has another answer to the same question that is equally true as far as it goes. Man, not God, suffers from his own sin and benefits from his own righteousness. Elihu says to Job,

> *Your wickedness affects a man,*
> *such as you,*
> *And your righteousness* **a son of man** (v. 8, emphasis mine).

In the course of a single sentence, Elihu swoops from one truth to another without making a connection. While God and His transcendence cannot be changed by human sin or righteousness, man in his immanence is the victim of sin or the beneficiary of righteousness. Equally insightful is Elihu's designation that human sin or righteousness impacts persons, *individually* (*"such as you"*) and *corporately* (*"a son of man"*) (v. 8). A corporate designation includes a class of people, a social institution, a nation, or a civilization. In this case, Elihu is referring specifically to the socio-economic class of the poor who are oppressed by the sins of the rich and the powerful. Thus, his second answer to the question, What's the use of being good? is to say that as far as human nature is concerned, individually and corporately, our sin or righteousness makes all the difference in the world.

Conservative Christians, in particular, stress the individual impact of sin or righteousness but shy away from the corporate impact of human behavior. While it is true that only individuals can sin and be redeemed, the consequences of sin and righteousness are public as well as personal. We often quote the proverb,

> Righteousness exalts a nation,
> But sin is a reproach to any people (Prov. 14:34).

To follow the responsibility for righteousness at the public level is quite another matter. It is not enough to assume that the redemption of individuals will automatically reform and renew the social structures that suffer from the consequences of sin. Nor can isolation from social issues be justified because the meaning of the "social gospel" has been distorted by liberal activists and liberation theologians. The continuing challenge for the church—conservative and liberal—is to find the balance between personal redemption and public renewal.

Elihu has a different problem. In answering the question, What's the use of being good?, he poses two separate answers, neither of which is satisfactory. On the one hand, to preserve the transcendent nature of God, Elihu not only makes Him untouchable by human sin and righteousness but also implies that He is indifferent. On the other hand, he limits the consequences of sin to the human situation, ignoring the eternal consequences and any intimate relationship between God and man. Of course, the truth lies in between. Eternal truth is always a paradox. God is immanent as well as transcendent. While His nature is not affected by human sin or righteousness, His heart is grieved by sin and pleased by righteousness. If only Elihu had heard God say to Satan, "Have you considered My servant Job, that there is none like him on the earth, a blameless and upright man, one who fears God and shuns evil?" (1:8).

Patience is required with Elihu. By posing the extremes between the nature of God and the nature of man, he reveals the limitations of God's revelation to his generation. The truth is suspended in paradox awaiting God's next word. Elihu is right at the same time that he is wrong.

In the same sense, What's the use of being good? is a right and wrong question. More often than not, religious experience begins with a human need that only God can meet. Jesus Himself does not hesitate to ask the two blind men sitting beside the roadway, "What do you want Me to do for you?" (Matt. 20:32). TV evangelists who stress physical healing ask this same question of sick and crippled people. Another TV evangelist signs off with the promise, "Something good is going to happen to you." Still another prominent preacher of the electronic church has built a ministry to millions on the promise that faith in God reverses Satan's trick of robbing Adam of his self-esteem. If we are honest, most of us will confess that our original religious impulse was self-serving, whether physical healing, financial recovery, self-respect, family reconciliation, or just plain old-fashioned fear of hell. The problem comes if there is no growth in faith beyond the self-serving impulse or if the whole fabric of faith is created out of the weakest thread of truth, namely, the benefits of being good.

Television is a medium that aggravates the problem because it is geared to the charismatic personality who must get the attention of people in a limited time-span. The temptation, then, is to reduce the gospel to a simplistic formula of faith, not unlike a television commercial that promises "instant relief" for ailing souls and a "macho image" for wimpish spirits. Most television evangelists are aware of this problem and struggle to find ways to nurture and disciple their converts. Few of them, however, recommend the ministry of the local church and thus create suspicions about their own empire-building and fund-raising motives. The criticism also extends to local churches that are equally competitive, to parish preachers whose sermons are equally self-serving, and to lay people whose expectations are equally immature. If contemporary Christianity remains trapped in a faith based upon benefits, we are nursing a generation of "milk-fed" believers who have nothing more to offer to those who suffer than Elihu has to offer Job.

Why Doesn't God Answer Prayer?

Thoughts string out of Elihu. With just the mention of the people who suffer from the consequences of sin, he shifts his focus from the lofty God of the heavens to the lowliest people on earth—people who *"cry out for help because of the arm of the mighty"* (v. 9).

At first, there seems to be little connection between Elihu's thoughts until we remember that he is still talking about the nature of God and the suffering of Job. In this case, he uses the cry of the poor for relief from depression to address Job's complaint, "Why doesn't God answer prayer?"

Who hasn't asked the same question? I have prayed for the healing of my mother who was in her mid-sixties when the doctor told me that she would die in nine months from acute leukemia. I have also prayed for the merciful death of my mother-in-law, who vegetates in her nineties after a lifetime in the parish ministry with her husband. God answered neither of my prayers. Why not? Elihu's answer is that the motive is wrong. Using oppressed people as the example, he says that God does not answer them because they pray for relief from suffering rather than for the presence of God. The tie-in between unanswered prayer and unprofitable righteousness now becomes evident. If prayer is the bargaining tool by which we can ask and get rewards for our righteousness, we pray amiss. Likewise, for the poor to pray for freedom from oppression, for Job to pray for relief from suffering, for me to pray for the healing of my mother or the peaceful death of my mother-in-law, as *ends in themselves*—the petitions are misguided.

Such a thought only adds to our frustrations. Is any human prayer without mixed motives? Only the Holy Spirit can help us, "For we do not know what we should pray for as we ought, but the Spirit Himself makes intercession for us with groanings which cannot be uttered" (Rom. 8:26).

The same Spirit inspires Elihu to state the highest motive for prayer in one of the most poetic passages in holy Scripture,

> *But no one says,*
> *"Where is God my Maker,*
> *Who gives songs in the night,*

Who teaches us more
than the beasts of the earth,
And makes us wiser
than the birds of heaven?" (35:10–11).

Countless sermons have been preached on this text. As a study of a purpose of prayer, a natural outline emerges. *In prayer, we are to seek first the presence of God.* To plead for His presence, asking, "Where is God, my maker?", does not mean that freedom from oppression, relief from suffering, or healing for broken relationships are illegitimate requests. It does mean that the presence of God is our first priority in prayer. Not unlike Jesus' admonition about our earthly pursuits and human needs, we are to seek first the presence of God.

Elihu's point is well taken. Most of our private and public prayers fail the test of seeking first the presence of God. We rush into prayer without adequate preparation of mind or heart. We assume that God has nothing to do but wait for us to return from our own pursuits and speak to Him. Then we greet God like a servant, repeat the formal words of worship, and speed on to our requests.

Even while writing these words early on Sunday morning, I hear a television preacher conclude his sermon by asking his congregation to sing the chorus:

They that wait upon the Lord
Shall renew their strength,
They shall mount up with wings as eagles,
They shall run and not be weary,
They shall walk and not faint,
Lord, teach us to wait on thee.

In the middle of the last note, the preacher flashes back to pronounce a hurried two-sentence benediction in which the tyranny of television timing can be felt. "Amen" is only half-way out of his mouth when the cameras cut away to a pre-taped two-minute commercial promoting a "give-away" of a religious object to raise funds. "Selling the program" stands higher on the scale of importance than "seeking the presence" of God. My criticism, however, is muted when I consider the time that I give and the emphasis that I put upon "seeking first the Kingdom of God" in my own prayers. As guilty as the television preacher, I realize that my prayer life would be revolutionized if I learned the lesson taught by E. Herman in her book, *Creative Prayer:*

> Prayer in most cases begins with personal petition. We ask benefits for ourselves and for those we love. Then we come to realize that the power of prayer lies not in the external benefit or even in the mutual or spiritual reinforcement that comes to us through it but in our communion with God. A new love takes possession of us, a new relationship tranfigures life, a new world dawns upon our unsealed eyes.[3]

"A new love . . . a new relationship . . . a new world." Few of us know the potential of prayer that begins with the spiritual discipline of "seeking first the presence of God" by asking, Where is God, my maker?

Second, in the presence of God, we sing songs in the night. Nighttime is the symbol of human sin and suffering. Anyone who has been kept awake by a burning conscience or an unmitigated pain knows the experience of staring out into the blackness, passing through an eternity of time, seeing ghosts in every shadow, nodding into a nightmare, jerking back to startled consciousness, and lying wide awake once again in the cold sweat of morbid fear. To sing a song of joy at such a time is not only ludicrous, it is impossible. At best we can "whistle in the dark" with the hope of bolstering our own courage and scaring the imaginary ghost away.

Elihu is right again as he admonishes Job. Only in the presence of God can we sing songs in the night. He fails, however, to remember that Job has known that experience of singing in the night. When the black curtain of catastrophe fell over his soul at the announcement of losing his wealth and his children, he sang,

> The LORD gave, and the LORD
> has taken away;
> Blessed be the name of the LORD (1:21).

But with the loss of his health and with the silence of God, Job has lost his song. We do not blame him because we would not be singing either. Yet, the truth remains, as Charles Haddon Spurgeon says in his well-known sermon taken from this text, "Songs in the night come only from God; they are not in the power of man."[4]

Each of us has met unforgettable people who sing songs in the night. Dorothy Kreider was one of the grandest and most gracious women my wife and I have ever known. She taught at Seattle Pacific University for many years, as the founder and builder of the Department of Home Economics. Everything she did flowed naturally from her teaching of home economics—the clothes she wore, the meals she served, the rooms she decorated, the nutrition she followed, and the receptions she hosted. Her spiritual graces were equally known by the praise of her heart, the twinkle in her eyes, and the laugh on her lips. Shortly after retiring from teaching, Dorothy had surgery to remove a maligant tumor the size of a grapefruit. The prognosis gave her no hope. Weeks, months, and then years of radiation and chemical therapy left her nauseated, emaciated, and weak. Yet, mustering her strength, she appeared at university and church functions to amaze her friends with a bright but realistic quip about her condition. On two occasions, she got out of bed to give unforgettable, often rib-tickling, tributes to two close friends who died. Another time in the later stages of the disease, she rallied her waning resources to bring the house down and the audience to its feet when an honorary doctor's degree was conferred upon her. As would be expected, Dorothy out-lived all medical predictions. Just a day or two before her death, her pastor asked if she wanted any visitors. True to form, Dorothy answered, "No, I think not; I would have to buy a new gown for the reception." Dr. Dorothy Kreider lived as one of God's choicest night singers.

What is the theme of the night songs that we can sing in the presence of God? Spurgeon says that we can sing of the day that is past, the night that is not all darkness, and the morning that is to come:

> Remember it was not always night with thee . . . remember that God who made thee sing yesterday has not left thee in the night. He is not a daylight God, who cannot know His children in darkness; but He loves thee now as much as ever: though He has left thee a little, it is to prove thee, to make thee trust Him better and serve Him more.[5]

Job has sung another night song. In his darkest hour, he gives the centuries the melodious line, "I know that my Redeemer lives" (19:25), and, out of the shadows of despair, he strikes the morning chord, "When He has tested me, I shall come forth as gold" (23:10). Count Job among the night singers.

Third, in prayer we see the mystery and the meaning of being human. Elihu identifies prayer as God's vehicle for distinguishing between the potential of human intelligence and animal instincts. Two differences are drawn. One is the human ability to learn and know. God, Elihu says, is the one

> *Who teaches us more than*
> *the beasts of the earth* (35:11).

Human beings and animals are both capable of learning. Animals, however, are limited by their instincts. Our family dog amazes us. Like Snoopy, the Peanuts cartoon character, our dog, Muffin, comes running at the first rattle of her supper dish when my wife is fixing dinner. With uncanny premonition, she scoots under the bed when just the thought comes into our son's mind, "It's time for Muffin's bath." As smart as she may seem, our dog is still a dumb animal. She learns by associating a stimulus, such as the rattle of the supper dish, with the response of being fed. Beyond that behavioristic level, she cannot wonder who she is, solve abstract problems, ponder the mystery of the unknown, worship her Creator, or build a library of her learning and communicate her knowledge to the next generation of Maltese puppies.

Humankind, however, is endowed with unique intelligence that is part of the Creator's image. Behaviorists, such as B. F. Skinner, try to explain human intelligence as simply a sophisticated extension of the rattling supper dish. Evolutionists add their theory that man's superior ability to learn is represented by the biological accident that made it possible for the human animal to touch the tip of the forefinger with the tip of the thumb, thereby forming pincers, a simple tool which the ape lacks. But is man just an ape grown smarter, a tool-making animal?

Elihu refutes such a thought by citing the knowledge that a person gains at prayer in the presence of God. For him, prayer is not an intellectually passive or sterile experience. Vigorous interaction between the mind of God and the mind of man takes place in prayer. A suffering person, in particular, will have a mind honed by pain. Existential questions are asked: Who am I? What does the experience of others teach us? How did this happen to me? When will I find relief? These questions soon pale, however, before the essential question, Why must I suffer? To further complicate the issue, add Job's innocence to the question and then ask as Rabbi Kushner does, "Why do bad things happen to good people?"

Elihu promises that God will teach us knowledge in prayer. Medical science, for example, is the result of someone asking the questions *who, what, when, where,* and *how* about physical disease. The miracles of modern medicine are answers to these questions. Yet, the mystery of the question *why* remains. To assume that human knowledge can answer the question *why* is to deny that the ultimate meaning of life is found only in God. Elihu has demonstrated how human reason leaves us suspended in the paradox of eternal truth. The mystery confounds us. Now, whether he knows it or not, Elihu is the voice of the Spirit, revealing that the mystery of human existence can only be accepted by prayer in the presence of God. Rather than demanding a bill of particulars as Job has done, Elihu advances the mystery of being human, not as a point of frustration but as a progressive adventure pushing back frontiers of human knowledge by faith.

Wisdom is knowledge made whole. Elihu is not repeating himself for poetic reasons when he states that God will also make us *"wiser than the birds of heaven"* (35:11).

Birds are reputed to be the wisest of God's nonhuman creatures. They soar on the wind and see from the heavens and sing on earth. Yet, their "bird's-eye view" is limited by their instincts. They see far and wide, but they cannot relate what they see to the understanding of God's purpose of creation. Such wisdom is preserved for the person at prayer in the presence of God. Lifted above mundane matters and expedient time, life is seen whole through the lens of God's will. The question *why* may not be answered immediately, but the evidence of God's providence, bringing together past experience and giving meaning to our life history, is enough perspective for our current circumstances to declare by faith, "God knows what He is doing." Life with meaning through faith, not life with all the answers, is the wisdom reserved for persons who pray in the presence of God.

According to Elihu, Job has been proud (v. 12), impatient (v. 14), and foolish (v. 15) in his complaining questions, "What's the use of being good?" and "Why doesn't God answer prayer?" For the sin of his pride, Elihu says that Job should repent; for the impatience of his demands, he should wait; and for the following of his words, he should close his mouth. The advice would not be bad except that Elihu forgets that Job's prosperity is not dependent upon Job's righteousness and Job's deepest desire is God's presence. Awkwardly, but step by step, Elihu is creating the climate in which God will speak and Job will listen.

Elihu leaves us with the dissatisfaction of unanswered questions. Or does he? The answers are not avoided as much as the questions are misguided. "What's the use of being good?" assumes that righteousness is motivated by rewards rather than by a relationship with God. "Though He slay me, yet will I trust Him" (13:15) is the commitment that renders the question invalid. Likewise, "Why doesn't God answer prayer?" assumes that God must respond on our terms. True prayer is to seek first and unconditionally the presence of God as an end in itself. Only in His presence comes the faith to deal with the mystery of suffering and the understanding of its meaning.

On the Purpose of Pain

In summarizing the arguments, Elihu reaffirms that God is just and will ultimately honor righteousness. Elihu believes that Job's suffering, therefore, must be explained by God's purpose to teach him the dangers of sin, the judgment upon the sinner, and the promise of prosperity for those who repent.

1 Elihu also proceeded and said:
2 "Bear with me a little, and I will show you
That there are yet words to speak on God's
behalf.
3 I will fetch my knowledge from afar;
I will ascribe righteousness to my Maker.
4 For truly my words are not false;
One who is perfect in knowledge is with you.
5 "Behold, God is mighty, but despises no one;
He is mighty in strength of understanding.
6 He does not preserve the life of the wicked,
But gives justice to the oppressed.

7 He does not withdraw His eyes from the righteous;
But they are on the throne with kings,
For He has seated them forever,
And they are exalted.
8 And if they are bound in fetters,
Held in the cords of affliction,
9 Then He tells them their work and their transgressions—
That they have acted defiantly.
10 He also opens their ear to instruction,
And commands that they turn from iniquity.
11 If they obey and serve Him,
They shall spend their days in prosperity,
And their years in pleasures.
12 But if they do not obey,
They shall perish by the sword,
And they shall die without knowledge.
13 "But the hypocrites in heart store up wrath;
They do not cry for help when He binds them.
14 They die in youth,
And their life ends among the perverted persons.
15 He delivers the poor in their affliction,
And opens their ears in oppression.
16 "Indeed He would have brought you out of dire distress,
Into a broad place where there is no restraint;
And what is set on your table would be full of richness.
17 But you are filled with the judgment due the wicked;
Judgment and justice take hold of you.
18 Because there is wrath, beware lest He take you away with one blow;
For a large ransom would not help you avoid it.
19 Will your riches,
Or all the mighty forces,
Keep you from distress?
20 Do not desire the night,
When people are cut off in their place.

21 Take heed, do not turn to iniquity,
For you have chosen this rather than affliction.
22 "Behold, God is exalted by His power;
Who teaches like Him?
23 Who has assigned Him His way,
Or who has said, 'You have done wrong'?

Job 36:1–23

Teaching God's Goodness

Elihu continues to walk around Job's complaint that he suffers at the hand of God even though he is innocent. In his first speech (chapter 33), he stopped to speak gently under the inspiration of the "breath of the Almighty" and showed Job the hope of redemption (33:4). In his second speech (34:35), Elihu takes the part of a scholar in the Wisdom School who traces through the maze of human reason to defend the justice of God and condemn Job's rebellion.

Elihu has yet to speak for himself. Several times in his first two speeches, he has implied that God's purpose in suffering is to "open the ears of men" (33:16) in order to teach them His ways. This theme now comes forward in Elihu's final address. Creating a classroomlike setting, he assumes the role of a teacher, still speaking on God's behalf, but drawing upon the resources of his own knowledge (36:2–3). Although Elihu has never had a course in teaching, either his intuition or the inspiration of the Spirit serves him well. As a final step in preparing the way for the Lord to speak, Elihu opens the way as a teacher who takes his student, Job, through the full cycle of an effective teaching-learning process in two classroom sessions.

Session 1: Learning from the *Goodness* of God
A. Presenting his teaching credentials (vv. 1–4)
B. Reviewing his subject (vv. 5–12)
C. Motivating his student (vv. 13–21)
D. Posing his questions (vv. 22–23)

Session 2: Learning from the *Greatness* of God
A. Advancing his subject (vv. 24–25)
B. Illustrating his lesson (36:26–37:13)
C. Questioning his learner (vv. 14–18)
D. Applying his teaching (vv. 19–24)

Session 1: Learning from the Goodness of God

Good teaching always breaks down a complicated subject into manageable parts. In keeping with that principle, Elihu's teaching is divided into separate sessions, even though the lessons and the learning process are not complete until the second session is finished.

Presenting his credentials. In one way or another, the credentials of good teachers are made known to the student. A Ph.D., for instance, does not guarantee good teaching, but it is still the "union card" for college professors. Student opinion, of course, is one of the best credentials a teacher can have. Over a period of time, the reputation of good teachers rises to the top. Students may take snap courses and choose soft teachers while in school, but after graduation they recommend the teachers who are tough, but fair, and scholarly, but human, with their students.

Because of his age and inexperience, Elihu suffers from the lack of established credentials as a teacher for Job and the assembled company of bystanders. Therefore, he sounds a bit arrogant, again, as he declares his qualifications for teaching.

His teaching will be *extensive:*
I will fetch my knowledge from afar (v. 3).
His approach will be *humble:*
I will ascribe righteousness to my Maker (v. 3).
His teaching will be *true:*
For truly my words are not false (v. 4).
His teaching will be *comprehensive* and *sincere:*
One who is perfect in knowledge is with you (v. 4).

Critics come down hard on Elihu's final claim to be *"perfect in knowledge."* His choice of words is unfortunate because he does not mean that he shares the omniscience of God. Still, there is reason to believe that his youthful self-confidence has gotten out of hand. To assume that his knowledge has the quality of "wholeness" implied in the word *perfect* seems to run counter to his promise of humility. *Sincere* is a far better word because it implies that he will speak the truth as he knows it without pretense or manipulation. To claim to know the whole truth puts Elihu in the camp of Eliphaz, Bildad, and Zophar, but to attest his sincerity separates him from the gymnastic twists of truth at which they were so agile.

Every person who teaches has something to learn from the professor who concluded a distinguished classroom career with a confession to his students. "Half of what I have taught you will be untrue in ten years," the professor said, "and to be honest, I have no idea which half it is." While those who teach the Word of God are assured of its unchanging nature, we must confess that our interpretation of the Word can be tainted by the bias of our humanity and the color of our culture. Some years ago, a preacher opposed men wearing neckties because they were "superfluous adornment" and a sign of pride. From the pulpit, he pronounced, "If you ever see me wearing a necktie, you will know that I am on my way to hell." A picture in my memory sees that man in his casket, wearing a dark blue four-in-hand tie, which he traded for the clerical collar several years before his death. As I paid my last respects to a good and faithful servant of Christ, the thought crossed my mind, "I'm glad that God doesn't take seriously everything that we preach as His truth. He has to have a sense of humor."

Reviewing his subject. Critics of Elihu use this passage as proof that he does nothing more than rework the wornout arguments of his three elder friends in defense of the justice of God. They are right, except that Elihu argues that God's purpose with those who suffer is not limited to retribution for sin, the position that Eliphaz, Bildad, and Zophar held so tenaciously. Elihu adds, *"He also opens their ear to instruction"* (v. 10).

If teaching is a purpose of God in suffering, it is essential that Elihu restate the case made by his friends with the insertion of this new element of truth. Rather than being just a youthful mimic of what he has heard from his elders, Elihu demonstrates a major principle of good teaching and learning, namely, review and repetition.

When I was a high-school principal, students often came for counsel on study habits. The simple formula "SQR-3" was recommended to them:

S = Study
Q = Question
R = Review
3 = Repeat three times.

Review and repetition are essential to sound learning. Therefore, as a teacher and an educator, Elihu's review and repetition of the case defending God's justice in a *teaching* rather than a *preaching* tone affirm his skills and help refute the charge that he is arrogant.

To refresh our own memory, Elihu's review follows this outline:

1. *God is mighty, but in His strength . . .*
   a. He despises no one (v. 5);
   b. He has understanding (v. 5);
   c. He does not preserve the wicked (v. 6); and
   d. He gives justice to the oppressed (v. 6).
2. *God watches and exalts the righteous* (v. 7), *but if they are afflicted* (v. 8) . . .
   a. He shows them their sin (v. 9);
   b. He opens their ear to instruction (v. 10); and
   c. He commands them to repent (v. 10).
3. *The righteous who suffer have a choice* (vv. 11–12) . . .
   a. if they obey and serve God, they will have prosperity and pleasure (v. 11); or
   b. if they do not obey God, they will perish by the sword and die without knowledge (v. 12).

In an awkward way, Elihu is struggling to move the argument from God's power through the teaching of suffering to God's goodness. The weight of his words is tipped toward the God who cares, watches, and teaches in order to reward those who obey and serve Him, rather than the God who is distant, indifferent, and swift-acting upon those who are wicked. Elihu's anger appears to have subsided, and, with the mellowing of the Spirit, we sense that he is not just preparing the way for God to speak to Job but he is gaining spiritual insights of his own.

Motivating his student. To this point, Job has remained untouched by the accusations of Eliphaz, Bildad, and Zophar. He has denied that he has any need that requires confession and submission before God. Without the need to be taught, Job has nothing to learn. Elihu knows, therefore, that he must create the need in Job as the motivation for learning what God wants to teach him.

In the teaching-learning process, motivation is the difference between success and failure. A master teacher with all the resources and the most favorable conditions for learning will fail unless the student is motivated by a need to learn. Conversely, strongly motivate a student and he or she will find a way to learn despite the circumstances. Every child of my generation heard the story of Abraham Lincoln borrowing books to read by candlelight, with snow and cold coming through the chinks in the log cabin's roof. For me the motivation worked. I was inspired to read by the promise of the great American dream that I, too, could become president!

Motivation is a highly personalized matter. Some people respond to praise; others to criticism. A master teacher knows each student well enough to personalize the motivation for learning. One study in education, for instance, shows that grades serve to motivate or discourage students with different personalities. If two students stand in the borderline between an A and B, the tendency of the teacher is to give them a B+ rather than an A– in order to motivate them to work harder. The study shows that an extroverted and aggressive student will take the challenge and work harder to get an A on the next report card. An introverted student who lacks self-confidence, however, will interpret the lower grade as a defeat and give up. Likewise, aggressive students respond to lofty, long-term goals that seem to be out of reach, while nonaggressive students need more manageable short-term goals for their success. With all students, however, there is one overriding principle: *appropriate praise is the most effective motivator for positive learning.*

Elihu is not so gentle with Job. While lifting the heavy hand of negative accusation that has failed to work with Job, he does not hesitate to use criticism to create a need for learning. Elihu's approach is consistent with everything that we know about the personality of Job—disciplined in righteousness, daring in business, dominant in family, and dauntless in spirit. Who else would have the nerve to confront God with an oath of innocence? A tough-minded man needs a tough-minded challenge.

Elihu's warnings are tough. He warns Job about the consequences of storing up wrath and harboring spite in his heart (v. 13). Spite can be a barrier, he says, against crying out for help and a catalyst for early death and perversion (v. 14). His warning, as severe as it may seem, is consistent with what we know about the psychology of bitterness. Persons can be literally "eaten up"—physically, emotionally, and morally—by hatred.

Another warning is given by Elihu when he sounds the alarm on Job's compulsion to make judgments as if he were God Himself (v. 17). According to Elihu, this is the attitude that has stopped God from delivering Job (v. 16) and the attitude that will make it impossible for God to redeem him (v. 18). Worse yet, God's justice will require His wrath to wipe out such an arrogant soul (v. 18).

The key to Elihu's warning comes next. Job's *self-sufficiency* is the reason why God can not teach him,

> *Will your riches,*
> *Or all the mighty forces,*
> *Keep you from distress?* (v. 19).

Job's refusal to cry for help, his penchant for pronouncing judgment, and his wealth and power are interpreted by Elihu as evidence of his self-sufficiency, which must be broken before God can lead him out into new knowledge and wisdom. Elihu pleads with Job not to desire death, which will mean the end of learning, or choose the way of the wicked as the alternative for affliction (vv. 20–21). Instead, he recesses the first session by leaving Job with three open questions to ponder about the power and the goodness of God:

> *Who teaches like Him?*
> *Who has assigned Him His way?*
> *Or who has said, "You have done wrong"?* (v. 22–23).

Through the mind of the Spirit in these three questions, Elihu has presented the learning plan from which God will teach.

On the Goodness of God

To conclude his case, Elihu breaks into a hymn of praise to the God of creation. Nature reveals the consistency of His mysterious ways. Autumn, with its rain and thunder, and winter, with its snow and storms, speak the goodness and justice of God. All lead to summer, when clear skies and warm sun leave no doubt about God's good purpose in the world.

> 24 "Remember to magnify His work,
> Of which men have sung.

25 Everyone has seen it;
Man looks on it from afar.
26 "Behold, God is great, and we do not know Him;
Nor can the number of His years be discovered.
27 For He draws up drops of water,
Which distill as rain from the mist,
28 Which the clouds drop down
And pour abundantly on man.
29 Indeed, can anyone understand the spreading of clouds,
The thunder from His canopy?
30 Look, He scatters His light upon it,
And covers the depths of the sea.
31 For by these He judges the peoples;
He gives food in abundance.
32 He covers His hands with lightning,
And commands it to strike.
33 His thunder declares it,
The cattle also, concerning the rising storm.
37:1 "At this also my heart trembles,
And leaps from its place.
2 Hear attentively the thunder of His voice,
And the rumbling that comes from His mouth.
3 He sends it forth under the whole heaven,
His lightning to the ends of the earth.
4 After it a voice roars;
He thunders with His majestic voice,
And He does not restrain them when His voice is heard.
5 God thunders marvelously with His voice;
He does great things which we cannot comprehend.
6 For He says to the snow, 'Fall on the earth';
Likewise to the gentle rain and the heavy rain of His strength.
7 He seals the hand of every man,
That all men may know His work.
8 The beasts go into dens,
And remain in their lairs.
9 From the chamber of the south comes the whirlwind,
And cold from the scattering winds of the north.

10 By the breath of God ice is given,
And the broad waters are frozen.
11 Also with moisture He saturates the thick clouds;
He scatters His bright clouds.
12 And they swirl about, being turned by His guidance,
That they may do whatever He commands them
On the face of the whole earth.
13 He causes it to come,
Whether for correction,
Or for His land,
Or for mercy.
14 "Listen to this, O Job;
Stand still and consider the wondrous works of God.
15 Do you know when God dispatches them,
And causes the light of His cloud to shine?
16 Do you know how the clouds are balanced,
Those wondrous works of Him who is perfect in knowledge?
17 Why are your garments hot,
When He quiets the earth by the south wind?
18 With Him, have you spread out the skies,
Strong as a cast metal mirror?
19 "Teach us what we should say to Him,
For we can prepare nothing because of the darkness.
20 Should He be told that I wish to speak?
If a man were to speak, surely he would be swallowed up.
21 Even now men cannot look at the light when it is bright in the skies,
When the wind has passed and cleared them.
22 He comes from the north as golden splendor;
With God is awesome majesty.
23 As for the Almighty, we cannot find Him;
He is excellent in power,
In judgment and abundant justice;
He does not oppress.
24 Therefore men fear Him;
He shows no partiality to any who are wise of heart."

Job 36:24—37:24

Session 2: Learning from the Greatness of God

A good teacher leaves time in the class period for questions and answers. Elihu concludes his first session with three questions for Job:

> Who teaches like Him?
> Who has assigned Him His way?
> Or who has said, "You have done
> wrong"? (36:22–23).

There is a pause. Elihu waits for Job's answer or rebuttal. His student remains silent.

Questions are the most delicate and effective instrument in the teaching-learning process. Poor teachers ask only rhetorical or closed-ended questions. The answer is obvious and there is no alternative for discussion. Master teachers, however, bring learning alive with open-ended questions that invite the exploration of alternatives and advance the learning process. Elihu's test questions at the close of session one are both open and closed. For example, he asks, *"Who teaches like Him?"* The only answer is *no one.* Yet, at the same time, Elihu is asking Job to open himself to the instruction of God.

A question is also a compliment to the mental ability of the learner. By leaving Job with questions rather than pronouncements, Elihu is inviting him to continue thinking about the subject and urging him to keep the field of inquiry open for the advanced lesson that is to come.

Job neither answers Elihu's questions nor refutes them. His silence may well speak his willingness to learn. At least that is what Elihu presumes as he moves into a more advanced lesson on God's purpose in human suffering.

Advancing his subject. In his first lesson, Elihu talked about the teaching of God in the context of His mighty power (36:5, 22). He now advances to the lesson that God teaches about suffering in His majestic works. Beginning with a proverb that Job would recognize and with which they would both agree, Elihu introduces his subject:

> *Remember to magnify His work,*
> *Of which men have sung.*

Everyone has seen it;
Man looks on it from afar (vv. 24–25).

Again, Elihu demonstrates his skill in teaching by citing the sources for his lesson. God's work is magnified in the hymns of praise that people sing, in the created universe that they see, and in the history records that they read or hear. From the beginning to the end of the Scriptures, there are *hymns of praise* magnifying the work of God. After Moses served as a file-leader for the children of Israel crossing the Red Sea, on the other side he became a song-leader for the nation in a hymn that begins,

I will sing to the LORD,
For He has triumphed gloriously! (Exod. 15:1).

In heaven, at the end of time, the bride of Christ will again sing the song of Moses, which has now become the song of the Lamb, beginning with the words,

Great and marvelous are Your works,
Lord God Almighty! (Rev. 15:3).

Hymns of praise are first and foremost in our witness to the work of God. Someone once said, "Let me write the songs for your people and I'll let you write their history." At the heart of American history, for instance, there is a hymn. After the Pilgrims survived their first disastrous winter in Plymouth Colony and reaped the harvest of their first planting, they walked through the golden fields of ripened corn, singing Psalm 24:

The earth is the LORD's,
  and all its fullness,
The world and those who dwell therein.
For He has founded it upon the seas,
And established it upon the waters (Ps. 24:1–2).

Creation itself is cited by Elihu as another learning resource that God uses to teach His ways. Whereas hymns of praise are sung only by those who exalt God, the works of creation are universal—seen by everyone in every generation. Elihu's insight coincides with the revelation given to the apostle Paul in his letter to the Roman church, "For since the creation of the world His invisible attributes are clearly seen, being understood by the things that are made, even His eternal power and Godhead, so that they are without excuse" (Rom. 1:20).

Human history joins the hymns of praise and the wonders of creation as a learning resource for teaching the meaning of God's majestic works. Since the beginning of time, people have kept a record of events that represent the rise and fall of their tribes, families, nations, cultures, and civilizations. Recognizing the evidence of history, whether transmitted by stories, artifacts, or written records, Elihu says, *"Man looks on it from afar"* (v. 25).

The word *"afar"* is the same word that Elihu uses to introduce his authority for giving this final speech. In each case, he is referring to a time perspective that reaches back into the ancient past and provides the accumulated evidence of God's work in human affairs. History is the antidote for repeating the errors of the past and interpreting the meaning of movements over a period of time. Sorry to say, human beings are slow learners. In the arms race, for instance, each new defense weapon against nuclear attack becomes a challenge for the superpowers to find an offensive weapon that will beat the system. Human history confirms human depravity. Each step of so phistication in military weapons has not taken us away from war but closer to annihilation. Throughout the same human history, however, the thread of redemption can also be traced. In the midst of gross sin, there is evidence of God's abounding grace; out of bitter hatred, there are facts of God's expanding love; against the prevailing pessimism, there is the evidence of God's pervading hope.

Out of my memory comes the story of an agnostic scientist. A friend tried to lead him to Christ, but failed. One day, the scientist showed his Christian friend his experiment with ants in a sandbox. To trace the ants' ability to search for food, the scientist put some bread crumbs in the corner of the sandbox that was opposite their anthill. Tortuously, the ants crisscrossed the dunes until they finally found the food. The scientist then moved the food to another corner directly on the diagonal from the anthill. Once again, the ants started retracing the maze that they had made on their first successful venture rather than taking the shortcut across the center of the sandbox. Finding no food in the original corner, they started their random search until they finally found it. Then, the scientist placed the next store of food just over a mound in the same corner as their anthill, but opposite the direction of their first march. Sure enough, the ants started out on their old path; failing to find food in the first corner, they retraced their steps to the second corner, found no food, and turned once again to the random hunt.

At this point, the scientist felt the frustration of seeing the ants struggle so hard when the food was so close at hand. He doubled his fists, gritted his teeth, and exclaimed, "Oh, if only I could show them the way!" The scientist's frustration gave his Christian friend the opening for which he had prayed. He explained that human history represented man's frustrating and often fruitless search for God, retracing old steps and repeating old sins. But, he said, God felt just as the scientist did while watching the human scene. While the scientist could do nothing about the ants' futility, his friend said that God in love sent His Son, Christ, to show us the way.

History, then, is the learning resource based upon experiential knowledge. It joins the intuitive knowledge that breaks forth into song and the empirical knowledge that comes from the observation of natural creation. Elihu says that each of these "ways of knowing" confirms the majesty of God's work. As a good teacher, Elihu does not limit his authority to a single source or a single way of knowing. In today's terms, he has established a liberal arts curriculum for his teaching. Hymns rising out of intuition represent the fine arts and the humanities, observations of creation represent the natural sciences, and historical description of human experience represent the social sciences. Without doubt, Elihu comes to his subject with breadth of field and depth of authority.

Illustrating his lesson. From among his three sources that reveal God's magnificent works, Elihu chooses the wonders of creation. Darkening skies, distant thunder, lightning flashes, and humid air turn his outdoor classroom into one grand audio-visual learning experience. Theoretically, Elihu says, God is so great that we cannot know or understand Him (36:26, 29). But wait. Perhaps pointing to the raindrops that are falling on their heads (vv. 27–28), he notes that every drop of rain, every pattern of clouds, every bolt of lightning, and every clap of thunder are expressions of God's creative power. Calling on his student's most vivid imagination, Elihu personifies the thunder as God's voice and the lightning as bolts in His hands. Rather than striking fear into the heart, the events of nature should lend confidence to the soul. See them, he says, as the symbols that God uses to communicate His character to His human creation. David wrote psalm after psalm extolling the greatness of God through His creation. Elihu and David might sing as a duet,

> Sing to the LORD with thanksgiving;
> Sing praises on the harp to our God,
> Who covers the heavens with clouds,
> Who prepares rain for the earth,
> Who makes grass to grow on the mountains (Ps. 147:7–8).

To know that God is the creator of all things is the keystone upon which Elihu builds his lesson. His line of thought is shattered, however, by a clap of thunder that leaves him trembling with his heart in his mouth (37:1). But instead of remaining rattled, he uses the interruption to dramatize his next point. Calling his listener's attention to the rumbling (v. 2) and roaring (v. 4) thunder of God's majestic voice, Elihu puts all of creation under the control of divine command. Snow (v. 6), gentle rain (v. 6), heavy rain (v. 6), whirlwind (v. 9), cold wind (v. 9), ice (v. 10), thick clouds (v. 11), and bright clouds (v. 11)—*"They may do whatever He commands them"* (v. 12).

Upon the keystone of knowledge that *God is the creator of all,* Elihu places the building block of truth that *God is in control of all* that He has created. Although it may be too glib, there is comfort in Robert Browning's oft-quoted lines from *Pippa Passes:* "God's on His Throne,/ All's right with the world." Far more profound is the insight of the psalmist who begins with the declaration that all creation is the handiwork of God and all creation responds to the law of the Lord. Thinking beings alone are led by these facts to the confession,

> Let the words of my mouth
> and the meditation of my heart
> Be acceptable in Your sight,
> O LORD, my strength and my
> redeemer (Ps. 19:14).

Perhaps Elihu is leading his student to that end. But for now, he continues to build upon the truth that *God is creator of all* and *controller of all* by adding the premise that *God has cause for it all* (37:13).

For the first time in all of the arguments that have been advanced to defend the justice of God, purpose is assigned to His works beyond rewards and punishments. Still using rain as his symbol for God's self-expression, Elihu states three reasons for God's creation and control of the gentle rain (prolonged suffering) and the wild storm (sudden calamity):

> *Whether for correction,*
> *Or for His land,*
> *Or for mercy* (v. 13).

"Correction" is the obvious and oft-repeated reason advanced by Eliphaz, Bildad, and Zophar. Their thoughts, however, are dominated by the thought of punishment, whereas Elihu has introduced persuasion through teaching as God's preferred method. *"Correction"* may well be a reason for suffering, but it is neither the exclusive nor the automatic reason. Elihu adds a thought that God may cause the rain to come for the good of *"His land"* (v. 13). Scholars disagree on the meaning of *"His land."* Some eliminate it altogether from interpretation, others join it with *"mercy,"* the third reason that Elihu gives for God sending rain upon the earth. My preference is to draw the contrast with *"correction,"* which is synonymous with punishment or teaching, and enlarge the passage to read, "for the love of His land." A new thought is then released, which is still true to the text. God sends the rain to "rescue" the land He loves, and thus returns us to Elihu's Spirit-guided thought in 23:24, when he sees suffering as an opportunity for God to show His grace by ransoming those whom He loves.

"Mercy"—the third cause behind God's creation and control of rain—is equally difficult to interpret. Two tangential meanings are suggested by scholars that compliment Elihu for his Spirit-guided insights. One interpretation is that God sends the rain just for His own good pleasure. If so, humans will never understand His purpose and He owes no one an explanation. The other interpretation, however, ties back to the idea of "covenanted loyalty" between brothers—a test that Eliphaz, Bildad, and Zophar failed according to Job (6:14–15). Now, Elihu may dimly perceive that the cause of Job's suffering

may be a "covenanted loyalty" test between God and Job that Satan has provoked. Job, himself, has already had a similar insight when he said,

> "But He knows the way that I take;
> When He has tested me,
> I shall come forth as gold" (23:10).

So, restating Elihu's reasons for suffering, they are to *correct those who have gone astray, rescue those whom God loves,* and *test the loyalty of persons who are in covenant relationship with God.* As in taking a multiple-choice test, we may need to answer "all of the above" to explain suffering; or we may still have to mark the box designated "I don't know." At least Elihu has increased the options and enlarged the field of our understanding.

Questioning his student. Elihu has made his point. It is time to test his student. Like a teacher asking Job to stand at attention, Elihu fires a series of questions that would make Socrates proud. In paraphrase, they are:

> Do you know *when* God dispatches
> His wondrous works? (37:15).
> Do you know *what* causes the light
> in His clouds to shine? (v. 15).
> Do you know *how* the clouds
> are balanced? (v. 16).
> Do you know *why* your garments
> are hot? (v. 17).
> Do you know *when* He quiets
> the earth with a south wind? (v. 17).
> Do you know *who* spreads out
> the skies? (v. 18).

A teacher's heart tingles with excitement when the full range of *when, what, how, why,* and *who* questions are asked. Good testing is always comprehensive and challenging. Once again, Elihu is commended as a person who speaks with the "breath of the Almighty." One is reminded of Jesus' promise, that when the Holy Spirit comes, "He will guide you into all truth" (John 16:13). By asking these critical, comprehensive, and challenging questions, Elihu passes the test of a good teacher who has the mind of the Spirit.

Applying his lesson. True to the form of good teaching, Elihu suggests that the time has come for their roles to be reversed: *"Teach us what we should say to Him"* (37:19). Job, however, has been struck dumb with the fear that he would be swallowed up by the power of God if he dared to speak again. Yet there is hope. Evidently, the storm is past and Elihu remarks on the bright, calm, and clear skies (v. 21), which are accented by the golden splendor of the north, perhaps the aurora borealis. *"Awesome"* and *"excellent"* are the words that leap to his lips as he sees in the golden splendor of the sky the unsurpassed glory of God, which hides His face but reveals His presence. Elihu thus brings Job full cycle to his own confession.

> "Behold, the fear of the Lord,
> that is wisdom,
> And to depart from evil is
> understanding" (28:28).

But more than that, Elihu denies that the *"wise of heart"* are those who gain God's favor (37:24). Now, we know Elihu's purpose in utilizing all his gifts as a master teacher. He has banished the half-god of human reason. Here he stops. God Himself will have to come to complete the lesson.

NOTES

1. G. A. Studdert-Kennedy, "Indifference," *The Best of G. A. Studdert-Kennedy* (New York: Harper and Bros., 1924), p. 15.
2. Jacques Ellul, *The Technological Society* (New York: Alfred A. Knopf, 1967).
3. E. Herman, *Creative Prayer* (Cincinnati: Forward Movement Miniatures, n.d.), p. 114.
4. Andrew Watterson Blackwood, ed., *The Protestant Pulpit* (Abingdon-Cokesbury Press, 1947), p. 116.
5. Ibid., p. 118.

CHAPTER EIGHT

God's Revelation/Job's Repentance

Job 38:1—42:6

In answer to Job's plea, God speaks, but in His own time and way. Rather than entering the fray as one of the disputants, God comes as God—speaking out of the whirlwind about the mystery of the universe. His first speech challenges Job to understand and to participate in the creation of the natural universe. Acknowledging his impotence and admitting his ignorance, Job submits in silence.

God's second speech begins with the admission that there are margins of sin and suffering that appear to be out of His control. Yet, these are the areas covered by the mystery of His grace in the creation of living things. As proof, He presents the leviathan and the behemoth, two of the most ludicrous—or better yet, comical—creatures of God's creation. Still, God loves them, cares for them, and finds joy in them. A higher level of faith breaks through for Job. For the first time, he sees the God of grace, who is not only just but loving and caring. Job is reconciled with God and ready for healing.

God—The Mystery of Creation

God does not directly answer any of the issues in the debate. He has no need to defend Himself. He does, however, obliquely address Job's initial question *why* from the perspective of His power at work in the natural universe. Does Job have the power to create and to understand heaven and earth, stars and sea, morning and night, light and darkness, snow and hail, flood and lightning, rain, dew, frost, and clouds? To think that these are the "mere edges" of God's power! Job is overwhelmed.

Without waiting for an answer, God adds the mystery of His living creation—the lion's cub, the mountain goat, the wild ass, the buffalo, the ostrich, the horse, the hawk, and the falcon. They are God's glory and in His care. Confessing that he is impotent and ignorant before the mystery of creation, Job repents with the realization that he cannot judge God or understand the moral order of the universe.

38:1 Then the LORD answered Job out of the whirlwind, and said:
2 "Who is this who darkens counsel
By words without knowledge?
3 Now prepare yourself like a man;
I will question you, and you shall answer Me.
4 "Where were you when I laid the foundations of the earth?
Tell Me, if you have understanding.
5 Who determined its measurements?
Surely you know!
Or who stretched the line upon it?
6 To what were its foundations fastened?
Or who laid its cornerstone,
7 When the morning stars sang together,
And all the sons of God shouted for joy?
8 "Or who shut in the sea with doors,
When it burst forth and issued from the womb;
9 When I made the clouds its garment,
And thick darkness its swaddling band;
10 When I fixed My limit for it,
And set bars and doors;
11 When I said,
'This far you may come, but no farther,
And here your proud waves must stop!'
12 "Have you commanded the morning since your days began,
And caused the dawn to know its place,
13 That it might take hold of the ends of the earth,
And the wicked be shaken out of it?
14 It takes on form like clay under a seal,
And stands out like a garment.
15 From the wicked their light is withheld,
And the upraised arm is broken.
16 "Have you entered the springs of the sea?
Or have you walked in search of the depths?
17 Have the gates of death been revealed to you?

Or have you seen the doors of the shadow of death?
18 Have you comprehended the breadth of the earth?
Tell Me, if you know all this.
19 "Where is the way to the dwelling of light?
And darkness, where is its place,
20 That you may take it to its territory,
That you may know the paths to its home?
21 Do you know it, because you were born then,
Or because the number of your days is great?
22 "Have you entered the treasury of snow,
Or have you seen the treasury of hail,
23 Which I have reserved for the time of trouble,
For the day of battle and war?
24 By what way is light diffused,
Or the east wind scattered over the earth?
25 "Who has divided a channel for the overflowing water,
Or a path for the thunderbolt,
26 To cause it to rain on a land where there is no one,
A wilderness in which there is no man;
27 To satisfy the desolate waste,
And cause to spring forth the growth of tender grass?
28 Has the rain a father?
Or who has begotten the drops of dew?
29 From whose womb comes the ice?
And the frost of heaven, who gives it birth?
30 The waters harden like stone,
And the surface of the deep is frozen.
31 "Can you bind the cluster of the Pleiades,
Or loose the belt of Orion?
32 Can you bring out Mazzaroth in its season?
Or can you guide the Great Bear with its cubs?
33 Do you know the ordinances of the heavens?
Can you set their dominion over the earth?
34 "Can you lift up your voice to the clouds,
That an abundance of water may cover you?
35 Can you send out lightnings, that they may go,
And say to you, 'Here we are!'?

36 Who has put wisdom in the mind?
Or who has given understanding to the heart?
37 Who can number the clouds by wisdom?
Or who can pour out the bottles of heaven,
38 When the dust hardens in clumps,
And the clods cling together?
39 "Can you hunt the prey for the lion,
Or satisfy the appetite of the young lions,
40 When they crouch in their dens,
Or lurk in their lairs to lie in wait?
41 Who provides food for the raven,
When its young ones cry to God,
And wander about for lack of food?
39:1 "Do you know the time when the wild mountain goats bear young?
Or can you mark when the deer gives birth?
2 Can you number the months that they fulfill?
Or do you know the time when they bear young?
3 They bow down,
They bring forth their young,
They deliver their offspring.
4 Their young ones are healthy,
They grow strong with grain;
They depart and do not return to them.
5 "Who set the wild donkey free?
Who loosed the bonds of the onager,
6 Whose home I have made the wilderness,
And the barren land his dwelling?
7 He scorns the tumult of the city;
He does not heed the shouts of the driver.
8 The range of the mountains is his pasture,
And he searches after every green thing.
9 "Will the wild ox be willing to serve you?
Will he bed by your manger?
10 Can you bind the wild ox in the furrow with ropes?
Or will he plow the valleys behind you?
11 Will you trust him because his strength is great?
Or will you leave your labor to him?
12 Will you trust him to bring home your grain,
And gather it to your threshing floor?

13 "The wings of the ostrich wave proudly,
But are her wings and pinions like the kindly stork's?
14 For she leaves her eggs on the ground,
And warms them in the dust;
15 She forgets that a foot may crush them,
Or that a wild beast may break them.
16 She treats her young harshly, as though they were not hers;
Her labor is in vain, without concern,
17 Because God deprived her of wisdom,
And did not endow her with understanding.
18 When she lifts herself on high,
She scorns the horse and its rider.
19 "Have you given the horse strength?
Have you clothed his neck with thunder?
20 Can you frighten him like a locust?
His majestic snorting strikes terror.
21 He paws in the valley, and rejoices in his strength;
He gallops into the clash of arms.
22 He mocks at fear, and is not frightened;
Nor does he turn back from the sword.
23 The quiver rattles against him,
The glittering spear and javelin.
24 He devours the distance with fierceness and rage;
Nor does he come to a halt because the trumpet has sounded.
25 At the blast of the trumpet he says, 'Aha!'
He smells the battle from afar,
The thunder of captains and shouting.
26 "Does the hawk fly by your wisdom,
And spread its wings toward the south?
27 Does the eagle mount up at your command,
And make its nest on high?
28 On the rock it dwells and resides,
On the crag of the rock and the stronghold.
29 From there it spies out the prey;
Its eyes observe from afar.
30 Its young ones suck up blood;
And where the slain are, there it is."

Job 38:1—39:30

Out of the Whirlwind

At last! The Lord comes. All of us who have felt the tedium and the tension, the anguish and the anger, the doggedness and despair of the Jobian drama—we are more than ready for God to speak.

The setting is significant. Elihu has concluded his speeches in one of those treasured moments after a storm when the splendor of a golden calm bathes the soul in glowing hope. Then, like an intruder in the tranquility, an isolated whirlwind spirals into view, sending tumbleweeds end over end in its wake.

Whirlwinds in the desert are not out of place. On the barren stretch of sand between Needles, California, and Hoover Dam, Nevada, the air burns with temperatures above one hundred and twenty degrees in the summertime. But against the visible waves of thermal heat, you can see the dust-filled cones of whirlwinds dipping and dancing over the desert floor. At one and the same time, they are partners with the desert, yet independent of it. God comes to us the same way—in sequence with our surroundings, but also with surprise. A burning bush, a ladder of angels, a still, small voice, a wheel in a wheel, a lofty throne, a solar eclipse, a sheet filled with animals, a trumpet sound—all announce the coming of the Lord. To our chagrin, God seldom, if ever, comes the same way twice. Attempts to fix the way He comes as doctrinally correct or spiritually superior are to put God in a box from which He will inevitably escape. Certainly, God does not come as Job expects. He tried to arraign God's appearance in a somber and orderly courtroom setting. Instead, he gets the sound of fury and the spin of chaos in a whirlwind.

Once again, we must stop to give credit to Elihu's claim that he spoke with the "voice of the Almighty." While the whirlwind out of which God spoke seems to come as an interruption, the actual transition is more like a natural line of progression from one scene to another. *"Then the* LORD *answered Job out of the whirlwind"* (38:1) suggests that Elihu prepared the way for God, and the voice of God followed in natural sequence with the voice of Elihu.

How much this sequence is like the role of the preacher in the pulpit. The sermon may begin with the sound of a human voice but only in preparation for the voice of God. As we say to our seminarians, "You do not preach until another Voice is heard." Elihu served the Spirit well.

God knows how to get our attention. How often have you heard the story about the soft-spoken Quaker who tamed a recalcitrant mule by hitting him over the head with a two-by-four? When asked to explain the contradiction between his violent act and pacifistic personality, the Quaker explained that before you can train a mule, "Thee must first get his attention." As a boy growing up, I remember just the opposite kind of training. My father never spanked or threatened me. One silent look from his eyes struck fear into my heart, stopped my protest, changed my direction, and modified my behavior. God has that same sensitivity to our individuality. Pompous, wordy, and defiant—Job needs a whirlwind.

So, like a voice out of a windstorm, God confronts Job with a question that arrests, indicts, tries, convicts, and sentences him:

Who is this who darkens counsel
By words without knowledge? (v. 2).

Job has spoken as if his innocence gives him direct access to the mind of God and as if his wisdom earns him an explanation from God. His greatest fault, however, is to presume that his own finite mind can comprehend the infinite mind of God. With such presumption, Job has been staggering along the borderline between limiting God's power and denying His justice. Notably, God does not condemn him for sin. Instead, He chides him for throwing up a barrage of empty words about a subject beyond his knowledge. *"Words without knowledge"* only smog the sky and keep him from seeing through to God's purpose.

The image of ack-ack guns, sending up a skyful of flak to protect the cities of London and Berlin during World War II, comes to mind. As an admission that the aircraft gunners could not turn back the invaders by aiming at the hundreds of planes droning over the cities, the defenders resorted to a strategy of desperation by shooting up a screen of smoke and shrapnel through which the bombers had to fly. Hits came by a gambler's chance rather than a gunner's aim.

God sees Job's words as a similar tactic. Bombarded by suffering beyond his comprehension or control, Job sends a screen of verbal scattershot to defend his ignorance and his impotence. Because his faith is too small to cover the contingency of the innocent suffering, Job projects the blame on God and, in so doing, creates a shadow of darkness over the mind of God through which he cannot see.

Words are a common defense for our insecurity. In an interview with a prospective field representative for a Christian organization, I asked one simple question that triggered a veritable fifteen-minute barrage of words. Only by interrupting could I ask a second question. Another fifteen-minute fusillade followed. The prospect missed all of the cues I gave—shifting in my seat, leaning forward as if to ask another question, raising a hand to make a suggestion, and even pleading *stop* with my eyes. Finally, a colleague inserted his own question. I almost choked with laughter when he asked in a matter-of-fact tone, "How do you rate yourself as a listener?" The candidate blushed red as if to understand and answered, "It is an area I have to work on." Then, believe it or not, with hardly a breath, he went on for another ten minutes until my impatience got the best of me, and I concluded the interview by standing up, shaking his hand, and saying, "Thank you for coming." More unbelievable yet, when he got his letter of rejection, he wrote back to ask, "What did I do wrong?" He failed to see that in representing the organization with friends in the field his verbiage would throw up a dark screen through which the purpose of a spiritual ministry could not be seen.

Was I unfair in not saying to the wordy candidate, "You talk too much?" God does not hesitate to confront Job bluntly about the same problem. He does not "swallow him up" as Job feared. Instead, He comes down to Job's level, meets him where he is, and adopts his tactic of asking questions. The gauntlet falls as God takes the initiative:

> Now prepare yourself like a man;
> I will question you,
> and you shall answer Me (38:3; 40:7).

Job has challenged God; now it is God's turn to challenge Job. He will test his knowledge and push his wisdom to its outer limits. God will be like the professor who told his class at examination time, "If anyone gets 100 percent on my test, it means that I have not examined the limits of your knowledge." God says the same thing to Job, "I will test the limits of your knowledge." *Creation* is the theme of the test and three specific questions are asked of Job:

1. Do you know the *sources* from which the universe began? (38:4–21).

2. Do you understand the *systems* upon which the earth depends? (38:22–38).

3. Do you appreciate the *specialties* by which the animals are distinguished? (38:39–39:30).

None of the questions purports to answer the ethical issues for which Job demands a response. Evidently, God has something else in mind.

Do You Know the Sources from Which the Universe Began?

With unsurpassed poetic beauty, God opens the examination with a series of questions about His work as the architect and engineer of the universe:

> *Where were you when I laid the foundations of the earth?* (38:4)
> *Or who shut in the sea with doors?* (v. 8)
> *Have you commanded the morning since your days began,*
> *And caused the dawn to know its place?* (v. 12)
> *Have you entered the springs of the sea?* (v. 16)
> *Where is the way to the dwelling of light?* (v. 19)

Time collapses on Job. His beginning does not precede the Creator of the universe. His existence does not give him power to limit the sea, command the dawn, probe the underworld, or discover the source of light. Yet, Job has asked the question *why* about his suffering. It is a legitimate question because it arises from his God-given curiosity. To ask *why* is to inquire about the "first cause" of creation. To know the answer is to be God Himself. Therefore, if the question *why* is twisted into Satan's promise that Adam and Eve can be as wise as God, natural curiosity can lead to sin and death.

Robert Oppenheimer, reputed to be the father of the atomic bomb, followed the scientist's curiosity when he said of the bomb, "It was so technologically sweet, it had to be invented." But after he heard about the devastation of Hiroshima when the bomb was dropped, he declared, "The physicists have known sin."

As the "Intermediate Adam," Job's curiosity has taken him into the same temptation. By demanding that God explain his suffering, Job assumes that he can be as wise as God. His first lesson must be that he is a created being with a brief history in time and space. As represented by the origins of the universe, Job will have to accept the tension of being able to ask *why* without the privilege of knowing all the answers. God is asking Job to trust Him.

Do You Understand the Systems upon Which the Earth Depends?

Without a pause, God's questions flow into a recital of the seasons of the earth. Winter's snow and hail fall as a time of trouble, stopping armies in their tracks (vv. 22–23). Spring floods followed by summer's thunderstorms bring rain to a parched land (vv. 26–27). In one case, God uses the snow and hail for the purpose of stopping war. In the other case, He brings rain to the wasteland to grow green grass for no apparent reason at all, except for His own good pleasure.

Behind the question *why* is always the question *how.* Sin is more than the desire to be as wise as God; it is also the urge to be as powerful as God. If the cause of suffering, for instance, can be broken down into explainable pieces, it is assumed that solutions can be found to control the problem. This is the path of scientific process that has made miracles so common among us. God is not condemning science by His questions about the systems of the earth which remain a mystery to the human mind and ultimately out of human control. He is saying that the human mind can take the world apart, but it cannot put it back together again.

Fred Smith, one of the most creative of Christian minds in this century, heard a well-known philosopher say, "Whatever man can undo, man can do." Fred answered, "I'd like to break an egg over his head and say, 'Now you *do* what I have *undone.*' " Like the good theology in the nursery rhyme of Humpty-Dumpty's fall, all of the king's horses and all of the king's men cannot put that delicate shell back together again.

The mystery of the control of creation is further illustrated by the answer a panel of economists gave to the moderator's final question on a television program, "What is the greatest influence upon the world economy?" As one, the economists answered, "The weather." After all of our efforts to manage money and stock markets in order to control the economy, the honest confession is that the weather—a factor completely out of human control—will determine bull markets and bear markets, prosperity and depression, deficits and surpluses.

The lesson is that God is in control of what he creates. Job cannot understand *why* God controls His creation as He does any more than Job can comprehend creation itself. To believe in God is to live with mystery. Yet, God assures Job that the seasons do not come and go by whimsy. The movements of the celestial constellations—Pleiades, Orion, Mazzaroth, the Great Bear (vv. 31–33)—are bound, freed, started, and guided at His command to control the seasons of the earth. In between the heavens and the earth, there are the clouds that contain the water, rain, and electricity for lightning—falling and flashing upon His command. Is it possible what God is bringing to Job's mind is the lightning that caused the fire, killing his sheep and his servants in the first round of Job's catastrophes? Is there any connection in the fact that God is speaking out of a whirlwind, the very force of nature that took the lives of his children? If so, God is not saying that He caused their deaths, but He is saying that the lightning was not out of His control.

A fine line of mystery divides creation, control, and causation in human suffering. If God is the Creator of all and the Controller of all, is He not then the Cause of all, including natural catastrophes and the consequence of human suffering? Insurance companies carry this theology of causation through to their policies, which define natural catastrophes—such as earthquakes, tornadoes, floods, and fire caused by lightning—as "acts of God." According to God's word to Job, they are and they are not. He creates all of the elements of nature and controls them through His laws, but this does not mean ipso facto that God causes them to favor some people and to destroy others. He may, of course, intervene in nature to bring about His blessing or His judgment, but this does not mean that every act of nature can be explained as divine intervention.

Once again, we are suspended in a paradox, best defined as "truth held absurdly." With Job, we must believe that God is the Creator of all, the Controller of all, and the Cause of all, but not the one who intervenes in natural law so that every evidence of prosperity or punishment can be interpreted as a cause-and-effect relationship initiated by God. This was the fatal trap into which Eliphaz, Bildad, and Zophar fell. They insisted that human reason could understand everything that happens to human beings by applying the cause-and-effect formula in which God automatically rewards justice and punishes wickedness. No room is left for God's grace or mankind's faith.

Do You Appreciate the Speciality by Which Animals Are Distinguished?

Creation involves three categories, each unique on its own level: *inanimate creation, animate creation,* and *human creation.* The faultline of evolutionary theory is not just the question of origins, Did life begin by intelligent design or random accident? The theory also presumes a continuous line of upward development through the categories of creation. It is assumed that out of inanimate creation came the animals and out of the animals came human beings. No one doubts that animals are made up of chemical elements or that humans share the nervous, respiratory, and visceral systems with animals. But does this mean that each level of creation is a direct extension of the other? The frustrated search for the "missing link" between animals and human beings illustrates the efforts to prove the theory.

In Genesis, the six days draw the lines of distinction among the three categories of creation. Human creation, especially, is singled out when God declares, "Let Us make man in Our image, according to Our likeness" (1:26).

God's creative act is as special as His words. In the complementary account of creation in the second chapter of Genesis, the commonality and the uniqueness of human beings is clearly stated in the scriptural record: "And the LORD God formed man of the dust of the ground, and breathed into his nostrils the breath of life; and man became a living being [soul]" (2:7).

God teaches Job the lesson of special creation with illustrations from the animal kingdom. A dozen different animals are mentioned: lion, raven, goat, onager, deer, donkey, ox, ostrich, horse, locust, hawk, and eagle. Each has the common characteristic of being a living animal, but each is made fearfully and wonderfully different. Lions and ravens are animals that need help in finding food for their young (38:39–41). Lions tend to wait in ambush for their prey to come, while ravens tend to flit around in search of seeds. In both cases, God cares for them.

For the first time in the theophanies of Job, God's care for His creation is specifically introduced. A sequence is unfolding. God is not only the Creator of all, but He cares about each of His created beings. James Herriot must have been inspired when he entitled his books about the animal kingdom—*All Creatures Great and Small, All Things Wise and Wonderful,* and *All Things Bright and Beautiful.*

Centuries earlier, God preceded him in the Book of Job as He creates verbal pictures of the animals He loves—the *unpredictability* of the birthing and development of goats and deer (39:1–4); the *freedom* of the foraging donkey and onager (vv. 5–8); the *stubbornness* of the working ox (vv. 9–12); the *foolishness* of the speeding ostrich (vv. 13–18); the *courage* of the warring horse (vv. 19–25); the *wisdom* of the migrating hawk (v. 26); and the *perspective* of the high-nesting eagle (vv. 27–30).

Note that each animal in God's menagerie is not only unique in itself, but within each animal are complementary gifts and flaws, graces and faults, charms and handicaps. The ostrich, for instance, is at once the fastest and the most foolish of the animal creation. Deprived of the simple wisdom of maternal instinct, she lays her eggs and abandons them. Motherhood is so fundamental with us that we tend to write off the ostrich as a cruel trick of nature and a waste upon the earth. God doesn't think or act as we do. Even in the ostrich, He notes the compensating value of its ability to survive by sheer speed, outrunning the fastest horse and rider.

God is paying Job the greatest compliment that a teacher can give a student. Instead of giving him answers, God only asks questions. Instead of stating conclusions, God presents only the facts. Induction, not deduction, is God's method of teaching. He might have pronounced His conclusion to Job and then presented the supporting facts as a deductive teacher. If He had done so, Job's fear of being "swallowed up" would have been realized. But God shows how much He cares for His creation by refusing to violate Job's freedom or insult his intelligence. He gives him assorted facts and counts upon him to make the connections, see the meaning, and apply his understanding to the next higher and more complex level of learning. Underneath the process, however, God is at work on faith development. Facts and faith go hand in hand. When we have the facts, we need no faith. But when the facts add to the mystery of the unknown, even greater faith is required.

Job has been suffering in the "no-man's-land" between known facts and his unknown future. By demanding that God answer his question *why,* he has assumed that God owes him the facts to explain his affliction and defend divine justice. Inadvertently, Job has started on the path that leads to humanism, agnosticism, and atheism. Nietzsche, the atheist, said, "He who knows the *why* can bear with any *how!*"

Why is the question for which Satan promised the answer to Eve in the Garden. To her, he said, "You will be like God, knowing good and evil" (Gen. 3:5). As the Intermediate Adam, Job is tempted with the same question. Throughout his contest with his friends and his God, he demands answers to the question *why.* In his own way, he feels that his innocence has earned him the right to be as wise as God, knowing good and evil.

God honors Job's spiritual potential as well as his human intelligence by ignoring the question *why* in His response. To answer the question is to speed the human mind down the dead-end street where Nietzsche ran until he hit the wall of atheism, which in turn spawned the atrocities of the Nazi regime. As evidence of His loving care, when Job asks *why* God answers *who.* Faith is never created out of facts that answer the question *why.* Only out of mysteries beyond human comprehension comes the trust in *who.*

JOB—SUBMITTING IN SILENCE

A conundrum begins to clear. "Why," we ask, "does God speak to Job without answering any of his questions?" The answer is that Job is casting a dark shadow between his mind and God's mind with the *why* of ethical questions about his suffering, which the human mind cannot comprehend or understand. We lack the perspective of God's view in *creating* the universe, *controlling* its forces, and *caring* about its creatures. Job needs to learn that the issue is not ethical, the question is not *why,* and the need is not understanding. The issue is spiritual, the question is *who,* and the need is trust.

1 Moreover the LORD answered Job, and said:
2 "Shall the one who contends with the Almighty
  correct Him?
 He who rebukes God, let him answer it."
3 Then Job answered the LORD and said:

4 "Behold, I am vile;
What shall I answer You?
I lay my hand over my mouth.
5 Once I have spoken, but I will not answer;
Yes, twice, but I will proceed no further."

Job 40:1–5

Job has two answers that he didn't expect to give. One is the answer to God's question, *"Who am I?"* He now sees the God who is purposeful in His creation, pervasive in His control, and personal in His care. The answers tell us about the gaps in Job's faith. His suffering has raised hidden doubts about God's purpose in creation, His power of control, and His personal interest in His creatures. At one and the same time, the question *why* reflects Job's deepest fears that all human beings know. Do we have doubts about God's purpose in our lives? Ask *why.* Do we have fears that He may not have control in every facet of our lives? Ask *why.* Do we have concerns about His personal interest in us? Ask *why.* These are the hidden and prior questions of trust that must be answered by an "I-Thou" relationship with God, not by a recitation of facts or reasons.

"Who am I?" is God's way of introducing Himself personally to us. For all his righteousness, Job has not met God in the depth and breadth of a relationship that includes the possibility of unexplained suffering.

The second question that God answers for Job is *"Who are you?"* By showing him the uniqueness of the animal creation and the complementary gifts and gaffs of the individual animals, God let Job draw the inference that he is a special creation of God above and beyond the animals, with untold capability for good and evil that escapes the limits of animal instinct and explores the realm of God's image through human intelligence. Yet with all this potential, human wisdom flounders on the shore of an uncharted ocean. At their best and at their highest, the miracles of human intelligence only open new vistas of mystery that prompt the breathless confession, I don't know, as the true expression of human wisdom. Hulme, in his book on Job entitled *Dialogue in Despair,* tells about a scientist who was asked to describe his research in one hundred fifty words. For his answer, the scientist wrote fifty times the three-word sentence, "I don't know."[1]

Job is a good, quick learner. After God puts question after question to him about His creation, His control, and His care, the challenge is repeated:

Shall the one who contends with the
Almighty correct Him?
He who rebukes God,
let him answer it (40:2).

Job's rehearsed speech, which he planned to give in the presence of God, sticks in his throat. Like Isaiah who saw the Lord high and lifted up, he can only cry,

Behold, I am vile;
What shall I answer You? (v. 4).

The snowman of self-righteousness melts before God in the confession, "I am unworthy," and in the admission, "I don't know." The impotence of Job's righteousness and the ignorance of his wisdom is exposed. Job is reduced to silence—the last thing he expected to do in the presence of God, but the first thing that he needed to do in order to save himself from another flurry of words with which he would try to defend himself.

My father used to tell about the Frenchman who spoke so excitedly with grand and sweeping gestures. "Cut off his hands," my dad said, "and he would be speechless." Job's verbal skills served a similar purpose. Words had become his strategic defense and his offensive weapon. After all, he had reduced Eliphaz, Bildad, and Zophar to silence. Before God, however, he is the one who is reduced to confession and silence. With his hand over his mouth, Job no longer relies on his own weapon of words. He is learning to listen to God, but hearing alone is not healing. God has more to say and Job has more to learn.

God—The Mystery of Grace

God is not yet finished. Passing by Job's repentance, God unveils the mystery of His grace. Two exceptions to the beauty and harmony of the created order are noted. One is the margin of evil that appears to be out of God's control—an apparent exception to His omnipotence. The other is the ridiculous animals—the behemoth or hippopotamus and the leviathan or crocodile—who appear to be out of harmony with the rest of creation. For these exceptions, God's grace is sufficient. For the first time, Job sees his suffering from the perspective of God's view. In a leap of faith, he shouts, "I see"—the beauty of God's power, the harmony of His creation, the justice of His ways, and the sufficiency of His grace. Job is more than reconciled to God—he is redeemed.

6 Then the LORD answered Job out of the whirlwind, and said:
7 "Now prepare yourself like a man;
I will question you, and you shall answer Me:
8 "Would you indeed annul My judgment?
Would you condemn Me that you may be justified?
9 Have you an arm like God?
Or can you thunder with a voice like His?
10 Then adorn yourself with majesty and splendor,
And array yourself with glory and beauty.
11 Disperse the rage of your wrath;
Look on everyone who is proud, and humble him.
12 Look on everyone who is proud, and bring him low;
Tread down the wicked in their place.
13 Hide them in the dust together,
Bind their faces in hidden darkness.
14 Then I will also confess to you
That your own right hand can save you.
15 "Look now at the behemoth, which I made along with you;
He eats grass like an ox.
16 See now, his strength is in his hips,
And his power is in his stomach muscles.
17 He moves his tail like a cedar;
The sinews of his thighs are tightly knit.
18 His bones are like beams of bronze,
His ribs like bars of iron.

19 He is the first of the ways of God;
Only He who made him can bring near His sword.
20 Surely the mountains yield food for him,
And all the beasts of the field play there.
21 He lies under the lotus trees,
In a covert of reeds and marsh.
22 The lotus trees cover him with their shade;
The willows by the brook surround him.
23 Indeed the river may rage,
Yet he is not disturbed;
He is confident, though the Jordan gushes into his mouth,
24 Though he takes it in his eyes,
Or one pierces his nose with a snare.
41:1 "Can you draw out Leviathan with a hook,
Or snare his tongue with a line which you lower?
2 Can you put a reed through his nose,
Or pierce his jaw with a hook?
3 Will he make many supplications to you?
Will he speak softly to you?
4 Will he make a covenant with you?
Will you take him as a servant forever?
5 Will you play with him as with a bird,
Or will you leash him for your maidens?
6 Will your companions make a banquet of him?
Will they apportion him among the merchants?
7 Can you fill his skin with harpoons,
Or his head with fishing spears?
8 Lay your hand on him;
Remember the battle—
Never do it again!
9 Indeed, any hope of overcoming him is false;
Shall one not be overwhelmed at the sight of him?
10 No one is so fierce that he would dare stir him up.
Who then is able to stand against Me?
11 Who has preceded Me, that I should pay him?
Everything under heaven is Mine.
12 "I will not conceal his limbs,
His mighty power, or his graceful proportions.

13 Who can remove his outer coat?
Who can approach him with a double bridle?
14 Who can open the doors of his face,
With his terrible teeth all around?
15 His rows of scales are his pride,
Shut up tightly as with a seal;
16 One is so near another
That no air can come between them;
17 They are joined one to another,
They stick together and cannot be parted.
18 His sneezings flash forth light,
And his eyes are like the eyelids of the morning.
19 Out of his mouth go burning lights;
Sparks of fire shoot out.
20 Smoke goes out of his nostrils,
As from a boiling pot and burning rushes.
21 His breath kindles coals,
And a flame goes out of his mouth.
22 Strength dwells in his neck,
And sorrow dances before him.
23 The folds of his flesh are joined together;
They are firm on him and cannot be moved.
24 His heart is as hard as stone,
Even as hard as the lower millstone.
25 When he raises himself up, the mighty are afraid;
Because of his crashings they are beside
themselves.
26 Though the sword reaches him, it cannot avail;
Nor does spear, dart, or javelin.
27 He regards iron as straw,
And bronze as rotten wood.
28 The arrow cannot make him flee;
Slingstones become like stubble to him.
29 Darts are regarded as straw;
He laughs at the threat of javelins.
30 His undersides are like sharp potsherds;
He spreads pointed marks in the mire.
31 He makes the deep boil like a pot;
He makes the sea like a pot of ointment.
32 He leaves a shining wake behind him;
One would think the deep had white hair.

33 On earth there is nothing like him,
Which is made without fear.
34 He beholds every high thing;
He is king over all the children of pride."
Job 40:6—41:34

"The God of Contingencies"

Submissive and silent, Job awaits God's response. No spoken acceptance of his confession is given or needed. By advancing to His next subject, God assumes that Job has learned his first lesson—he is small before the bigness of God; his knowledge is limited in time and scope; and his words are symbols of his security rather than his wisdom. Like a hungry baby bird reaching upward with its mouth wide open, Job is ready and eager to learn again.

God begins by letting Job know that He has another subject in mind. Out of the whirlwind, God repeats His challenge:

Now prepare yourself like a man;
I will question you,
and you shall answer Me (40:7).

Still in a confrontational mood, God goes straight to the point with four questions that pick up on Job's earlier demands:

Would you indeed annul My judgment?
Would you condemn Me that you may be justified?
Have you an arm like God?
Or can you thunder with a voice like His? (vv. 8–9).

In paraphrase, God is asking:

Do you *refute* My wisdom?
Do you *condemn* My justice?
Do you *doubt* My power?
Do you *reject* My voice?

Once again, God sets the agenda for His teaching. The subject is the justice and the power of God. Time after time, Job has raised questions about God's moral government which permitted him to suffer even in his innocence. From his viewpoint, God has to be either unfair in His justice or limited in His power. Job has raised the ethical questions and moral issues upon which faith or fatalism turns. In his opening address, God ignored these issues. His first task was to soften the heart and open Job's mind for learning beyond human wisdom. Sweeping generalizations about the physical universe and special examples from the animal kingdom show Job the mysteries of God's creation, control, and care which he can never fully comprehend. When Job admits his limited wisdom and drops his verbal guard, he is ready to face the tougher questions that God will ask.

Consistent with His character, God continues to honor the personhood and respect the intelligence of Job by asking him questions and letting him draw the conclusions. Job has acknowledged that the wisdom of God's general and special creation is beyond the time or scope of his understanding. God now asks him to understand the apparent *exceptions* in His power and wisdom that perplex and confound the wisest of the wise among human minds.

In management circles, the "critical incident" has been identified as the factor that distinguishes between effective and ineffective executives. Any job has routine matters that almost anyone can handle. Executives earn their money, however, when they must make crucial decisions that determine the destiny of their people and their organization. Such decisions arise out of "critical incidents" for which there is no company policy or standard practice. When Harry Truman said, "If you can't stand the heat, get out of the kitchen," he was referring to the decisions on "critical incidents" that the president of the United States is called to make. Critical incidents in the careers of American presidents include Truman's firing of General Douglas MacArthur, Dwight D. Eisenhower's priority for the space program, John F. Kennedy's blockade of Cuba, Lyndon B. Johnson's bombing of Hanoi, Richard Nixon's failure to destroy the tapes, Jimmy Carter's attempt to free the Iranian hostages, and Ronald Reagan's risk on the "Star Wars" system.

Suppose, for example, that the president of a corporation is informed that a vice-president is suspected of embezzlement. How does he handle the volatile situation? All of the accumulated experiences of a lifetime are needed to weigh all the evidence, balance responsibilities for the individual and the institution, consider the long-term consequences for all parties, and still make a fair and clean decision. The issue is a "critical incident." The decision makes the difference between an effective and an ineffective executive.

Three exceptions to the moral order of the universe, which God created and controls, are presented to Job as "critical incidents." To begin, God asks Job to change roles and assume that he has in his hands the power of God. Now, as the new executor of the universe, Job must make decisions on three "critical incidents":

> Would you *crush the wicked?* (vv. 8–14).
> Would you *create the useless?* (vv. 15–24).
> Would you *control the hostile?* (41:1–34).

In each case, power is the issue and justice is the principle with which Job must deal.

Would You Crush the Wicked?

Job has complained about the apparent inconsistency of God letting him suffer while the wicked prosper. Indirectly, God admits that this is a problem with which He also struggles. Strict justice, not unlike the kind in which Eliphaz, Bildad, and Zophar believed, dictated swift punishment for the wicked and abundant prosperity for the righteous. Certainly, such action is within His power. Why then, does He not crush the wicked to prove that He is just? Job, who has questioned God's justice, is asked what he would do if God's power were in his hands. God imagines that Job would

> *Disperse the rage of your wrath;*
> *Look on everyone who is proud,*
> *and humble him.*
> . . . .
> *Tread down the wicked in their place.*
> *Hide them in the dust together,*
> *Bind their faces in*
> *hidden darkness* (40:11–13).

If Job would do this, God agrees to bow before him, confess his greatness, and acknowledge his power to save himself (v. 14). In other words, Job would prove to be the omnipotent God of justice, but something would still be missing. He would not be the God of grace who delays His judgment in order to save the wicked. Later on, this attribute of grace will become flesh and blood in the person of Jesus Christ. As an intimation of that time, God is showing Job His grace in a situation where justice rules and when He owes the wicked nothing but punishment. Yet, He does not destroy them as Job might wish because of His genuine love for His creation.

Whenever human beings have the power to play God and use that power to punish the wicked, evil triumphs. The Spanish Inquisition and the Holy Wars are horror stories in human history. Prompted by the motive to punish evil in the name of Christ, they concocted greater evil than the sins they sought to punish. In the Garden of Gethsemane, when the Roman guard came to arrest Him, Jesus rebuked Peter for brandishing the sword and cutting off the Roman servant's ear, "Put your sword in its place, for all who take the sword will perish by the sword" (Matt. 26:52).

Job is quick to understand the point. If he exercised swift and certain justice upon the wicked, he too would die because he has acknowledged that he is not without sinful nature. What appears to be God's injustice, then, is in reality the patience of redeeming grace.

Would You Create the Useless?

God illustrates this question with a graphic portrayal of the behemoth, perhaps the animal better known to us as the hippopotamus. At best, the monstrous animal is a riddle of creation. He eats grass like an ox, but is not an ox; he has strength in his hips, his stomach, and his thighs, and yet he is useless for work. He is blessed with a tail like a tree, bones like bronze, and ribs like iron (vv. 17–18).

But for what purpose? The hippopotamus has no place among the birds and beasts of earlier listing because it has no unique function or special quality that sets it apart in the animal kingdom. The hippopotamus is ugly and useless.

Humor is a part of God's grace. The hippopotamus is a ludicrous creature who fouls up a neat and orderly universe in which everything makes sense and everything makes a contribution. Not the hippo. It is a maverick best known for crashing through the jungle, upsetting the harmony of nature, or sinking up to its bulbous eyeballs in a muddy riverbed. If the hippopotamus has a reason for being, it is to keep us laughing at the ludicrous in ourselves as well as in the universe.

God has another view of the hippopotamus. Is His tongue in His cheek when He tells Job how much He prizes the hippopotamus?

> *I made* [him] *along with you* (v. 15).
> *He is the first of the ways of God* (v. 19).

God is not kidding. The big, dumb, ugly, useless animal called the hippopotamus is a special object of God's care. Whether feeding on the mountains, playing in the fields, lying under a lotus tree, or letting the river gush into his eyes, nose, and mouth, the beast is a tranquil picture of playful trust.

Beauty and function are not the conditions of God's grace. Among the contingencies of His creation are ugly and useless creatures or circumstances for which the purpose seems unknown.

Among the frequent cries that surround the suffering of the innocent soul are "What a waste!" and "How senseless!" Very legitimately, Job feels the same way about his suffering. But then, God gives him the opportunity to assume the power and answer the questions, "Would you create the ugly and useless?" and "Would you do away with all creatures or circumstances for which there is no obvious purpose?" Some suffering would disappear if the useless were erased from the earth, but what would be lost? Learning the lesson from the hippopotamus, there would be no need for the humor of God's grace, and because each of us has some of the ugly and the useless in us, there would be no need to trust God.

To judge the value of persons or events on their utilitarian merits is another dangerous doctrine that must be avoided at all costs. One of the first stirrings of moral decadence in a civilization is to devalue or destroy persons who are not deemed useful to the culture. Girl babies who could not contribute to the "macho" image of Rome were tossed out in the street after one look by the father. Eskimo and Indian societies sent their elderly into the wilderness to die when they could no longer fight, work, or move with the tribe. Our society may be on the borderline of such decadence. The premium upon utilitarian values is so high that uselessness may be among the motives behind abortion without cause. A baby who restricts freedom, requires unselfish attention, costs $200,000–$300,000 to raise, and offers nothing useful in return may be an unwanted child.

If this attitude persists as a characteristic of our culture, a major moral crisis may be in the making. People over the age of sixty-five are the fastest-growing segment of our population, and, of that category, people over one hundred years old are the fastest-growing segment of all. To this time, however, we have failed to utilize effectively the skills and experience of the aged. If utility is equated with worth, we will have to find a meaningful function for the elderly or face the dilemma of living wills, negotiated deaths, suicide pacts, and varied forms of euthanasia.

On another level, a society that is dominated by utilitarian values has little appreciation for the creative arts or recreative play. A sculpture or a symphony may have value only in themselves, but they are the "grace notes" that are prized by great societies and devalued by declining civilizations.

Learning from a hippopotamus may seem to be a bizarre way to appreciate what appears to be ugly and useless in the realm of God's creation. But without the hippopotamus, we would lose another example of God's loving grace for an undeserving creature. With Job, we learn to laugh and cry when we realize that there is some of the ugly and the useless in each of us. Never again can we see water gushing up to the bulgy eyes, over the pointy ears, and out of the snubby snout of a hippopotamus resting on a riverbed without seeing a prized creature of God's creation and a precious example of God's grace.

Would You Control the Hostile?

At the other extreme of creation is the leviathan, an amphibious monster of land and sea, which may be the animal we know as the crocodile. In contrast with the playful trust of the useless hippopotamus, the crocodile is a creature of violent hostility. God uses the crocodile to symbolize the forces of evil that exist for one persistent and malicious purpose in the universe—to oppose the will of God. In the most vivid and complete portrait of any of the animals, God details every incorrigible characteristic of the crocodile in a chapter that might be entitled, "Everything You Always Wanted to Know about Crocodiles but Were Afraid to Ask." The horny, hostile monster is described as uncatchable, unfeeling, untrustworthy, unmanageable, unplayful, undesirable, unhospitable, and unethical (41:1–6).

Attempts to capture or control the crocodile are vain. Furthermore, wisdom suggests that it is foolish to aggravate the crocodile because of all the beasts of the earth, he is the most ferocious of all. What is the difference between a crocodile and an alligator? According to an attendant at a zoological park, the crocodile will attack people without provocation while the alligator will strike only as provoked.

It takes God to subdue the crocodile. Where human beings fail, He can control:

> *Who then is able to stand against Me?*
> *Who has preceded Me,*
> *that I should pay him?*
> *Everything under heaven is Mine* (vv. 10–11).

No doubt remains. All of the forces of evil, no matter how fierce, are not outside of God's command. Why, then, doesn't God wipe evil from the face of the earth? This is the question that is posed to Job. God asks,"If you had the power to subdue evil, would you do it?" Sin would end, suffering would cease, and God's justice would be vindicated. But what would be lost? Once again, the answer is *human freedom* and *divine grace.* Job might have been relieved of suffering, but he could not have been redeemed from sin. In the symbol of the crocodile, God makes a choice. He prefers a loving relationship with His creation more than a perfect world. Thus, He permits evil to exist until he has fulfilled His redemptive purpose. Saints as well as sinners will be victims of evil, but out of suffering, God will work His good purpose.

God has more to say about evil. With descriptive overkill, He introduces Job to the biological details of the crocodile:

limbs that are mighty and graceful (v. 12);
skin that cannot be removed and a ferocity that will not respond to a double bridle (v. 13);
jaws that cannot be opened and teeth that cannot be counted (v. 14);
scales that are like a coat of armor (v. 15);

sneezings that flash with light and eyelids that lift like the dawn (v. 18);
breath that resembles fire (v. 19);
strength that centers in the neck (v. 22);
flesh that defies penetration (v. 23); and
a heart that is as hard as stone (v. 24).

All of the human weapons that are arrayed against the crocodile will fail:

sword, spear, dart and javelin bounce off him (vv. 26–27);
iron is as straw and bronze is as rotting wood (v. 27);
arrows do not faze him and slingstones are like stubble against him (v. 28); and
darts are like straw and javelins are a laugh to him (v. 29).

Once the crocodile is aggravated, however, he

slashes the mire with pointed marks (v. 30);
makes the deep boil like a pot and turns the sea into seething ointment (v. 31); and
leaves a shining wake behind him (v. 32).

Nothing on earth is like him—fearless, ferocious, and formidable. Symbolizing Satan, the crocodile *"is king over all the children of pride"* (v. 34). Among God's creatures, he is the epitome of evil.

God has brought Job full cycle to the issue of evil in the universe. He permits evil in order to reveal His grace, but He will not provoke evil by exercising His power. Contrary to the opinion of Rabbi Harold Kushner that God is limited in His power to heal, Job is taught that God in His wisdom will not always act to subdue evil if a greater evil is the result or if His redemptive purpose is sacrificed. Only an administrator of justice can understand the dilemma of making moral decisions in which the choice is for the lesser evil as well as the greater good.

Elton Trueblood, one of my mentors in philosophy and faith, shook me up the first time that I met him. He accepted the invitation to be our commencement speaker at Spring Arbor College when I was president. When we met for breakfast prior to the commencement service, Trueblood said that he had to miss an important Monday morning class to give the commencement address. "I had to choose," he said, "between lesser evils. Would my students missing the class suffer more than the audience not hearing me speak?" At the time, I reacted against this negative outlook because I wanted every decision to be made in the context of the greater good, not the lesser evil. Later, I learned that Trueblood's realism put a perspective on decision-making that I had missed. Our decisions for the greater good can result in the greater evil. To impose Christian values on a sinful society, for instance, may be consistent with the greater good, but, more often than not, the long-term consequence is a greater evil. Furthermore, in practical decision-making as an administrator, another of my mentors in the university presidency, Dr. Charles Odegaard, often said, "Whenever I make an executive decision, I must ask who it is that I will alienate." Through the symbol of the crocodile, God is teaching Job that He does not always act to punish short-term evil because the long-term consequences may be a greater evil.

God has introduced Job to the most profound and perplexing problem of the universe. Without direct references, He has invited him into the inner sanctum of heaven's council, where He accepted the challenge of Satan to test the faith of His servant Job. Evil is the ultimate contingency of the universe which God permits in order to show His grace, and He will not provoke long-term evil for a short-term good. No higher compliment could be given by God to Job than to unveil this truth with the confidence that His servant will understand. A ferocious creature as incorrigible as the crocodile is God's way of explaining the existence of evil as an opportunity for His grace.

The God of the orderly creation and the God of the disorderly contingency has now introduced Himself to Job. He does not answer the plaintiff's question *why,* but He does address the ultimate question *who.* When it comes down to the rub of our fears, we are afraid that some corner of creation is out of God's control. No conundrum is greater than the suffering of the innocent. This is why God addresses Himself to Job's fear rather than answering His questions of fact. Unless we have all of the facts of the omniscient mind—back to the origins, systems, and distinctions of creation—our fears will remain. If, however, we are confident that there is no contingency or creature outside the command of the God who cares, we can bear the pain of suffering and live with mystery. Unencumbered trust is God's goal for His servant Job.

Job—Seeing through Suffering

As quickly as the whirlwind appeared, it vanishes. The voice of God is gone, finishing on a strange note; not a call to faith, but a statement of fact about the crocodile as the symbol of evil in the world,

> On earth there is nothing like him,
> Which is made without fear.
> He beholds every high thing;
> He is king over all the children of pride (vv. 33–34).

God has revealed the character of Satan—fearing no one on earth, lording it over the high of the earth, and presiding over the pride in human hearts.

Job is left with a decision. Can he affirm his faith in God knowing that Satan is still permitted to work evil in the world? Can he put his trust in God who will not answer his question *why?* Even more personally, can he believe in God who will give him no promise of immunity from the mysterious accidents of nature or from the deliberate actions of Satan whose obsession is to make him curse God and die?

> 1 Then Job answered the LORD and said:
> 2 "I know that You can do everything,
> And that no purpose of Yours can be withheld from You.
> 3 You asked, 'Who is this who hides counsel without knowledge?'
> Therefore I have uttered what I did not understand,
> Things too wonderful for me, which I did not know.
> 4 Listen, please, and let me speak;
> You said, 'I will question you, and you shall answer Me.'

5 "I have heard of You by the hearing of the ear,
But now my eye sees You.
6 Therefore I abhor myself,
And repent in dust and ashes."

Job 42:1–6

For Job, the question is no longer *why* but *who.* This is a two-sided question that every person must answer, whether suffering in innocence or devastated by sin: *Who am I?* and *Who is God?*

Spiritually, the answer to the first question is a *confession of need;* the answer to the second question is an *affirmation of faith.* Job does not disappoint us.

Who Am I?

When God first spoke to Job out of the whirlwind, he asked the question "Who is this?" (38:2). Now, in a human confession of need, Job repeats the question and answers, "Who am I?" He makes a humble confession of need: I am *weak* (42:2), I am *unwise* and *wordy* (v. 3), and I am *unworthy* (v. 6).

Job needs to confess each of these deficiencies. Although he has not sinned, his pride has taken him perilously close to blasphemy when he demands that God come down to his level of power and understanding. God must have had him in mind when He closed His speech with the warning about Satan, "He is king over all the children of pride" (41:34). Job gets the message. His pride in his own righteousness has taken him within a hair's breadth of Satan's control. Therefore, before he can affirm his faith, he must confess his pride.

My mother used to say, "Confession is good for the soul." Job is not confessing either the overt sins of the rich of which Eliphaz accused him (22:2–11) or the hidden sins of the hypocrite which Bildad tried to uncover (8:11–18). He is confessing his reliance upon the power of his own righteousness and the wisdom of his own knowledge. In part, Job is a victim of his background. Schooled in the oral tradition and mastered by self-discipline, the strength of his background could have been a weakness in his faith.

Tragedy dogs the steps of people who have let religious tradition or self-discipline become their barrier to God. A friend of mine who is dying of cancer still blames his fundamentalist background for keeping him from God. If he is to be healed in spirit, if not in body, he must confess that he has used his background as an excuse for his cynicism. Without his confession, Job would have fallen into the same cynical mire. He had followed every fundamentalist step toward faith—living blamelessly and uprightly, fearing God and shunning evil (1:1). By all human counts, he was righteous and wise. His suffering, then, becomes the pivot upon which he can grow in faith or sink in cynicism. Job chooses to grow. Confessing that he is weak, unwise, wordy, and unworthy, Job progresses to an affirmation of faith that is big enough to include the question, Why do the innocent suffer?

Who Is God?

If a person never goes beyond asking "Who am I?", fatalistic despair is inevitable. After a lifetime of asking "Who am I?", the humanist Walter Kauffman summed up his philosophy of life by saying, "Just do the best you can, and, if possible, face death with a smile."

If Job had stopped with the confession that he was weak, unwise, wordy, and unworthy, the book that bears his name would be lost among other literary tragedies.

In modern literature, the works of Elie Wiesel represent that kind of tragedy. Wiesel, who coined the word *holocaust,* suffers all of the wounds of a child who somehow survived both Auschwitz and Buchenwald. Wiesel said, "So heavy was my anguish that in the spring of 1945 I made a vow: not to speak, not to touch upon the essential for at least ten years. Long enough to unite the language of humanity with the silence of the dead."[2]

Today, his books such as *Night, The Jews of Silence, One Generation After,* and *The Fifth Son* still carry the theme of his first book, when he broke the silence: "A child watches the hanging of another child: 'Where is God? Where is He?' . . . And I heard a voice within me answer: 'Where is He? Here He is—He is hanging here on this gallows.' "[3]

Wiesel cannot separate the murder of the innocent from the martyrdom of faith. Ever so slowly, such as with the birth of his own son, Wiesel is beginning to believe again. He, with Job, balances upon the pivot that can turn to festering cynicism or affirming faith. The pivot is the suffering of the innocent.

Only the redeeming grace of God can bring us through tragedy to an affirming faith that covers every contingency—known and unknown, useful and useless, good and evil. This is not a flippant statement of faith; it is a fact of life. To limit ourselves to the question "Who am I?", whether for ourselves or for humanity, will ultimately lead to the martyrdom of faith. Only by asking the companion question "Who is God?" can faith be resurrected, expanded, and affirmed.

Critical scholars find redundance in Job's first confession of submission and silence and his second confession of weakness, lack of wisdom, wordiness, and unworthiness. They fail to understand the full meaning of the gospel that Jesus proclaims at the announcement of His public ministry, "Repent and believe the Gospel." In his confession, Job *repents;* in his affirmation, Job *believes.* A creed of faith can be written out of the affirmations that Job speaks in response to the question "Who is God?"

I know that *Your power* can do anything for me, and that *Your purpose* will be accomplished for me (42:2),
I know that *Your will* is good for me (v. 3),
I know that *Your presence* is real to me (v. 5), and
I know that *Your grace* is given to me (v. 6).

Two words are key to understanding Job's affirmation of faith. One is the word *"wonderful"* (v. 3), the other is the word *"sees"* (v. 5).

Eliphaz, Bildad, Zophar, and Elihu expressed the grandest of poetic eloquence in their hymns of praise to the power and majesty of God. None of them, however, used the word *"wonderful"* to exalt His works. At the thought of His presence, they quaked with "fear." Now we know why. *Fear* is the logical response to the justice of God; *wonder* is the experiential response to the grace of God. Mystery, wonder, and grace are inseparable. God expects us to marvel at the mysteries of His creation. More than that, He wants us to enjoy the wonders of His creation with Him. But most of all, He wants us to see the wonder of His grace and the mystery of His creation. Adults tend to fear mystery but children find glee in the unknown. So when Job speaks of *"things too wonderful for me,"* he is like a child reveling for a moment in the wonders of God. Elizabeth Akers Allen wished for such a moment when she wrote,

> Backward, turn backward
> O time, in your flight
> Make me a child again
> Just for tonight.[4]

Rachel Carson is best known for her book *Silent Spring,* in which she foresees the pollution of nature by the use of pesticides. A lesser-known book, which I prize, is entitled *A Sense of Wonder.* With her nephew Roger at her side, Miss Carson explores the beach and woods through the eyes of a child. In one of the most beautiful passages in contemporary literature, she writes,

> A child's world is fresh and beautiful, full of wonder and excitement. It is our misfortune that for most of us that clear-eyed vision, that true instinct for what is beautiful and awe-inspiring is dimmed and even lost before we reach adulthood. If I had influence with the good fairy who is supposed to preside over the christening of all children, I should ask that her gift to each child in the world would be a sense of wonder so indestructible that it would last throughout a life, as an unfailing antidote against the boredom and disenchantment of later years, the sterile preoccupation with things that are artificial, the alienation from our source of strength.[5]

If only Rachel Carson had known God. Her sense of wonder led her to the threshold of His presence, but she died before she finished her book or declared her faith. Job, however, crosses the threshold of wonder into the very presence of God. In the wonders of creation, he catches a glimpse of the grace of God. With the writer of the Proverbs, he worships as he wonders:

> There are three things which are too wonderful for me,
> Yes, four which I do not understand:
> The way of an eagle in the air,
> The way of a serpent upon a rock,
> The way of a ship in the midst of the sea,
> And the way of a man with a virgin (Prov. 30:18–19).

Before this experience, the power of God in creation provoked in Job the fear that is reputed to be the "beginning of wisdom." Now, he advances in faith as a sense of wonder leads him into the presence of Wisdom itself. Like a child who is at home with the wonders of creation, if Job were alive today, he would smile, nod his head, and join in the chorus of George Beverly Shea's well-known song,

> There's the wonder of sunset at evening,
> The wonder of sunrise I see;
> But the wonder of wonders that thrills my soul
> Is the wonder that God loves me.

Seeing is the other word that opens up our understanding of Job's affirmation of faith. Elihu, in his second speech, introduced us to the "inner ear" of human reason,

> For the ear tests words
> As the palate tastes food (34:3).

Job, exemplar of the Wisdom School, confesses that he has relied upon the same teaching-learning process in his approach to God: *"I have heard You by the hearing of the ear"* (42:5).

The teaching of his elders and the logic of his mind had served as Job's way of knowing God. Out of the same oral tradition as Eliphaz, Bildad, and Zophar, Job had only extended their line of thinking on the straight line of human reason. They had become fixed in the tradition of orthodoxy that equated suffering with sin and prosperity with righteousness. Job had not really refuted their position; he had only extended it by continuing to conceive God within the limits of his own mind. Taking a "me-He" rather than an "I-Thou" approach to God, Job demanded an answer from God on human terms. While protesting his innocence, Job was really demonstrating his arrogance. He spoke only with the authority of what he had heard about God from the oral tradition and what he had thought about God in his own mind.

No wonder that God came to Job out of a whirlwind. A breakthrough is needed before Job's faith can be transformed from hearsay to experience. Job's own testimony is witness to that breakthrough: *"But now my eye sees You"* (v. 5).

Throughout Scripture, the "eye" symbolizes the spiritual perception that comes from a life-changing encounter with God. While no mortal man can actually "see" God and live, it is possible to know His person and His presence so intimately that one can say, *"My eye sees You."*

Malcolm Muggeridge is a severe critic of television, because he says that it makes us *see* as spectators, not as participants. Edmund Blake's verse supports Muggeridge:

> This Life's dim windows of the soul
> Distorts the Heavens from Pole to Pole,
> And leads you to believe a lie,
> When you see with, not through, the eye.[6]

Job's self-confessed wordiness blurred his view of God—His person, His presence, and His purpose. Once he clapped his hand over his mouth and confessed his ignorance, he began to see clearly through to the person, presence, and purpose of God. All of the wonders of creation began to make sense. They are not just accidents of nature, or displays of power, but expressions of a person—God Himself. Through the seeing of the eye, Job's world comes together. He has perspective. Usually, we think of perspective as the ability to see the larger scene so that the parts of the picture fit into a meaningful whole. We forget that perspective is gained only by "seeing through" to the center point to which all other parts are related.

In my office are three original color prints of geometric figures done by Brian Halsey, a Christian artist. Each print is perfect in symmetry. To appreciate them, however, you must "see through" to the center point from which all of the patterns and figures emerge. To help lead your eye to the point of perspective, the artist uses variations of the same color to focus the brightest light at the center from which all lines diverge in relationship to the center point and to each other. It is no surprise to learn that Halsey entitled the series "Creation." God is the point of perspective, and His creation is in perfect unity with Him. After "seeing through" to the perspective of the prints and appreciating the perfection of every line, it is easy to understand how God stepped back to view His own creative work and said, "It is good."

Job "sees through" to God. No longer does he rely upon tradition or hearsay about God; he knows God for Himself. No longer does he have to depend upon human reason to define the nature of God; he has been in the presence of God. No longer does he have to tremble in fear before the power of God; he has seen the grace of God. No longer does he have to demand an explanation for every mystery; he has put his trust in God. Through the perception of the soul, Job sees the answer to the question, Who is God? *He is the God of grace.* With the Bishop of Cambrai, Job can now say, "Smite or heal/ Depress or build me up/I adore Thy purposes without knowing them." Better yet, he can add experience to insight and speak again the grand affirmation of his faith, "Though He slay me, yet will I trust Him" (13:15).

He can sing his hope with new meaning,

> I know that my Redeemer lives,
> And He shall stand at last on the earth;
> And after my skin is destroyed,
> this I know,
> That in my flesh I shall see God (19:25–26).

Job can now bear his suffering through his seeing,

> He knows the way that I take;
> When He has tested me,
> I shall come forth as gold (23:10).

Knowing the answer to the question *who,* Job no longer needs to ask the question *why.*

Why then does Job conclude his response to God by bowing and repenting once again? The answer is that one who "sees through" to the great grace of God bows humbly and repents sincerely. By bowing, grace lifts him; by repenting, grace liberates him. So, like the phoenix bird rising out of the dust and ashes with the colors of the sun, God will lift Job to his feet and set him free—reconciled, restored, and ready to serve others with new-found grace. Job has "seen through" to God.

NOTES

1. Hulme, *Dialogue in Despair,* p. 142.
2. Elie Wiesel, *Time* magazine, March 18, 1985, p. 79.
3. Elie Wiesel, *Night/Dawn, The Accident* (New York: Hill and Wang, 1972), p. 10.
4. Elizabeth Akers Allen, *Saturday Evening Post,* May 1960.
5. Rachel Carson, *A Sense of Wonder* (New York: Harper and Row, 1956), pp. 42–43.
6. Malcolm Muggeridge, *Christ and the Media* (Grand Rapids: Wm. B. Eerdmans, 1977), p. 62.

CHAPTER NINE

Epilogue: God's Redemption/Job's Restoration

Job 42:7–17

Eliphaz had predicted that if Job repented, he would be restored to prosperity and even become an intercessor for his friends. Little did he realize that he and his friends would be the ones in need of Job's intercession. In the end, God condemns them for not speaking the truth to Job about Him, orders their sacrifices for repentance, and gives them hope only if Job intercedes for them. To their credit, they obey and Job prays. God then doubles all of Job's possessions in the act of restoration—doubles his herds, doubles his sons, doubles his years, and doubles his generations. Only his daughters are not doubled.

Job is now a man of grace. He prays for his friends who failed him, accepts gifts from his kin and townsfolk who ostracized him, and gives an inheritance to his daughters (an exception to the tradition of his time and culture).

What an epitaph! Because of grace, it reads, "So Job died, an old man, satisfied with life."

> 7 And so it was, after the LORD had spoken these words to Job, that the LORD said to Eliphaz the Temanite, "My wrath is aroused against you and your two friends, for you have not spoken of Me what is right, as My servant Job has.
>
> 8 "Now therefore, take for yourselves seven bulls and seven rams, go to My servant Job, and offer up for yourselves a burnt offering; and My servant Job shall pray for you. For I will accept him, lest I deal with you according to your folly; because you have not spoken of Me what is right, as My servant Job has."

9 So Eliphaz the Temanite and Bildad the Shuhite and Zophar the Naamathite went and did as the LORD commanded them; for the LORD had accepted Job.

10 And the LORD restored Job's losses when he prayed for his friends. Indeed the LORD gave Job twice as much as he had before.

11 Then all his brothers, all his sisters, and all those who had been his acquaintances before, came to him and ate food with him in his house; and they consoled him and comforted him for all the adversity that the LORD had brought upon him. Each one gave him a piece of silver and each a ring of gold.

12 Now the LORD blessed the latter days of Job more than his beginning; for he had fourteen thousand sheep, six thousand camels, one thousand yoke of oxen, and one thousand female donkeys.

13 He also had seven sons and three daughters.

14 And he called the name of the first Jemimah, the name of the second Keziah, and the name of the third Keren-Happuch.

15 In all the land were found no women so beautiful as the daughters of Job; and their father gave them an inheritance among their brothers.

16 After this Job lived one hundred and forty years, and saw his children and grandchildren for four generations.

17 So Job died, old and full of days.

Job 42:7–17

GRACE FOR GRACE

Reconciliation and restoration are the harmonious themes that bring the epic of Job to its grand finale. Our first reaction is that the ending is too good, too neat, too unreal. Only fairy tales end with the line, "And so they lived happily ever after." In real life, physical suffering, interpersonal alienation, social disgrace, the barren womb, and material poverty may well continue even after "seeing through" to the person of God, living in His presence, and trusting in His purpose.

Many critics of the Book of Job feel this way about the epilogue, in which Job is reconciled with his foes, his friends, his family, and restored to health, wealth, and fame. Either they excise the ending from the book or treat it as an editor's addendum to make the story "come out right." For those who excise the ending, Job is left in the dust and ashes abhorring his unworthiness and repenting of his wordiness. For them, God is either unjust or powerless. If He is unjust, God dies on the ash heap with Job. If He is powerless, Job has only his own resources upon which to find the strength to rise again.

In that case, the ending of Job must be rewritten, as Rabbi Kushner has done in his book *When Bad Things Happen to Good People.* Having concluded that God is limited in His power to deal with the suffering of the innocent, Kushner shifts the burden of love to the person who suffers. In the conclusion of his book, he asks,

> Are you capable of forgiving and accepting in love a world which has disappointed you by not being perfect . . . ?
>
> Are you capable of forgiving and loving the people around you, even if they have hurt you and let you down by not being perfect . . . ?
>
> Are you capable of forgiving and loving God even when you have found out that He is not perfect . . . ?
>
> And if you can do these things, will you be able to recognize that the ability to forgive and the ability to love are the weapons God has given to us to live fully, bravely and meaningfully in this less-than-perfect world?[1]

In the stageplay *J.B.,* Archibald MacLeish also rewrites the ending of the Book of Job.[2] The play draws to its conclusion when J.B.'s wife says to him, "You wanted justice, didn't you? There isn't any . . . there is only love."

God and Satan, observing the scene, are both baffled. They ask,

> Who plays the hero, God or him?
> Is God to be forgiven?
> Isn't He? Job was innocent,
> You may remember.

The curtain falls as J.B. forgives God, and his wife reflects upon human love as their only hope,

> The candles in the churches are out,
> The stars have gone out in the sky,

Blow on the coals of the heart
And we'll see by and by.

Contrast these revised endings of the Book of Job with the final thoughts of Philip Yancey in his book *Where Is God When It Hurts?* After struggling with the same issue as Kushner and MacLeish, but as a Christian who accepts the epilogue of the Book of Job, Yancey answers his own question, "Where is God when it hurts?"

> He has been there from the beginning. . . .
> He has watched us reflect His image. . . .
> He has used pain, even in its grossest forms, to teach us. . . .
> He has let us cry out and echo Job. . . .
> He has allied Himself with the poor and suffering. . . .
> He has promised supernatural strength to nourish our spirit. . . .
> He has joined us . . . hurt and bled and cried and suffered.
> He has dignified for all time those who suffer. . . .
> He is with us now. . . .
> He is waiting. . . .
>
> Where, O death, is your victory?
> Where, O death, is your sting?[3]

Or, consider the unsurpassed eloquence of C. S. Lewis as he concludes his own Jobian journey in *A Grief Observed.* After his wife, Joy, died an early and painful death, he shouted his rage, confessed his doubts, cried his loneliness, and vented his bitterness against God. Then, with Job, he discovered a new dimension of faith that reconciled him to God as he accepted the death of Joy:

> How wicked it would be, if we could, to call the dead back! She said not to me but to the chaplain, "I am at peace with God." She smiled, but not at me. *Poi si torno all' sterna fontana.*[4]

The difference is not textual; it is theological. Until we ourselves "see through" to the God of grace, the ending of the Book of Job makes little sense. Rather than redemption, we read revenge. Job, for instance, gets his vengeance upon Eliphaz, Bildad, and Zophar when God vents His wrath against them (42:7) and vindicates Job by making him the intercessor for their sins (v. 8). The contradiction is further aggravated when God makes Job twice as rich as he was before (v. 10). Along with riches comes the return of his friends, who abandoned and ostracized him when he lost his fame and fortune. Job's health and family are restored so that he lives a long and fulfilling life as an esteemed patriarch, fathers fourteen sons and three daughters who are the most beautiful in all the land, sees four generations of his children, and dies as he wished—in his bed, surrounded by his family, and fully satisfied with his years (29:18–20).

If divine justice is the standard by which we judge the restoration of Job, Eliphaz, Bildad, and Zophar are right in contending that sin causes suffering and righteousness produces prosperity. Therefore, when Job repents in dust and ashes, God restores him just as Eliphaz promised:

> If you return to the Almighty,
> you will be built up;
> . . . .
> Yes, the Almighty will be your gold (22:23–25).

Wait. Why then is God angry with Eliphaz and his friends, condemning their counsel, ordering their sacrifice, and making Job their intercessor? The contradiction is insoluble. Unless grace intervenes, we have our choice—humanism, cynicism, or atheism.

Grace is defined as *unmerited favor.* It cannot be inherited or earned. It is the gift of unconditional love. Yet, neither grace nor love is mentioned in the ending of the Book of Job. Critics might feel better if the book concluded with the single sentence of God's response to Job's repentance on the ash heap, "So Job found grace in the eyes of the Lord and died in peace."

The ending would still not be satisfactory because God's message for us in the Book of Job would not be complete. Job's restoration is essential to that message, not for Job's personal prosperity, but for his spiritual maturity. In response to Job's repentance in dust and ashes, God shows him His love and gives him His grace. Despite the fact that Job has nothing to offer God and God owes him nothing but justice, he rises from the ash heap forgiven, accepted, and restored by God. This is grace at work! How do we know that Job is forgiven, accepted, and restored by God? The proof is in the grace that Job gives to his foes, his friends, and his family. Grace received is grace to be given.

The Grace That Forgives Our Foes

Job was first introduced to us as a father who prayed for his family. Now, after God comes to him with the grace of intercession, Job is able to intercede for his three friends who became his foes. God begins by addressing Eliphaz as the senior member of the company. In no uncertain terms, He speaks His wrath against them for misrepresenting Him. God also makes it clear that Job, despite his anger and his arrogance, spoke the truth. To reinforce the point, God speaks of *"My servant Job"* three times in his brief encounter with Eliphaz. Even then, we see grace at work. God owes Eliphaz, Bildad, and Zophar nothing. Still, He chooses to speak to them and offers them forgiveness. The test, however, is for Job. Will he be able to intercede for the friends who have become his foes? Justice says *never.* Grace says *yes.*

Strong prophetic leanings toward Christ are in this passage. Job, as the Intermediate Adam, not only resists the temptation to curse God and die, but he prefigures the Spirit of Christ who interceded for his enemies on the cross with the prayer, "Father, forgive them, for they do not know what they do" (Luke 23:34).

Jake DeShazer, one of the Doolittle flyers who bombed Tokyo in a daring World War II raid, spent thirty months in a Japanese prison camp. During this time, he suffered every brutality short of death itself. Yet, he found Christ in his prison cell and lived to be liberated at the end of the war. Returning home, he enrolled at Seattle Pacific College (now University) with one thought in mind. He wanted to return to Japan and preach Christ to his captors. Eventually, Jake's testimony led two of the guards who tortured him to seek Christ. Later, he stood shoulder to shoulder, brother to brother, with Commander Fuchida who led the attack on Pearl Harbor. He, too, found Christ after hearing Jake's testimony. If you knew Jake as I do, you would agree that he is the most unlikely person to command an audience or win a convert. But oh, how the grace of God flows through his hesitant words and his humble presence. He can even forgive his enemies.

God puts Job to the same test. Is he willing to intercede for his enemies? To pray for them is to forgive them. Job's response must be unconditional. He cannot do it to win the favor of God; certainly, he has no guarantee of riches. After the way that Eliphaz, Bildad, and Zophar treated him, they do not deserve it. But he to whom grace is given does not stop to ask questions. When Eliphaz, Bildad, and Zophar ask Job to pray for them, he does. God hears Job's prayer, holds His anger against his friends, and accepts their sacrifice. Job is not yet restored. Perhaps he prayed from the ash heap. If so, when the sweet savor signaled that God had accepted Eliphaz's, Bildad's, and Zophar's sacrifice, Job himself might have felt the strength of God's healing touch surge through his being. Standing to his feet and shaking off the dust and ashes, isn't it possible that Job, Eliphaz, Bildad, and Zophar locked arms and walked away reconciled to God and to each other?

Elihu is the missing person in the picture. His name is not mentioned along with Eliphaz, Bildad, and Zophar. Yet he too had said he spoke for God. As we remember, there are those who say that Elihu's speeches contribute nothing to the Book of Job. He is perceived as a wordy, hot-headed kid who mimics his elders by mouthing what they have already said. At best, God is ignoring him; at worst, he is only a figment of some editor's imagination.

Elihu deserves a better fate. The absence of his name in the epilogue may also mean that he spoke the truth when he claimed to have "the breath of the Almighty" for his understanding (32:8). Is it possible that he also fulfilled his claim to be Job's spokesman before God? (33:6). If so, the absence of his name in the epilogue is a silent witness on his behalf. Like John the Baptist, he served as a voice crying in the wilderness, "Prepare ye the way of the Lord." Also, like John, when the work of preparation is done, he disappears from the scene. Elihu and John the Baptist deserve the distinction of being forerunners for God. Their time is brief and their style is rough, but they speak the truth in the Spirit. Hail the ministry of forerunners!

Grace That Accepts Those Who Abandon Us

Those who argue that Job's restoration to prosperity after his repentance vindicates the doctrine of justice proclaimed by his three friends' need to follow the sequence of restoration more closely. Job's wealth is not restored after his repentance. We read: *"**And** the* LORD *restored Job's losses* **when** *he prayed for his friends"* (42:10, emphasis mine).

The conjunction *"and"* connects Job's restoration to his act of intercession, and the adverb *"when"* sets the timing for the beginning of the restoration simultaneously with his prayers. God honors Job for his grace, not for his righteousness.

We first met Job as the "greatest of all people of the East" (1:3). The adage "If you want to make a fortune, go into a business that has a reputation for dishonesty and be honest" could appropriately have been applied to Job. We reason that his impeccable ethics earned him a fortune as an entrepreneur on the lawless frontier of the East. Nothing of Job's suffering changes his reputation. Try as they might, Eliphaz, Bildad, and Zophar failed miserably in their attempts to accuse Job of the sins of the rich and powerful. In fact, Job's call for witnesses against him led to their downfall. When none appeared, they were reduced to silence.

Add the grace of forgiveness to the ethics of a righteous man. The doubling of Job's wealth is no longer mysterious or miraculous. With an open line of credit, a newfound love for people, a loose hold on riches, and a singular desire to glorify God, instant wealth would come to Job. But Job's wealth is not the point of the story. His grace is tested once again. As soon as he regains his fortune, the fickle dame of fame woos him again. Relatives and friends who had abandoned him in his poverty and pain suddenly reappear at his doorstep to eat his food, console and comfort him, and give him gifts of silver and gold (v. 11).

As a president in Christian higher education for a quarter of a century, I find fund raising indispensable to my role. Early in my career, I met wealthy individuals and foundation executives who are among the saddest and loneliest people I know. One way or another, almost every human contact relates to their wealth or power to give away money. Often I have wondered if anyone sees these people as persons rather than as dollar signs. Consequently, I have determined that fund raising must be secondary to ministry. If I cannot be a friend and a minister to those from whom I ask money, I do not want the money. In one case, this conviction has kept me from asking for anything from one of the wealthiest men in America. He is my friend. Everyone asks him for money. But he is my friend, and I cannot violate that friendship.

Job's problem is similar. The motive of his relatives and friends is obvious. They want to be able to say, "I know Job, the greatest man in the East." To curry his favor, they bring him a piece of silver and a ring of gold. Without doubt, they demean him as a person and devalue him as a soul. Their purpose is to use him for their own glory.

The scene is reminiscent of the crowd hailing Jesus as the King when He enters Jerusalem riding on an ass's colt. With the shouts of "Hosanna," they give Him their praise; with the waving of the palm leaves, they offer Him their possessions; with the laying of their clothes on the ground, they relinquish to Him their power. With all of that, their motives are still self-serving. Within days, Jesus is arraigned, tortured, mocked, and condemned to a criminal's death. Where is His loving family, His loyal friends, and His lauding crowd? Gone—as quickly as His fame.

The relatives and friends who abandoned Job when he lost his fame and fortune do not deserve a whit of his time and attention. Justice would be served if he threw the silver and gold in their faces and slammed the door. *But grace holds no grudges.* When God accepts Job He does not remind him of his anger for which He could have struck him dead or his accusations which bordered on blasphemy. Job is no better than his relatives and family who use him for their own purposes. He tried to use God to justify himself. So, as a recipient of grace whom God accepts, Job demonstrates the same grace by accepting the comfort and the gifts of his relatives and friends who had abandoned him.

Margaret Mead, the anthropologist, received a $25,000 award for her contribution to science. As a part of the celebration, the trustees of the Pacific Science Center in Seattle, Washington, hosted her for dinner. As one of the trustees, I remember her response when she was given a gift wrapped in silver foil with a white ribbon. While opening it, she stopped and mused aloud, "Every time I open a surprise gift, I am reminded of the final task that is given to British diplomats. They have to say 'Thank you' for a gift they do not want." Of course, the sterling silver replica of the Seattle Space Needle was a gift that Margaret Mead wanted, but I have never forgotten the lesson. Training in diplomacy can teach us to say *thank you* for a gift we do not want, but only the grace of God can prompt us to say *thank you* for a gift from relatives and friends who abandoned us when we needed them most.

The doubling of the wealth is not the real story of Job's restoration.

By accepting those who abandoned him, Job witnesses to the grace of God at work in his life. As God accepted him after he turned against God, Job can now accept others who do not deserve acceptance from him. In this, he prefigures the Christ who appeared before His frightened disciples after the resurrection, breathed on them, and said, "Receive the Holy Spirit. If you forgive the sins of any, they are forgiven them; if you retain the sins of any, they are retained" (John 20:22–23). It takes grace to do that!

Grace That Gives to Those Who Are Disinherited

How do you double perfection? Before catastrophe struck, Job's health, wealth, and family were perfect in number, kind, and quality. Now, in the restoration, the Lord blesses him with double his wealth (42:12), double his sons (v. 13), double his years (v. 16), and double his generations (v. 16). Grammatical structure of the text suggests that Job's sons were doubled even though most translations read *"seven sons."* Only his daughters do not double. He lost three daughters to a whirlwind and regained three in the restoration. Yet for some reason they are special. The author of Job takes the time to name them (v. 14), extol their unsurpassed beauty (v. 15), and inform us that Job gave them an inheritance along with their brothers (v. 15).

Their names are intriguing. *Jemima* means "turtledove," *Keziah* is translated "cinnamon," and *Keren-happuch* is another name for "horn-of-paint." The song of a turtledove, the smell of cinnamon, and the sight of cosmetics that were carried in a hollow horn—each signifies the simple beauty of Eastern womanhood in ancient times. Perhaps it is their beauty that favors them with their father, but beauty alone would not cause Job to give them equal shares of his fortune with their brothers. In the patriarchal society, daughters received no inheritance unless there were no sons. Later the tradition became law, when God commanded Moses, "If a man dies and has no son, then you shall cause his inheritance to pass to his daughter" (Num. 27:8).

Why then does Job break with tradition? His daughters neither expect an inheritance nor, according to tradition, deserve one. Grace has to be the answer. As God has blessed Job with double wealth that he doesn't expect or deserve, he in gratitude shares his fortune with all whom he loves. Grace plays no favorites. Neither tradition nor law can limit its out-working. In a patriarchal age, grace gives to women; in an adult culture, grace gives to children; in an affluent society, grace gives to the poor; in a "macho" world, grace gives to the weak; in a Jewish nation, grace gives to Gentiles; in a Christian community, grace gives to the sinner.

Job's gift of grace for his three daughters prefigures Christ's gift of salvation for all who are spiritually disenfranchised. Without overworking the analogy, Job's sons represented the Israelites, legitimate heirs of salvation. The doubling of their numbers as part of Job's restoration fulfills the promise of God to Abraham, "I will multiply your descendants as the stars of the heaven and as the sand which is on the seashore" (Gen. 22:17).

We who are Gentiles do not share this promise of multiplied generations. Neither do we stand in the line of heirs who have a claim on a spiritual inheritance. As with Job's daughters, we would come to our share of the inheritance only if there were no sons who laid the first claim. Daughters and Gentiles are like the dogs who get the crumbs that have fallen from the table after the family has eaten. In Christ, however, the gift of grace is given to us all. Thus, Job's daring decision to break tradition and to project himself into a prophetic role far ahead of his time has to be an act of grace.

Men and women who explore a new frontier of faith through grace are always ahead of their time. History has to catch up with them. E. Stanley Jones, after whom we named our School of World Mission and Evangelism at Asbury Theological Seminary, is an example. He was a "world Christian."

Long before we coined such trendy expressions as *third world, Spaceship Earth, global village,* and *crosscultural communication,* Dr. Jones's preaching and teaching encompassed all of these world dimensions. Critics accused him of contaminating the gospel by relating Christ to the "context" of the culture where he ministered. Yet today, "contextualization" is considered imperative to effective missions and evangelism. No wonder that E. Stanley Jones's books and sermons are being rediscovered in this generation. History is catching up with him.

The Book of Job ends with the epitaph, *"So Job died, old and full of days"* (42:17).

Our hero dies well. Despite the fact that he came through suffering without sin, became a model of God's grace, and prefigured the resur rection of Christ in his restoration, Job died as all humans do. The quality of his days, however, is his own final testimony. God doubles his years so that he lives to be two hundred and ten years old—

three times his promised three-score-and-ten! In a culture that honored fathers and age, Job's epitaph tells us that he became a patriarch without peer in the land of the East.

The length of Job's life, however, is secondary to its quality. We read again, *"So Job died, old and **full of days**"* (emphasis mine), which tells us that he celebrated the joy of living to the very end. Grace does that for us. Our bodies will age and we will die, but grace is the quality of spirit that is renewed with youthful vigor every day. Whether we want to admit it or not, Americans are an aging, graying people. Persons sixty-five years and older will soon be the majority segment of our population. In that aging segment, the fastest-growing group is made up of people who are one hundred years or older. Yet, if you ask people how they perceive the elderly, their response will tend to be identified with a nursing home or a shuffleboard court. The truth is that the aged are shunted aside in this society. We do not give them the honor that is due them and they do not expect to contribute to the advancement of a fast-moving, youth-oriented, high-tech culture. Their loss is our loss. As John Naisbitt writes in *Megatrends,* "We are drowning in a sea of information but starving for knowledge."[5] Simply put, we lack the perspective of experience that transforms information into knowledge and knowledge into wisdom. By denying the elderly the role of the wise in a nation fraught with moral conflict, we are not only denying the meaning of the past but degrading the value of the people who have given us our heritage. We must return to the wisdom of the proverb:

> The silver-haired head is a crown
> of glory,
> If it is found in the way of righteousness (Prov. 16:31).

Job is a modern as well as an ancient model of the silver-haired statesman whose grace and wisdom are indispensable to the life of the society.

So ends the journey of Job. It began with a *ring of righteousness*—sounded by self-discipline and tested for perfection. It ends on a *note of grace*—sensitized to suffering and tuned to trust.

His epitaph might well be rewritten:

And so Job died, old and ***full of grace.***

NOTES

1. Harold S. Kushner, *When Bad Things Happen to Good People* (New York: Avon Books, 1981), pp. 147–48.
2. Archibald MacLeish, *J.B.* (Boston: Houghton Mifflin Co., 1956), pp. 140ff.
3. Yancey, *Where Is God When It Hurts?* pp. 182–83.
4. Lewis, *A Grief Observed,* p. 189.
5. John Naisbitt, *Megatrends: Ten New Directions Transforming Our Lives* (New York: Warner Books, 1982), p. 24.

Bibliography

Andersen, Francis I. *Job: An Introduction and Commentary.* London; Downers Grove, Ill.: Inter-Varsity Press, 1976.

Baker, Wesley C. *More Than a Man Can Take: A Study of Job.* Philadelphia: Westminster Press, 1966.

Barnes, Albert. *Notes on the Old Testament Explanatory and Practical: Job.* Grand Rapids, Mich.: Baker Book House, 1950.

Bennett, T. Miles. *When Human Wisdom Fails: An Exposition of the Book of Job.* Grand Rapids, Mich.: Baker Book House, 1971.

Blackwood, Andrew Watterson, Jr. *Devotional Introduction to Job.* Grand Rapids, Mich.: Baker Book House, 1959.

———. *Out of the Whirlwind: A Study of Job.* Grand Rapids, Mich.: Baker Book House, 1959.

Carlisle, Thomas John. *Journey with Job.* Grand Rapids, Mich.: Wm. B. Eerdmans, 1976.

Carstensen, Roger N. *Job: Defense of Honor.* New York: Abingdon Press, 1963.

Dimnent, Edward D. *The Book of Job: The Poem. An Epic Version in English.* New York: Fleming H. Revell, 1937.

Dhorme, Edouard. *A Commentary on the Book of Job.* Nashville: B. T. Nelson, 1964.

Duquoc, Christian, and Casiano Floristan, eds. *Job and the Silence of God.* Edinburgh: T. & T. Clark; New York: Seabury Press, 1983.

Ellison, H. L. *From Tragedy to Triumph: The Message of the Book of Job.* Grand Rapids, Mich.: Wm. B. Eerdmans, 1958.

Ewing, Ward B. *Job, A Vision of God.* New York: Seabury Press, 1976.

Fowler, James W. *The Stages of Faith.* New York: Harper and Row, 1976.

Frost, Gerhard E. *The Color of the Night: Reflections on the Book of Job.* Minneapolis: Augsburg Publishing House, 1977.

Froude, J. A. *The Book of Job.* London: n.p., 1854.

Garland, D. David. *Job: A Study Guide.* Grand Rapids, Mich.: Zondervan Publishing House, 1971.

Gillaime, Alfred. *Studies in the Book of Job.* Leiden: E. J. Brill, 1968.

Glatzer, Nahum N. *The Dimensions of Job: A Study and Selected Readings.* New York: Schocken Books, 1969.

Gordis, Robert. *The Book of God and Man: A Study of Job.* Chicago: University of Chicago Press, 1965.

Habel, Norman C. *The Book of Job.* London; New York: Cambridge University Press, 1975.

Hulme, William Edward. *Dialogue in Despair: Pastoral Commentary on the Book of Job.* Nashville: Abingdon Press, 1968.

Johnson, L. D. *Out of the Whirlwind: The Major Message of Job.* Nashville: Broadman Press, 1971.

Janzen, J. Gerald. *Job.* Atlanta: John Knox Press, 1985.

Jordan, W. G. *The Book of Job: Its Substance and Spirit.* New York: Macmillan Publishing Co., 1929.

Jung, C. G. *Answer to Job.* London: Routledge and Paul, 1954.

BIBLIOGRAPHY

Kahn, Jack H. *Job's Illness: Loss, Grief and Integration: A Psychological Interpretation.* Oxford, N.Y.: Pergamon Press, 1975.

Kallen, Horace M. *The Book of Job as a Greek Tragedy.* New York: Hill and Wang, 1959.

Kent, Herbert Harold. *Job, Our Contemporary.* Grand Rapids, Mich.: Wm. B. Eerdmans, 1967.

Kushner, Harold S. *When Bad Things Happen to Good People.* New York: Avon Books, 1981.

Levenson, Jon Douglas. *The Book of Job in Its Time and in the Twentieth Century.* Cambridge, Mass.: Harvard University Press, 1972.

Lewis, C. S. *A Grief Observed.* New York: Bantam Books, 1961.

MacBeath, Andrew. *The Book of Job: A Study Manual.* Grand Rapids, Mich.: Baker Book House, 1966.

Massy, Cecil Hugh. *The Gospel in the Book of Job.* London: Skeffington, 1908.

Morgan, G. Campbell. *The Book of Job.* New York: F. H. Revell, 1909.

Morrow, Ord L. *Puzzles of Job.* Lincoln, Neb.: Back to the Bible, 1965.

Murphy, Roland Edmund. *The Wisdom Literature: Job, Proverbs, Ruth, Canticles, Ecclesiastes, and Esther.* Grand Rapids, Mich.: Wm. B. Eerdmans, 1981.

Patrick, Dale. *Arguing with God: The Angry Prayers of Job.* St. Louis: Bethany Press, 1977.

Pope, Marvin H. *Job.* Garden City, N.Y.: Doubleday, 1965.

Robinson, Theodore Henry. *Job and His Friends.* London: SCM Press, 1954.

Rowley, Harold Henry. *Job.* Grand Rapids, Mich.: Wm. B. Eerdmans, 1976.

Rowley, H. H., ed. *Job.* London: Nelson, 1970.

Sanders, Paul S., ed. *Twentieth Century Interpretations of the Book of Job: A Collection of Critical Essays.* Englewood Cliffs, N.J.: Prentice-Hall, 1968.

Singer, Richard E. *Job's Encounter.* New York: Bookman Associates, 1963.

Snaith, Norman Henry. *The Book of Job: Its Origin and Purpose.* Naperville, Ill.: A. R. Allenson, 1968.

Stewart, James. *The Message of Job.* London: Independent Press, 1959.

Studies in the Book of Job: A Biblical Drama Illuminating the Problem of the Ages. New York: Scribner, 1906.

Tournier, Paul. *Creative Suffering.* New York: Harper and Row, 1981.

Ward, William B. *Out of the Whirlwind: Answers to the Problems of Suffering from the Book of Job.* Richmond: John Knox Press, 1958.

Weitzner, Emil. *The Book of Job: A Paraphrase.* New York: n.p., 1960.

Wiesel, Elie. *Night/Dawn, The Accident.* NewYork: Hill and Wang, 1972.

Yancey, Phillip. *Where Is God When It Hurts?* Grand Rapids, Mich.: Zondervan Publishing House, 1977.